ROMANTICISM AND ANIMAL RIGHTS

In England in the second half of the eighteenth century an unprece-
dented amount of writing urged kindness to animals. This theme was
carried in many genres, from sermons to encyclopedias, from scientific works to literature for children, and in the poetry of Cowper,
Wordsworth, Coleridge, Clare, and others. *Romanticism and Animal
Rights* discusses the arguments writers used, and the particular meanings of these arguments in a social and economic context so different
from the present. After introductory chapters, the material is divided
according to specific practices that particularly influenced feeling or
aroused protest: pet keeping, hunting, baiting, working animals, eating them, and the various harms inflicted on wild birds. The book
shows how extensively English Romantic writing took up issues of
what we now call animal rights. In this respect it joins the growing number of studies that seek precedents or affinities in English
Romanticism for our own ecological concerns.

DAVID PERKINS is Marquand Professor, Emeritus, at Harvard University. He is the author or editor of nine books including *The Quest
for Permanence, Wordsworth and the Poetry of Sincerity, English Romantic Writers, A History of Modern Poetry*, and *Is Literary History Possible?*

This series aims to foster the best new work in one of the most challenging fields within English literary studies. From the early 1780s to the early 1830s a formidable array of talented men and women took to literary composition, not just in poetry, which some of them famously transformed, but in many modes of writing. The expansion of publishing created new opportunities for writers, and the political stakes of what they wrote were raised again by what Wordsworth called those 'great national events' that were 'almost daily taking place': the French Revolution, the Napoleonic and American wars, urbanization, industrialization, religious revival, an expanded empire abroad and the reform movement at home. This was an enormous ambition, even when it pretended otherwise. The relations between science, philosophy, religion and literature were reworked in texts such as *Frankenstein* and *Biographia Literaria*; gender relations in *A Vindication of the Rights of Woman* and *Don Juan*; journalism by Cobbett and Hazlitt; poetic form, content and style by the Lake School and the Cockney School. Outside Shakespeare studies, probably no body of writing has produced such a wealth of response or done so much to shape the responses of modern criticism. This indeed is the period that saw the emergence of those notions of "literature" and of literary history, especially national literary history, on which modern scholarship in English has been founded.

The categories produced by Romanticism have also been challenged by recent historicist arguments. The task of the series is to engage both with a challenging corpus of Romantic writings and with the changing field of criticism they have helped to shape. As with other literary series published by Cambridge, this one will represent the work of both younger and more established scholars, on either side of the Atlantic and elsewhere.

For a complete list of titles published see end of book.

ROMANTICISM AND ANIMAL RIGHTS

DAVID PERKINS

Harvard University

CAMBRIDGE
UNIVERSITY PRESS

PUBLISHED BY THE PRESS SYNDICATE OF THE UNIVERSITY OF CAMBRIDGE
The Pitt Building, Trumpington Street, Cambridge CB2 1RP, United Kingdom

CAMBRIDGE UNIVERSITY PRESS
The Edinburgh Building, Cambridge, CB2 2RU, UK
40 West 20th Street, New York, NY 10011–4211, USA
477 Williamstown Road, Port Melbourne, VIC 3207, Australia
Ruiz de Alarcón 13, 28014 Madrid, Spain
Dock House, The Waterfront, Cape Town 8001, South Africa

http://www.cambridge.org

First published 2003

Printed in the United Kingdom at the University Press, Cambridge

Typeface Adobe Garamond 11/12.5 pt.   *System* LATEX 2$_\varepsilon$ [TB]

A catalogue record for this book is available from the British Library

Library of Congress cataloguing in publication data
Perkins, David, 1928–
Romanticism and animal rights / by David Perkins.
p. cm. – (Cambridge studies in Romanticism; 58)
Includes bibliographical references (p. 175) and index.
ISBN 0 521 82941 0
1. English literature – 19th century – History and criticism.   2. Animals in literature.   3. English
literature – 18th century – History and criticism.   4. Animal welfare – Great
Britain – History – 18th century.   5. Animal welfare – Great Britain – History – 19th century.
6. Animal rights – Great Britain – History – 18th century.   7. Animal rights – Great
Britain – History – 19th century.   8. Human–animal relationships in literature.
9. Romanticism – Great Britain.   I. Title.   II. Series.
PR468.A56P47   2003   820.9′362′09034 – dc21   2003046082

ISBN 0 521 82941 0 hardback

For Morle, Midget, Musch, Lite, Silkey,
Poldi, Tommy, Tonio, Pronto, and Louie

Contents

Preface

Fellow feeling for animals, compassion, kindness, friendship, and affection are expressed in every time and place and culture, in primordial artifacts, Egyptian tombs, Homer's description of the old dog Argos, as much as in Henry Moore's 1980 drawings of sheep. Perhaps no argument for kindness to animals was ever made that had not already been made long before. In England, however, in the latter part of the eighteenth century, there was a change, a gradual, eventually enormous increase in the frequency of such expressions. Kindness to animals was urged and represented in sermons, treatises, pamphlets, journals, manuals of animal care, encyclopedias, scientific writings, novels, literature for children, and poems. There were also, of course, writings on the other side, defenses of traditional practices, such as bullbaiting, but they were far less numerous than the literature I foreground. To what extent all this writing registered or helped bring about a general change of mind, and to what extent it contributed to developments in the actual treatment of animals, are questions that cannot be answered with much certainty. I pursue them briefly in a moment, but the literature itself, the discourse, is my primary subject.

There was a close connection between the cultural world we call Romanticism, with its ideals of sympathy, sentiment, and nature, and the tender attitudes expressed in writing about animals. But these ideals might also be said to characterize what we call the Enlightenment, as might the practical, reforming benevolence that was strongly evident in this discourse, and the nexus I focus on might be called Enlightened as well as Romantic. The other half of my title, "animal rights," is hardly more precise, for the phrase has become a catch-all for any protest against cruelty to animals. A headline in today's newspaper reports "British Researchers on Animal Rights Death List." Whether or not the terrorists who made this list believe that animals have rights is unknown, for even if they were motivated only by pity and rage, they would still be called "animal rights activists." Accordingly,

I adopt the phrase "animal rights" as a shorthand term for kindly attitudes
to animals and pleas for reform in the treatment of them.

The place of focus is Great Britain, and given this already large ter-
rain, there is no attempt to expand further into colonies and possessions
overseas, or into the United States, although this would permit some interesting comparisons. The period of time to which the book attends is 1750
to 1830 with occasional excursions into earlier or later moments. Within
this period, the amount of writing that concerns or touches significantly on
animals approaches the numerical sublime. I do not in the least attempt to
survey all this, but notice only the portion that is relevant to animal rights,
an amount of writing that is still unmanageably much.[1] After preliminary
chapters of a more general kind, the material is divided according to specific
practices that particularly influenced feeling or aroused protest: pet keeping, hunting, baiting, working animals, eating them, and the various harms
inflicted on wild birds. To represent the spread of Romantic attitudes on
these topics, many authors are cited, but to me the individual case is more
interesting and in some ways more revealing than an array of quotations
from different sources. For this among other reasons, I have included in
most chapters longer readings of single authors or texts. These are contex-
tual readings in the sense that the texts are viewed amid other discourses on
their subject and close readings in the sense that the texts are considered in
detail. Robert Burns, William Cowper, Christopher Smart, Thomas Day,
Sarah Trimmer, John Aikin, Letitia Barbauld, William Wordsworth, John
Clare, Samuel Taylor Coleridge, Charles Lamb, and many others could be
described as animal lovers, even as immoderate ones. What, then, motivated
their attitude? What did they deplore, what hope for in human relations
with animals? Cumulatively, the book shows, I hope, how extensively
English Romantic writing took up issues of animal rights. In this respect
it joins the growing number of studies that seek precedents or affinities in
English Romanticism for our own ecological concerns.

Reading these descriptions of animal suffering at the hands of humans,
these protests against it, I interpret them more or less literally. In other
words, I emphasize that the concern was for animals, for their woes, more
than it was, in most of the texts I cite, for the socially subordinated humans
that animals might represent figuratively. Writings about animals in the
eighteenth century spread nets of figuration to allude also and variously to
children, women, servants, the lower classes, slaves, colonialized peoples,
and other races. Such tropes were age old. When such figurative meanings
are not obvious in the texts, they can be interpretively supplied. Persons who
are especially interested in one or another of these groups naturally develop

such readings. Thus G. J. Barker-Benfield, discussing women authors of the eighteenth century, argues that when they wrote about animals, they were referring to their own situation: the contribution of sentimental fiction to "revolutionary attitudes toward animals was a kind of surrogate feminism."[2] Carol J. Adams argues that "animals' oppression and women's oppression are [and were] linked together."[3] Moira Ferguson thinks that in the texts by women that she discusses, the situations of women, colonialized peoples, the working class, and the poor were all linked together and represented in discourse about animals.[4] Similarly allegorical readings easily suggest themselves with reference to other social groups. I pursue such readings myself on occasion. But to all such reading there is the objection that it crowds the stage and divides the spotlight. Whatever social group animals and their treatment are said to figure becomes the real center of concern, displacing the animals. If this is not a further exploitation of animals, it at least diverts attention from their suffering. Most of the authors I quote took up this suffering as a humanitarian cause in its own right.

Though this study deals with writings that are now more or less two hundred years old, the feelings and arguments they express are still with us, still sometimes controversial and even, in some cases, hotly and freshly so. The arguments deployed pro and con were much the same as they are now. The main exception was a once persuasive argument from religion that is now much less current. But in applying this material to the present day, the reader should keep in mind that the same or closely similar arguments may have dissimilar meanings in a social, cultural, and economic context of utterance that has changed enormously.

Given that my subject matter, though historical, is still controversial, the reader may wish to know where I am on questions of animal rights, from what standpoint the book is written. My purpose in this paragraph is only to confide, not at all to argue, which would require vastly more pages. I do not believe that creatures, including human ones, have natural rights. In an earlier part of my life I worked on a small farm and I have kept pets for years. Thus I know from experience as well as from books that emotions directed to animals may be very intense and are likely be in conflict with each other. However great the affection we have for our animals, we still generally intend to eat, work, cage, or at least dominate them, and even hunters are likely to say that they feel a tug of the heart toward their victims. Romantic authors generally assumed that the best thing for animals was to be far from humans, living their wild lives without interference. This Romantic opinion seems correct, though as a wish it is Utopian. I do not share the further Romantic belief that nature (or God) suffuses the natural

Preface

lives of animals with happiness, but at least in the wild they can follow their
instincts freely, as they cannot in zoos, pens, cages, and houses. Moreover,
even if human relations with animals involved no harms or hindrances
to them, we would still, I think, confront perplexing moral questions, at
least in situations such as pet keeping and farming, where we live with
animals. A relationship cannot be morally healthy that is utterly unequal,
the one dominant, the other helpless and vulnerable. And however much we
interact with animals, we have at best only a limited understanding of them.
Just as they, I presume, can relate to us only as though we were somewhat
peculiar cats, dogs, horses, cows, or parrots, we inevitably humanize them.
We have no other basis than ourselves for interpreting their behavior and
emotion, no basis, certainly, that serves immediately in daily life. Projective
self-deception takes place in all human relationships, but when it becomes
obvious and extreme, we are entitled to view it ironically. As a pet keeper
with moral qualms, I am inconsistent, like most of the authors in this
book, and I compromise principles with practicalities. But I strongly favor
kindness to animals, much more than exists at present, and, in short, can
confess of myself what Byron says of Don Juan:

> He had a kind of inclination, or
> Weakness, for what most people deem mere vermin,
> Live animals: an old maid of threescore
> For cats and birds more penchant ne'er displayed,
> Although he was not old, nor even a maid.[5]

I come now to the historical significance and consequences, if any, of this
discourse. My purpose is only to remind, briefly, of difficulties in addressing
such questions. Because so much more writing than in the past urged
kindness to animals, it seems reasonable to suppose there was a changed
climate of opinion in the later eighteenth century. The writers, in other
words, were not speaking only for themselves but for many other persons
who were subject to similar influences and harbored similar sentiments. And
certainly many social, economic, and cultural developments underlie this
literature, enabling and evoking it, and the literature itself was, of course,
an additional factor in disseminating concern for animals. The impression
that there was a changing climate of opinion is supported by the gradual
waning or suppression in this period of cock-throwing, bullbaiting, and
similar sports of the common people. Eventually bills to prevent various
abuses of animals were brought in Parliament and in 1822 the first was
passed. Thus the writings I take up can be said to testify and contribute to
sentiments that gradually had practical results.

But if there was a climate of opinion, it is not easy to say where it pervaded or who were its social bearers. So far as I have been able to discover in the secondary literature, there were not pronounced differences by region.[6] Modern conceptions of class seem not to apply very well to eighteenth-century England.[7] But contemporaries recognized, of course, a "middling sort," and if we locate this sort within families having incomes between £100 and £1,000 a year, they would make up between 15 and 25 percent of the population around 1800.[8] This group would include many lawyers, doctors, clergy, farmers, merchants, shopkeepers, craftsmen, and the like, and it was from such families that most writers emerged. Several, however, belonged to the gentry, such as Shelley and Byron, and some, such as Robert Burns and John Clare, were from lower positions on the social scale. Of course one might argue that in becoming writers their social identification altered; they would be perceived, compared, and talked about with other writers. Beyond the writers themselves, animal sympathizers would probably be found more among the genteel or respectable middling sort than among the low and poor and more in towns than the countryside. But Methodists were preaching kindness to animals, and villagers kept pets as much as anyone else. A further difficulty is that concern for animals varied according to the usual inconsistency of human nature and also according to interests. A person might deplore one thing and see nothing wrong with another that, to different minds, seemed just as cruel. Wordsworth wrote movingly against hunting but was an enthusiastic angler, for which Shelley attacked him.[9] Fox hunters denounced bullbaiting and horse racers drovers. All this writing was done with quills plucked from live geese.

Moreover, it is hard to disentangle the impact of literature and of sentiment from other causes that were also in operation. The practical reforms that can be cited might have come about anyway. Cock-throwing and bullbaiting attracted crowds, and these were often rowdy. In the sixteenth and seventeenth centuries such amusements of the people had been attacked by Puritans as occasions of drinking, gambling, swearing, and idleness. Methodists, evangelicals, and others continued this criticism in the eighteenth century. For such reasons and also because they were imbued with ideals of refinement, genteel persons in towns generally avoided such scenes by 1800. Moreover, as the towns grew larger, the magistrates were more concerned and challenged to maintain public order. Industrial production, though still relatively localized in 1800, required that expensive factories and machines not stand idle. The need for a sober, disciplined, and reliable workforce furnished another objection to bullbaitings and the like. Thus benevolent sentiment about animals could be co-opted, so to speak, and we could describe it *à la* Foucault as part of a disciplinary effort directed against the lower orders. Indeed, exactly this was said about it in Parliament. A typical expression of the magistrates may be quoted from the Norwich Court of the Mayorality, which in 1759 ordered that constables patrol the streets to enforce a ban on Shrovetide cock-throwing, "in just abhorrence of the cruel practice . . . and to prevent such disorders as usually arise therefrom."[10] Similarly the magistrates of Stamford affirmed in 1788 their intention to suppress the annual, November 13 bull-running in their town, "a custom of such unparalleled cruelty to an innocent animal, and in all respects a Disgrace to Religion, Law, and Nature."[11] Reading such statements, it is hard to know whether sentiments of humanity or concern for law and order were the primary motivation, and it is certainly possible that the former were put forward to ornament the latter. Historians usually explain such reforms as took place in the treatment of animals as the joint working of many factors, of which a changing attitude to animals was one.[12]

Neither is it clear that there was, on the whole, more kindness shown to animals in 1830 than in 1750, though there was more lip-service about it. Though bullbaiting and cock-throwing were on the wane, horse racing and cockfighting flourished, as horse racing does to the present. For these amusements were patronized by the gentry, which had the political strength to protect them, as of course they did hunting, which gathered more support than ever in the period I discuss. Fox hunting especially increased then. "There were 69 packs of hounds in Britain in 1812 and 91 in 1825."[13] As for the conditions and treatment of work and farm animals, and of those driven to markets and slaughtered, there was probably mitigation in some respects and greater harshness in others. The description given by Lewis Gompertz of these matters in 1829 does not suggest that amelioration had taken place.[14] Roy Porter was probably thinking of coach horses, among other things, when he suggested that "society's victims wrung fresh pity and guilt because they were being more savagely exploited than before."[15] In 1830 wild birds were still netted in vast numbers to be eaten or to become parlor pets in cages. If the perspective is extended to the present day, there is still no clear vista of improvement. I would not know how to weigh the sufferings of contemporary hens in batteries and hogs in hog cities against those of their ancestors in 1800, except that now vastly more animals are involved. Modern scientific breeding for the production of eggs, milk, and meat has produced monsters – chickens, for example, with breasts so large that the animal falls over if it tries to stand. Abuses of animals are less visible to most people than they were in 1800, but they are known and tolerated, and the fact does not argue a radical increase in human sympathy with animals. What alleviations time has brought to animals seem mostly the results of a changing economy and technology.[16] Railways and motor cars ended the woes of coach horses. There were no anesthetics in the eighteenth century, so vivisection was carried on without it. Before refrigeration, only live meat could be fresh, and cattle, sheep, and geese were driven from far to the London markets. That the abusive exploitation of animals now has a political and polemic opposition is a legacy to us of the writings I discuss.

Acknowledgments

In working on this project I had much aid from the late W. J. Bate, who took a wonderfully generous, supportive interest in it. I am also grateful to my friend Jens Rieckmann for many perusals, to Marilyn Butler and James Chandler, the general editors of the series in which the book is published, and to two anonymous readers for the Press – vigilant, knowledgeable, and helpful were they all. Portions of the book appeared in different versions in *Blake Quarterly, Eighteenth Century Life, English Literary History, Harvard Review, Modern Language Quarterly, Nineteenth-Century Literature, Texas Studies in Literature and Language,* and *Studies in Romanticism,* and I thank the editors of these journals. I also owe much to students in a course on this material at the University of California, Irvine.

I

In the beginning of animal rights

On October 18, 1772, church-goers in the parish of Shiplake, in Oxfordshire, were startled to hear a sermon on Proverbs 12. 10: "A righteous man regardeth the life of his beast." They had not expected their polite and learned vicar, James Granger, to dwell on horses and cows. The sermon "gave almost universal disgust . . . as a prostitution of the dignity of the pulpit."[1] When Granger published his sermon, it again proved unpopular. By January 1773, only a hundred copies had been sold. However, it was favorably reviewed in the *Monthly Review* and the *Critical Review* – a "sensible discourse," said the *Monthly*, a "seasonable and useful sermon," said the *Critical* – and his publisher, Davies, assured Granger that "every body speaks well of it."[2] Granger had wealthy, influential friends and a wide acquaintance among the learned. (He had compiled a *Biographical History of England*, 1769, which had involved much correspondence.) In the trouble with his congregation, his Bishop was induced to visit Shiplake and support him.

What had Granger said: a "righteous man" thinks himself "allied" to animals; the "meanest creature . . . has an equal right with himself to live"; in killing an insect "a man destroys what neither he, nor all the united powers of the world can ever repair"; England is "the Hell of Horses," and "there is no country upon the face of the whole earth . . . where the beast is so ill treated, as it is in our own."[3] These are the most extreme passages. The sermon is generally a sober discourse.

Granger was hardly the first in this vein. The poetry of his time habitually urged kindly sentiments towards animals. His reasoned arguments can mostly be found in John Hildrop's 1742 *Free Thoughts Upon the Brute Creation* and in other earlier discourses. Moreover, preachers, moralists, and philosophers as far back as the Schoolmen and as recently as John Locke and his followers had frequently urged kindness to animals, though generally more for the sake of society than for that of the creatures. Two sermons had been published anonymously in 1761 urging *Clemency to Brutes*.[4] They also were favorably reviewed in both the *Monthly Review* and the *Critical Review*, and the latter says that the sermons have had a good effect, though for many readers the subject is "seemingly mean and trivial."[5] Not long after Granger's sermon, Humphry Primatt, a Cambridge graduate and retired clergyman, published his *Duty of Mercy and Sin of Cruelty to Beasts* (1776). Warned, perhaps, by Granger's experience, Primatt confessed himself "well aware of the obloquy to which every man must expose himself, who presumes to encounter prejudices and long received customs. To make a comparison between a man and a brute, is abominable; to talk of a man's duty to his horse or his ox, is absurd; to suppose it cruel to chase a stag, or course a hare, is unpolite; to esteem it barbarous to throw at a cock, to bait a bull, to roast a lobster, or to crimp a fish, is ridiculous."[6] Nevertheless, the *Critical Review* affirmed that Primatt's work was "entitled to the warmest approbation";[7] it was excerpted and reprinted in the United States in 1802, and has won Primatt favorable mentions ever since.[8]

On May 8, 1796, James Plumptre, vicar of Great Gransden in Huntingdonshire, preached before the University of Cambridge, with Prince William of Gloucester among the hearers, on "The Duties of Man to the Brute Creation." Since the Sabbath had been ordained for cattle as well as for humans (Exodus 20.8–10; 23.12), Plumptre considered it a "NATIONAL SIN" that horses were used on this day.[9] Otherwise his sermon was timid, and continually supported itself with biblical texts, yet, even so, it was not well received. "The subject," he explains, "was then considered by many as trifling, and beneath the dignity of the pulpit, and especially that of the University. It was suggested to the preacher by the repeated perusal of *Cowper's Task*." The reactions to Granger and Plumptre suggest that they were in advance of their hearers. But when Plumptre published the work in 1816, he noted in a Foreword that since 1796 much had been done "to interest the minds of the public at large on the subject."[10]

I

A few instances may illustrate the sentiments about animals that Romantic writers could harbor and assert from the 1790s through the 1820s. Samuel Taylor Coleridge remarked in an 1805 notebook that he felt pain "from having *cursed* a gnat that was singing about my head."[11] A few years before he had written poems of pity for a young ass and of supernatural vengeance for the shooting of an albatross. According to Byron's mistress, Teresa Guiccioli, "the dread of treading on an ant makes him go out of his way."[12] In a gesture of both affection and misanthropy, to which I return, Byron provided in his will of 1811 that he should be buried beside his dog Boatswain. Later, in *Don Juan*, Byron attacked hunting. "If a Sparrow come before my Window," said John Keats in an 1817 letter, "I take part in its existince and pick about the Gravel."[13] Percy Bysshe Shelley would purchase crayfish from the street vendors in order to return them to the Thames.[14] In "The Sensitive Plant" (1820), Shelley's poem about a garden, aphids and worms are picked unharmed off the flowers and carried in a weed-lined basket to the woods.[15] In 1824 Charles Lamb felt intense remorse because he had once "set a dog upon a crab's leg that was shoved out under a moss of sea weeds, a pretty little feeler. – Oh! Pah! How sick I am of that."[16] Lamb was among the many town dwellers who boiled with indignation at the cruelty of donkey drivers: "I have often longed to see one of those refiners in discipline himself at the cart's tail . . . laid bare to the tender mercies of the whipster."[17]

Obviously the cause of animals evoked negative emotions – misanthropy, righteousness – as well as sympathetic ones, and I return to this later on. For the moment, the point is only how great the change in attitude might be, at least among the sentimental elite. Animals for centuries had been viewed as brutes, as bundles of lust, greed, and ferocity, incapable of self-control, without reason. Whatever impulses people feared in themselves could be projected on them, so that a bearbaiting might be unconsciously a scapegoating. Descartes, whose opinion was influential, had taught that animals were mere organic machines; if you whipped them, he said, there was no central consciousness in which the pain could be felt.

But increasingly the creatures were redescribed. By 1775 they might incarnate a pristine innocence, a spontaneous joy in life that adult human beings lacked. They were credited with moral virtues: the dauntless courage of the fighting cock, the fidelity of the dog, candor, integrity, innocence. The parental care of robins was extolled, and the mild peace of the herds. To a radical such as William Blake, appalled by middle-class convention, even animal wildness might be redemptive: "Every Wolfs & Lions howl / Raises from Hell a Human Soul."[18] In short, people might now project not their *id* but their ideals into animals. Moreover, in poems and in literature for children it became common to present animals as individuals, each with its unique character and life history. In the discourse of the age animals could be said to have rights, much as humans have, to life, to justice, to their natural happiness, though such assertions of course remained highly controversial. God, it was often proved, loves *all* his creatures, and so accordingly must we.

The many humanitarian movements of the eighteenth century mobilized generally similar supporters, arguments, and tactics. Whoever was for rescuing slaves, prisoners, foundlings, and other human victims was likely to feel a kindred impulse with respect to animals, and many an animal lover also supported other humanitarian causes. But the latter part of this statement requires two qualifications. For many persons, animals offered themselves as a conscience-appeasing surrogate for human sufferers, whose relief they were less ready to champion, perhaps because it might involve or symbolize a riskier alteration of the social order. In terms of practical politics, so to speak, it was clear that the baited, plucked, ridden, hunted creatures could not threaten their masters as humans might and lately had in the French Revolution. If animals had rights, they could not enforce them. The mouse in Burns's famous poem "To a Mouse" is an example, and we shall consider it in a moment.

    That the victims were animals introduced a moral or psychological complexity not present in other reform movements. The others affirmed solidarity with mankind. But the cause of animals appealed also to the pathologically shy, to the alienated, to the misanthropic, to those who, for whatever reason, had difficulty in identifying with other human beings. In a circle of reactions, compassion for animals nourished misanthropy. Human beings, "fellow men," were the displacers, abusers, tormentors, and destroyers of the creatures you sympathized with, were the enemy. In fact, you were the enemy merely because you were human, because you existed. This state of mind, in which human beings reject mankind, was and still is intensified by the Romantic idealization of nature, of an ideal nature conceived as opposite to civilized society. The comparison of nature and man might be rueful that we are not natural, but it could also be satiric and openly misanthropic. In his inscription for Boatswain's monument, in the garden of Newstead Abbey, Byron affirmed the moral superiority of dog to human nature. Boatswain, he wrote, "possessed Beauty without Vanity, Strength without Insolence," and "Courage without Ferocity." Humans, by contrast, were "vile":

> To mark a Friend's remains these stones arise;
> I never knew but one, – and here he lies.[19]

    Animals conventionally viewed as repulsive offered particularly challenging tests of sympathy, and writers seized upon them. The best-known example is the water snakes in Coleridge's "Rime of the Ancient Mariner." At first they appear slimy to the mariner, a foulness in the rotting sea, but then he sees them as beautiful and happy, and a spring of love for them gushes from his heart.

Thomson, Cowper, and Blake, among others, addressed compassionate verses to worms and snails. But insects offered writers the largest opportunity for instructive, provocative, prejudice-dispelling displays of sympathy, and an abundant discourse availed of them. Robert Burns's well-known "To a Louse" is partly a poem of this kind. Since most people viewed insects, as they still do, as insignificant, disagreeable, or dangerous, they had no fellow feelings with insects, no affectionate attitudes to them. They are the nearest to aliens that we encounter. Overcoming this distance, poets redescribed insects in human terms. One of the best known examples is Catherine Ann Dorset's poem to the coccinellid beetle:

> Oh! Lady-bird, Lady-bird, why dost thou roam
> So far from thy comrades, so distant from home?[20]

Perhaps the most wonderful of these redescriptions comes in a passage of William Blake's *Milton* (1800–04) that envisions gnats as "Children of Los":

> Thou seest the gorgeous clothed Flies that dance & sport in summer
> Upon the sunny brooks & meadows: every one the dance
> Knows in its intricate mazes of delight artful to weave:
> Each one to sound his instruments of music in the dance.[21]

Children were (and are) likely to torment insects. In combating this behavior, one could teach sympathy and possibly more – the conquering of antipathy to the different, foreign, and exotic; the appreciation of God's (or nature's) goodness to all creatures; the beauty of things. I quote Thomas Percival, a Manchester physician who wrote forty books; he included a section on "Cruelty to Insects" in *A Father's Instructions* (1784): the sensations of insects "are at least as exquisite as those of animals of more enlarged dimensions." Witness the millipede that rolls into a ball at the "slightest touch." The implication, of course, is that such creatures are susceptible of pain in a degree proportionate to their extreme sensitivity to touch. It is "inhuman to crush to death a harmless insect, whose only offence is that he eats the food which nature has provided for his sustenance."[22]

At about the same time as Percival was writing, Thomas Day, a philanthropic gentleman farmer, was conducting two imaginary youths, Harry Sandford and Thomas Merton, through a course of education somewhat modeled on Rousseau's *Émile*. The young Sandford twirled "a cockchafer round, which he had fastened to a long piece of thread." But "as soon as his father told him that the poor helpless insect felt as much, or more than he would do, were a knife thrust through his hand, he burst into tears and took the poor insect home, where he fed him during a fortnight upon fresh leaves; and, when perfectly recovered, he turned him out to enjoy liberty and the fresh air."²³ Some fifty years later William Drummond, a poet, Dissenting minister, and controversialist, advised mothers that "Instead of starting with feigned or real disgust at the sight of a spider, she will call her child to mark its racing speed, its thread most 'exquisitely fine,' and 'its delicate web, which brilliantly glistens with dew.'" Thus repulsion and fear would be lost in wonder.²⁴ The phrase "exquisitely fine" recalled lines of Alexander Pope that were repeatedly cited in writings about insects:

> The spider's touch, how exquisitely fine!
> Feels at each thread, and lives along the line.²⁵

Flies, the most familiar and annoying of England's insects, evoked astonishing feats of sympathy along with some ordinary ones. I quoted Blake's verses about the midges; in *Songs of Experience* (1789–94) he addressed a house fly, as I suppose it was:

> Am not I
> A fly like thee?
> Or art not thou
> A man like me?²⁶

In *Evenings at Home* (1792), a book for children, John Aikin and Letitia Barbauld briefly suggested a fly-centered view of mankind. When a child asks, "What were flies made for?" her father replies, "Suppose a fly capable of thinking, would he not be equally puzzled to find out what men were good for?"²⁷ Thus sympathy might tend to deprive humans of special importance and status among the creatures. Wordsworth also wrote a poem of sympathy for a fly, and James Thomson reminded his readers to rescue them from spiders' webs: the shrill buzz "asks the helping hospitable Hand."²⁸ Uncle Toby's fly, in Lawrence Sterne's *Tristram Shandy*, was another of the many that were ostentatiously spared or whose death was regretted. With Shandyan paradox, the tender-hearted Toby is a soldier. When he catches a fly, he famously says,

Go – says he, one day at dinner . . . I'll not hurt thee . . . I'll not hurt a hair of thy head: – Go, says he, lifting up the sash, and opening his hand as he spoke, to let it escape; – go, poor devil, get thee gone, why should I hurt thee?²⁹

Spiders are notoriously victims of cultural prejudice, are symbols of evil and death in many an ancient and modern writing. But in this period it might not be so, and the repugnance to be overcome seems sometimes to have called forth extremes of sentimental redescription. In William Blake's *Vala*, the "blind and age-bent" Enion pities a spider that was eaten by a bird:

> His Web is left all desolate, that his little anxious heart
> So careful wove: & spread it out with sighs and weariness.[30]

In Sarah Trimmer's *Fabulous Histories*, a children's story about a family of robins, the exemplary Mrs. Wilson would not destroy the webs of spiders: "I should not myself like to have the fruits of my industry demolished, nor my little ones taken out of my arms, or from their warm beds, and crushed to death."[31] Robert Southey wrote an affectionate poem about a spider, which begins,

> Spider! thou need'st not run in fear about
>   To shun my curious eyes;
> I won't humanely crush thy bowels out,
>   Lest thou shouldst eat the flies;
> Nor will I roast thee, with a damned delight
> Thy strange instinctive fortitude to see,
>   For there is One who might
>   One day roast me.[32]

Charles Lamb was "hugely pleased" by this poem: "I love this sort of poems, that open a new intercourse with the most despised of the animal and insect race."[33] Which brings me to Robert Burns's "To a Mouse."

II

No poem of compassion for animals is more widely loved and quoted than this one. Since mice were regarded as vermin, the poem belongs to the kind already mentioned, in which the poet evokes sympathy for a despised species. Of itself the gesture is appealing, for it bespeaks a kind heart and a liberal mind free from prejudice. Moreover, the poem liberates from restrictions of convention and social class and binds into a universal fellowship. Significantly, the fellowship is not with all other human beings but with all living things, this being an easier fellowship to accept.

"To a Mouse" is the first expression of Romantic sympathy for animals that I pause to analyze. There is necessarily an imperfect fit between the generalizations of cultural history and the particular events they cover. Though "To a Mouse" is movingly compassionate, the grounds of its feeling for the mouse are not what would have been expected in Burns's time. Burns does not idealize the animal as nature. He does not rely on usual arguments then, such as God's love for His creatures. Since the speaker is a poor ploughman, the poem undermines the self-flattering assumption of many readers that the poor were heartless and brutal. Instead, Burns views humans and animals as "fellow mortal[s]" (line 12), alike exposed to accident, loss, old age, and death.[34]

In the older criticism of Burns, his attitudes to animals have been explained as typical of a small farm in his time and place.[35] But as the speaker says in "To a Mouse," most ploughmen would have smashed the small creature "Wi murd'ring pattle" (line 6). This ploughman, being a poet, feels affectionate toward the mouse. Nevertheless, in turning up its nest with the plough, he has done it harm, and Wordsworth, for example, might have opened a misanthropic ecological perspective in which man is intrusive and destructive in the natural world. Since Burns's ploughman feels that man, too, is a vulnerable natural creature, the mouse ultimately becomes a figure of himself. Meanwhile, he talks to the mouse, a poetic device and also a common habit of pet owners. He addresses it with the intimate pronoun and an affectionate diminutive ("Mousie"). He thinks he knows what it feels. He attributes human capabilities (foresight) and emotions to it, and imagines it as quasi-human. For example, it builds a "house." Although in law and grammar one could not "murder" an animal, one could this mouse (line 6), a point that further humanizes it. Humorously the speaker subjects the mouse to the human moral code, by which it fails (it is a thief, line 13), and protectively he apologizes for it, taking its side. This humanizing of the small creature is the usual, universal basis of emotional reactions to animals; we react to what we have attributed.

All his kindness and charm make the speaker quite as sympathetic as he makes the mouse. Moreover, the speaker is attractive as a stock Romantic figure of the poet: intimate with nature, alone, sensitive, melancholy, emotional. The exclamations and interjections in his speech dramatize how strongly he is moved. His dialect supports the illusion of spontaneous talk rather than literature. (As a formal device, the dialect also defamiliarizes his language, some of which would be flat in standard English.) As a ploughman, a rustic, the poet speaker is presumably uneducated, in other words, he could be seen at this time as an untutored product of nature, an original genius. Burns emphasized this on the title page and in the Preface of his 1786 volume that included "To a Mouse." The role of peasant poet made him especially interesting to readers and boosted his sales.

The speaker of Burns's poem was no doubt as much a fictional creation as the mouse who speaks in Letitia Barbauld's "The Mouse's Petition."[36]

Composed fourteen years earlier than "To a Mouse," Barbauld's poem is similar in some of its themes. Barbauld notes, as Burns does, that the mouse steals very little, only "scattered gleanings" (line 17), or, as Burns puts it, "A daimen-icker in a thrave" (line 15; an occasional grain in the straw), and both poems suggest that a compassionate heart would not deny so small a boon. Barbauld also deploys the famous phrase, "mice and men," or "men like mice" in her version. It might seem that in inventing a mouse as the speaker, Barbauld chose the more daring strategy, but as the speaker, her mouse cannot plausibly picture itself in much detail. Possibly for this reason Barbauld lacks the ample, realistic description that brings the mouse vividly before the imagination of Burns's reader, and of course her reasoning mouse cannot create the lyric illusion that was important to Romantic poetry – the illusion of the presence of the speaker and of the reality of the occasion. Barbauld's mouse is much more an abstraction, the "pensive captive" or "prisoner" who urges the commonplaces of this role, though mindful of a mouse's special smallness, pitifulness, and insignificance. The humor, force, and paradox of Barbauld's poem lie in attributing the pleas of a prisoner to a mouse in a cage.

Incidentally, unless we feel that Barbauld, as a woman, especially sympathized with an animal in a cage, the differences between the two poems do not reflect gender differences of the poets. Just what, in the ideology of the age, were thought to be typical differences between the sexes in mental capacities, character, and temperament, is a complicated, controversial question, but by any view then current Barbauld's poem would have been considered at least as "manly" as Burns's. Her mouse speaker is an intellectual; it cites ancient philosophy in arguing for the universality of mind and possibly for metempsychosis (lines 29–36), and praises the "philosophic mind" much as Wordsworth, using Barbauld's phrase, would later in his Immortality Ode. When it appeals to sentiment, it does so in an argumentative, didactic way:

> The chearful light, the vital air,
> Are blessings widely given;
> Let nature's commoners enjoy
> The common gifts of heaven.
>
> The well taught philosophic mind
> To all compassion gives;
> Casts round the world an equal eye,
> And feels for all that lives.
>
> (lines 21–28)

Though a ploughman, Burns's speaker is more personal, impulsive, and emotional.

Neither Barbauld nor Burns intuit divine life immanent within the small creature. Their naturalism differentiates their poems from many of the later, high Romantic poems on animals, though naturalism is not quite the right word for an attitude that mingles objective perception with sentiment and strong sympathy. If pantheistic, divine being is not in animals, one need not assume that they are happy, and one can freely see in them the fates of man. Thus Barbauld's mouse, alluding to the trap, remarks that "men like mice" may fall into "unseen destruction" (line 45), and Burns sighs that "The best laid plans o' Mice and Men, / Gang aft agley" (lines 39–40).

The ground of Burns's sympathy for animals is, to repeat, a feeling of shared existential suffering. The speaker is, he tells the mouse, its "poor, earth-born companion, / An' fellow-mortal" (lines 11–12). Would you call yourself the companion of your dog, or your dog the companion of you? The least that can be said of Burns's reversal of expectation is that it shows, as a gesture, the speaker's strong desire to put himself on the same level as the mouse and thus kindly to reassure it. Though rhyming with "Man's dominion," the word "companion" tends to belie it. Etymologically, the mouse is a companion (*com-panis*) in that it eats the speaker's bread – or grain. It is a companion because it lives in the same place and undergoes similar experiences. The adjective "poor" picks up all the senses in which the mouse is an object of pity – weak, impoverished, vulnerable, frightened, mortal – and carries these senses from the mouse to the speaker, who is no less mortal than the mouse, and is, as the final stanza reveals, full of apprehensions. The last word in the poem is "fear." (I note below that the speaker would also be poor in a material sense, though much less so than the mouse.) "Fellow mortal" is a variant of the usual term, "fellow man," and mobilizes similar connotations of sympathy, equality, and likeness. The word "mortal" in the place of "man" brings out that the likeness is not in kind but in fate.

"Earth-born" tends to close religious perspectives on existence, and they are not opened elsewhere in the poem. But to have denied human immortality would have been unusually defiant in Burns's time and materially unprofitable. Safely orthodox interpretation is not difficult. When Wordsworth spoke of himself, in "Resolution and Independence," as a "Child of earth," like a hare (line 31), and two years later, in "Intimations of Immortality," as "heaven-born" (line 122), he need not have seemed inconsistent, since a human being was both mortal and immortal. So also, in some opinions, were animals. There was a minor controversy over this point, and I describe it in a later chapter. Barbauld raises this question, and, as I read her poem, she leaves the answer open, and also leaves ambiguous whether even humans are immortal.

> Or, if this transient gleam of day
> Be *all* of life we share,
> Let pity plead within thy breast
> That little *all* to spare.
>
> (lines 37–40)

This may suggest that humans and mice share mortal life but only humans live hereafter, or, less probably, that for both species there is only "this transient gleam of day." In Burns's "To a Mouse," to assume that the "earth-born," "fellow-mortal" ploughman feels himself destined, like the mouse, only to earthly life makes a more radical, provocative, and pathetic poem.

Is the speaker a democrat? The question arises not simply because other lyrics by Burns were assertively democratic for their time: "The rank is but the guinea's stamp, / The Man's the gowd for a' that" ("Song – For a' that and a' that," 11, 762, lines 7–8). In the relations of animals and humans, the latter obviously exercise dominance, whether as hunters, farmers, drivers, or keepers of pets. This might be denied in poems that described dangerous, wild, or free animals, such as Blake's tiger, Shelley's skylark, or Mary Anne Browne's "The Wild Horse," and the power of such poems lies partly in the reversal of hierarchy. But the general dominance of man meant, as I noted, that poets could use animals to represent subordinated persons in the human social structure.

Hence a contemporary might well have seen in "To a Mouse" a benevolent attitude of the upper toward the lower, the rich toward the poor – a model of how dominion should be. Like most pleas of the age for reform through compassion, such a poem is addressed, obviously, to comparatively well-off readers, helps them to feel complacent, and poses no revolutionary threat. If the mouse figures the human poor, the power relations between the ploughman and the small, frail, pitiful animal are completely reassuring. The poem insists on the poverty of the mouse in its "housie" (line 19); the "wee-bit," "silly" nest with its rudimentary structure ("heap") and materials ("leaves an' stibble") figures the hapless creature as a wretched cottager. When the ploughman says the mouse is "turn'd out" from its house, he uses the verb that applied frequently in this age of enclosures to human tenants.[37] Like Goody Blake in Wordsworth's "Goody Blake and Harry Gill," the mouse is driven by necessity to steal (a nice touch in the poem rhymes "thieve" with "live"), and unlike Wordsworth's wealthy farmer, Harry Gill, Burns's sensitive ploughman understands and forbears. Not only will he never miss, he says, the small takings of the mouse, but he will "get a blessin wi' the lave (remainder)" (line 17), for if you give to the poor, you receive a blessing. Even when the ploughman affirms that he too is poor and a fellow-mortal, the statement implies hierarchy. For it is compassionate and reassuring only if said by a superior to an inferior. If said by the low to the high, it would be radically democratic, leveling. However poor the ploughman may be, he is obviously better off than the mouse, and thus can kindly afford to grant the mouse his "daimen-icker."

The final stanza of the poem has lately evoked contrasting responses. For Carol McGuirk the "conclusion contradicts the spirit of the poem," is illogical and self-pitying.[38] For Seamus Heaney it enacts a reversal, a sudden emergence to consciousness of the feeling of vulnerability. The mouse, says Heaney, "gradually becomes a sibylline rather than a sentimental element in the poem."[39] Identifying with the mouse, I wish that Burns had not written the stanza. In it the superior claims to be worse off than the inferior. He distances himself from the mouse by repeating a scientific commonplace of his time: humans, it was often said, are motivated by memory and foresight, while animals live only in the present – "The present only toucheth thee" (line 44).[40] In various writers this distinction served, somewhat inconsistently, to ground claims that animals are happier than humans and also that humans are superior to animals. In Burns the mock-envious turn contradicts lines 25–28 and also undermines the phrase "Mice and Men," in which it was asserted that both mice and men make "schemes" (line 39) for the future. As McGuirk asks, "if the 'present only' touches the field mouse, how can she have been said to have 'schemes.'"[41]

The phrase "mice and men" comes with such effect partly because it brings to mind and summarizes the parallels between these species as the poem has depicted them. In a formalist analysis, the phrase is one of several doublings ("grief an' pain," "snell an' keen," etc.) in the poem at lines 5, 24, 25, 31, 34, 35–36, 41, 48. In the structure of such phrases, the second term is either a repetition of the first ("house or hald" [dwelling]) or an intensifier ("guess an' fear"), and in either case the effect is to prolong and weight the adversity that the phrase names. Such spreading or intensifying of adversity reaches its climax in "mice and men," formally because of the alliteration, and thematically because the doubling joins kinds that are usually kept distinct, so that adverse vicissitude is seen as a universal fate.

Just this universalizing power has made Burns's lines proverbial:

> The best laid schemes o' Mice an' Men,
> Gang aft agley.

If the statement were only that human schemes go wrong, it would be banal. The inclusion of the alliterative mice converts mischance into something to which all existence is exposed, and thus raises broody, sublime emotions about the tragic way of things. And just this drains away the social/political implications raised earlier in the poem. If "fellow-mortal" means a fellow-ship in mortality, even the rich can be called "poor" in an existential sense. Thus in the career of Burns's poem, compassion for the mouse becomes pity for the poor, then pity for all existence, and finally is withdrawn from the mouse in order to be bestowed on the self.

III

Though age-old, the suffering of animals at the hands of humans gradually became visible, so to speak, in the course of the eighteenth century. Just why is a question that gradually this book tries to answer. We may notice at the start two recent suggestions. In an interesting essay, Norbert Elias interprets the effort to check violence to animals as a psychological extension of the same effort between human beings. "That the sensitivity with regard to violence came to affect animals was characteristic of the irradiation of feeling beyond the initial target which is a general feature of conscience-formation." The mitigating of violence between humans, Elias says, took place in connection with "the growth, or with the growing effectiveness of, the monopolization of physical force by the representatives of [the] country's central institutions." To limit violence in the struggles for political power was also desired, and was possible because in England the same social class formed the rival parties, which thus shared a basic consensus.[42] In an even broader speculation James Turner thinks that the developing ethos of kindness to animals is explainable, at least in part, by "the stresses of modernization" and particularly by the industrial revolution. This brought people from the agricultural world into cities, where they were less dependent on animals for their bread. It also fostered a greater sensitivity to suffering in general by creating new forms and occasions of it. These were felt as the old forms of suffering under the ancien régime had not been, for the latter had been accepted as natural.[43]

Once it began to be seen, the torment of animals was a constant, intimate, pervading fact that strongly motivated because it appalled. "The

imagination of a man of much sensibility," as John Lawrence put it, "is perpetually haunted with horrid ideas" of the torments inflicted on animals.[44]
I do not want to be gruesome, but the reader must have some sense of
this suffering. The simple fact that people depended on animals for trans-
port of themselves and their goods opens an immense vista of animal woe.
John Gay's *Trivia* (1716) describes a common scene in the London streets
throughout the eighteenth century and later:

> Here laden Carts with thundring Waggons meet,
> Wheels clash with Wheels, and bar the narrow Street;
> The lashing Whip resounds, the Horses strain,
> And Blood in Anguish bursts the swelling Vein.[45]

The American Quaker, John Woolman, refused to use stagecoaches when
he was traveling in England. He had learned from other Friends that their
fearful journeys often killed or blinded the horses. For the same reason
he would not use the public mails.[46] In 1809 Lord Erskine, speaking in
Parliament, alluded to the common sight of post "horses panting – what
do I say! Literally dying under the scourge."[47]

I quote a few contemporary reports of what went on. These were not
exceptional occurrences. Neither were they relatively hidden from most
eyes, as now are hog cities and hen batteries, habitat loss and environmental
pollution. Instead, they were routine happenings, familiar to everyone,
possibly your own acts. The *Every-Day Book*, a journal, recalled in 1835
"a common practice" between 1790 and 1800. Selling fruit, fish, and the
like through city streets, a costermonger drove a cart with a horse or, more
probably, a donkey. In order to drive it more easily,

the costermonger was accustomed to make wounds for the express purpose of
producing torture . . . On each side of the back bone, at the lower end, just above
the tail, he made an incision of two or three inches in length through the skin,
and beat into these incisions with his stick till they became open wounds, and
so remained, while the ass lived to be driven to and from market, or through the
streets of the metropolis.[48]

Scientific experiments on animals had long been common and had led
to important discoveries. When these involved vivisection, they might be
denounced in the strongest terms. Though a pleader for animal rights,
John Lawrence, to quote him again, allowed most human uses of animals
so long as the procedures were as kindly as possible. But vivisection, he
thought, was different. Granted that the "experimental tortures" are for "the
furtherance and improvement of science." They are morally intolerable.[49]
If we consider that the work merely of butchers was thought to foster in
them a brutal, socially dangerous state of mind, we can easily understand

that vivisectionists might be figures of horror – a doctor "more dreadful," said Samuel Johnson, "than the gout or stone."[50] The experiments were incomparably more painful than they now usually are because there was as yet no anesthesia. In the opinion of the *Monthly Review*, Albrecht von Haller had "produced more misery, by his experiments to distinguish irritability and sensibility, than all the tyrants that have existed from the creation of the world." Those who "busy themselves, for years together, in pouring aquafortis upon the brains of living animals, . . . should consider that misery is an evil in proportion to its degree, and not in proportion to the rank which the suffering animal is supposed to hold in the scale of beings."[51] There were no legal controls, and any amateur or crackpot could perform any experiment he liked so long as the victim was his property.[52] A common parlor demonstration of amateur scientists was to put a small animal under a bell jar and gradually exhaust the air with a vacuum pump.

For a hunting scene, one cannot do better than quote the famous wood-engraver, Thomas Bewick, who recollects the first time he felt a twinge of regret. The year would have been 1775, when Bewick was twelve years old, and

Caught the Hare in my Arms, while surrounded by the Dogs & the Hunters, when the poor terrified creature screamed out so pitously, like a child, that I would have given any thing to save its life; in this however I was prevented, for a Farmer, well known to me, who stood close by, pressed upon me & desired I would give her to him, & from his being better able (as I thought) to save its life, I complied with his wishes; this was no sooner done than he proposed, to those about him to have a 'bit more sport with her' and this was to be done by his first breaking one of its legs, and then again setting the poor Animal off, a little before the Dogs.[53]

In fox hunting it was important that foxhounds not turn aside to pursue a hare. Peter Beckford, in his celebrated *Thoughts Upon Hunting* (1781), which was used as an instruction manual, tells that to train the dogs a hare should be thrown into their pen and the dogs whipped as they approach it.[54] It was also necessary to teach dogs not to pursue sheep, and William Somerville, in *The Chase* (1735), a poem much praised by Beckford, explains that this might be done by tying a puppy to a ram. After this "horned companion" has butted the puppy for a while and dragged it "trembling o'er the rugged ground,"

> Then spare not thou
> The twining whip, but ply his bleeding sides
> Lash after lash, and with thy threatening voice,
> Harsh-echoing from the hills, inculcate loud
> His vile offence.[55]

The torments of the slaughterhouse and the kitchen may be represented by a passage from John Lamb, brother of Charles, on the preparation of eels for the table. It comes from a pamphlet John Lamb wrote to answer a celebrated speech in Parliament by William Windham, who, as I discuss below, opposed Lord Erskine's 1809 bill for the prevention of cruelty to animals.

> If an eel [were] ignorant of man's usual practice, he would conclude that the cook would so far use her reason as to cut off his head first [so that he would feel no pain] . . . but if the woman were immediately to stick a fork into his eye, skin him alive, coil him up in a skewer, head and all, so that in the extremest agony he could not move, and forthwith broil him to death . . . with what fearful indignation might he inveigh against the unfeeling metaphysician that . . . [opposed] the Cruelty Prevention Bill.[56]

The woes of every animal were similarly dwelt on, from the stags, foxes, hares, otters, and pheasants that were hunted; the wild birds whose nests were plundered or who themselves were trapped, caged, and often blinded to improve their singing; the horses, oxen, and donkeys that were overloaded, over ridden, over driven, whipped, goaded, and starved; the bulls, badgers, otters, and occasionally more exotic animals that were baited, and the dogs that were mauled in the process; the pigs, calves, lambs, turkeys, geese, and other animals that were slaughtered in ways that disregarded pain and sometimes with particular torments to improve their culinary appeal; and the animals in vivisection, in air pumps, and in other scientific experiments.[57]

IV

Until 1822, when Parliament passed a bill to "Prevent the Cruel Treatment of Cattle," there was almost no legal protection of animals, and even after this bill, there was uncertainty and legal controversy as to what animals were covered. In a shocking instance of wanton cruelty to a cow, in 1784, the judge had declared himself unable to interfere because, as Arthur Moss summarizes the case, "animals had no rights that the law could protect."[58] According to John Trusler, "in the year 1790, a fellow was convicted of lacerating and tearing out the tongue of a horse, but there being no evidence of his . . . doing it with a view to injuring [the owner], this diabolical wretch, not having violated any then existing statute, was discharged without punishment."[59] Abuse of animals could be punished under the common law, "usually as a common nuisance," Robert W. Malcolmson explains, but in the absence of a statute, prosecutions were rare.[60] Although struggles in Parliament and in the courts of law are not the subject of this study, I briefly summarize early debates in Parliament because they were a prominent part of the context of literary pleas for animal rights.

The first bill to be brought in Parliament was introduced by Sir William Pulteney in 1800 to end bullbaiting. In this "sport" a bull was chained to an iron ring and dogs were set upon it. Incidentally, the "bulldog" quality formerly claimed for the English character refers to the canines bred and trained for this sport. Once the dog had fixed its teeth in the bull, it held on until "either the Dog tears out the Piece he has laid Hold on, and falls, or else remains fix'd to him, with an Obstinacy that would never end, if they did not pull him off."[61] The baiting might continue, sometimes for days, until the bull died. In other instances the same bull would be baited in one town after another, with much profit to its owner, for you were proud of your dog, and would pay a fee to exercise it. You might even place a bet on it. Though in earlier centuries bullbaitings had entertained persons of all social ranks, by 1800 respectable persons were less likely to attend them. As I remarked in the Preface, they had long been criticized as occasions of drinking, gambling, and idleness. Sir William Pulteney appealed to this reprobation in introducing his bill: the "cruel and inhuman" practice "drew together idle and disorderly persons; it drew from their occupations many who ought to be earning subsistence for themselves and families. It created many disorderly and mischievous proceedings and furnished scenes of profligacy and cruelty."[62] But bullbaitings were age old, could be thought a traditional right, like fairs and other gatherings for pleasure of the common people, and were very much enjoyed by them in towns and villages. William Howitt reports that in 1800, after Parliament rejected the petitions to end bullbaiting, "nothing was so common as to see the bulls led through the villages adorned with ribbons, and bearing on their necks large placards of – 'SANCTIONED BY WYNDHAM AND PARLIAMENT.' "[63]

For Sir William Pulteney's bill had been formidably opposed in Parliament by William Windham and George Canning, two notables in Pitt's government. With the exception of Sheridan, Windham was "the ablest speaker in the House of Commons," according to William Hazlitt; his opinions, Hazlitt added, were predictably the opposite of common ones. "If a thing had been thought cruel, he would prove that it was humane; if barbarous, manly."[64] Both statesmen argued against interfering in the ancient customs of the people. The bill, they said, was an insult to the English character, for "cruelty, or the thirst of blood, is not in the nature nor in the habits of Englishmen."[65] Bullbaiting, they said, was not crueller than other practices, such as overdriving oxen, which it was not proposed to outlaw. In this connection they fell on hunting, the diversion of the rich, on which Sir William Pulteney's bill was silent. (For otherwise, its chances with the Parliamentary squires would have been nil.) If, said Canning, members were so protective of their own sports, why would they wish to outlaw the sports of the poor? Bullbaiting, he added, "inspired courage, and produced a nobleness of sentiment and elevation of mind."[66] The bill was defeated by two votes, even though, as George Nicholson remarks, "petitions in favour of it were signed by long lists of the most respectable names of the nobility, gentry, clergy, freeholders, and manufacturers, as well as magistrates."[67]

In a next try, in 1809, the "British Cicero," Lord Thomas Erskine, a Scottish lawyer, a supporter of the campaign against slavery, and a former Lord Chancellor, introduced a bill for the Prevention of Cruelties to Animals. There are several anecdotes from this time in which respectable persons check, reprimand, punish, or themselves beat a coachman or carter who was beating a horse. One such story, which may stand for all, is told of Lord Erskine, who saw, on a day when he was enjoying Hampstead Heath, "a ruffian beating a wretched horse, he promptly remonstrated and was met with the reply, 'Can't I do what I like with my own?' 'Yes,' was the prompt answer. 'And so can I; this stick is my own,' and, ignoring his judicial position and status at the bar, he thereupon gave the scoundrel a good thrashing."[68]

I believe these stories are mostly apocryphal, but the mere telling of them testifies to feelings that horses should not be beaten and that the hero intervenes. The rescuer in these anecdotes is always of higher social rank than the beater. That the beater can safely be beaten illustrates the awful power of class at this time. I return later to the idea, which was frequently stated, that the genteel and respectable were pure of cruelty while the lower orders were imbued with it. Moral and political zeal might be energized on behalf of animals by this idea, but it allowed opponents of animal rights to present themselves as champions of the people.

Lord Erskine's bill provided that "any person who shall maliciously wound or with wanton cruelty beat or otherwise abuse any horse, mare, ass or ox shall be deemed to be guilty of a misdemeanour."[69] Penalties under the bill would have fallen chiefly on coachmen, carmen, grooms, and agricultural laborers, on persons who managed work animals, and William Windham, again opposing the bill, was able to say that it "should be entitled, A Bill for harrassing and oppressing certain classes among the lower orders of the people." Windham argued that though cruelty to animals was deplorable, it was not a fit subject of legislation. The offense was not exactly definable. "You inflict pains and penalties, upon conditions which no man is able previously to ascertain." Windham again satirized the exclusion of hunting, by which the House of Commons "in its wild career of humanity" must exhibit itself "as the most hardened and unblushing hypocrites that ever shocked the feelings of mankind." Reform, he concluded, must be left to morality and social opprobrium.[70] The bill was defeated by ten votes.

When in 1822 Parliament passed a bill to prevent cruelty to cattle, Richard Martin, its introducer, could say that "there was not a pulpit in London that had not spoken in a pronounced manner in approbation" of the bill.[71] Martin, a colorful Parliamentarian from Ireland, tried again unsuccessfully to end bullbaiting and dogfights in 1823, tried but failed to protect dogs and cats in 1824, and tried unsuccessfully on behalf of horses in knacker's yards, though all these and other measures were passed in the course of the nineteenth century.[72] The Society for the Prevention of Cruelty to Animals was founded in 1824, and became the Royal Society under Victoria's patronage in 1840.

2

Grounds of argument

I

This chapter surveys the arguments that were made on behalf of animals two hundred years ago. They were similar to our own, and in some cases very dissimilar. Cruelty to animals had been condemned by moralists in classical antiquity, the middle ages, and the early modern period, though the reason was seldom sympathy for animals. The impulses it expresses were thought to be dangerous to society, to other human beings. Francis Hutcheson, professor of moral philosophy at Glasgow university, echoed the traditional statements in 1755: "frequent cruelty to brutes may produce such a bad habit of mind as may break out in like treatment of our fellows."[1] Thanks to John Locke, whose psychological theories were widely accepted, the argument acquired a developmental perspective. Giving close attention to the origin of ideas and attitudes in early experience, Locke urged that "Children should from the beginning be bred up in abhorrence of killing and tormenting any living creature . . . and indeed, I think people from their cradle should be tender to all sensible creatures." He saw a close connection between childish "Tormenting and Killing of Beasts" and adult hardness of heart toward our "own kind."[2]

Locke's writings helped inspire an unremitting stream of warnings: childish cruelty must not be tolerated, not to insects, not to birds, not to small animals, not to pets, not to each other. In Locke's time and long after, let us remember, schoolboys might bite off the heads of sparrows, tie cats together by the tail or set them on fire, regularly stage cockfights, celebrate Shrove Sunday by throwing sticks at roosters (magistrates were trying to suppress this by the 1760s), and even whip rams to death. To judge from the admonitions, equally heartless enjoyments might be allowed smaller children. For example, the *Monthly Review* summarized in 1767 an anonymous *Discourse concerning Compassion due to the Brute-Creation . . . designed for the Use of Little Children*:

Cruelty to any thing that God has endued with feeling, is the worst depravity of human nature; and it is always with inexpressible concern that we see the seeds of this vice thoughtlessly sown by unfeeling parents, nurses, &c. and habits of barbarity rooted in the tempers of infants, by giving them little animals, birds and insects, to play with, and torment, by way of amusement . . . and when they come to riper years, they too easily lay aside compassion, even when *their own species* are the objects of it.[3]

In the 1772 sermon I mentioned earlier, James Granger more pithily admonished his congregation that the Roman emperor Domitian "began with killing flies, before he made such a havoc of his own species."[4] In 1791 Mary Wollstonecraft translated the *Moralisches Elementarbuch* of Christian Gotthilf Salzmann (1744–1811), a German pedagogue who authored more than a hundred books and founded a philanthropic educational institute. In this work, which Wollstonecraft Englished as *Elements of Morality, for the Use of Children*, the young Charles catches a field mouse. He is going to cut off its ears and tail, but Mr. Jones intervenes. "Fie," he says, "For shame. He who can torment a little harmless animal, has certainly a bad heart. He accustoms himself by degrees to cruelty, and at last he will find a savage joy in it: and after tormenting animals, will not fail to torment men."[5] So also Joanna Baillie, in the 1826 pamphlet she wrote for Hampstead schoolchildren. "No girl who can prevent her brother . . . from such bad practices, should neglect to do so."

They may be the means of preserving them from after disgrace, and even from a shameful end: since children who have been accustomed to be cruel to animals, will, we may well suppose, feel less horror afterwards in wounding or murdering a fellow creature; and the histories and confessions of many miserable wretches, who have finished their lives upon a gallows, prove this to be the case.[6]

That children who torment animals come to a bad end was vividly illustrated by Hogarth in a sequence of four engravings entitled the "Stages of Cruelty" (1751). In these, as Baillie perhaps recollected, a cruel boy becomes a murderer as an adult, is hanged, and ends as a corpse dissected in an anatomy demonstration. Commenting on this sequence in 1800, John Trusler explained that the protagonist "began by torturing a helpless dog, he then beat out the eye of an unoffending horse, and now, under the influence of that malignant, rancorous spirit, which by indulgence is become natural, he commits murder." "These gradations," Trusler went on, "are natural, I had almost said inevitable; and that parent who discovers the germ of barbarity in the mind of a child, and does not use every effort to exterminate the noxious weed, is an accessory to the evils which spring from its baneful growth."[7] One might even recommend cruelty in order to extirpate it. In Dorothy Kilner's *Life and Perambulation of a Mouse* (1780), a story for children, the young Charles is severely beaten by his father for tying a mouse to a string and teasing a cat with it. (The involutions of cruelty in this story are dizzying – cat to mouse, child to cat, father to child – and again open a perspective on unconscious energies and motives that might be enlisted in the campaign for animals.)[8] George Nicholson, perhaps picking up an anecdote told by John Lawrence, suggested that if a boy were tearing a fly to pieces, "a few hairs jerked" from his head might have "the most durable effects," particularly if accompanied by reasonings.[9]

Hogarth designed his "Stages of Cruelty" to impress the common people, the lower classes. In families of higher rank, where contemporary literature for children was likely to be read, to threaten the gallows would have been extremely inappropriate, improbable, and insulting. In children's literature, then, a typical punishment is simply that the cruel child has no friends as an adult. Coleridge's Ancient Mariner suffers a similar social isolation, though in a more extravagant form. In Thomas Day's *History of Sandford and Merton* the fate of a particularly malicious boy leads Mr. Barlow to point the moral: "Nobody is loved in this world, unless he loves others and does good to them."[10] In Sarah Trimmer's *Fabulous Histories*, Edward plundered the nests of birds, threw cats from the roof, and tied a dog and cat together. He went on, at school, to torment younger boys. By the time he was an adult, he had become so self-centered, egoistic, and hard-hearted that he was "despised by all with whom he had any intercourse." He had never learned to sympathize.[11] Mary Wollstonecraft told a story about a man who was cruel to animals and taught his children to behave in the same way. "The consequence was, that they neglected him when he was old and feeble; and he died in a ditch."[12]

People who pleaded for kindness to animals insisted on their likeness to humans. For obviously – or so it seemed to many persons – the closer animals were to being human, the less one could hunt, pluck, and eat them with a good conscience. That there is an essential difference between humans and animals still was unquestionable to most thinkers, though there were skeptics. But science and philosophy were narrowing the gap and thus furnishing arguments to reformers.

In discussions of animal intelligence, the traditional superiority of human beings was affirmed, but there was difficulty in pin-pointing exactly what it was. Most scientific opinion in the eighteenth century agreed with John Locke that "Brutes have Ideas, and that they reason, tho' they are not capable of comparing and comprehending these ideas."[13] They form shorter trains of association, said David Hartley; in other words, their thoughts are less complex and more predictable.[14] Animals, it was said, have fewer ideas, less power of attention, and inferior memories, and David Hume added that they are less susceptible "of the pleasures or pains of the imagination."[15] They derive, said John Lawrence, "little or no benefit from analogies."[16] But such differences were not in kind of intelligence but only in degree, a point pressed by animal sympathizers such as Lawrence. "If by the term *instinct*," he declared, "we mean to convey any other idea than that of an inferior degree of reason, we have only contrived a veil to obscure the face of truth."[17] It was both more difficult and more necessary to locate a difference in kind, one that would radically separate human from animal intelligence. Lawrence, to cite him once more, was one of several persons who pointed out that "human reason ... [has] nearly as great inequality between man and man, as between man and beast."[18]

Many British philosophers also agreed with Locke that animals do not abstract from immediate experience and form general ideas. For this reason, Locke said, "they have no use of Words, or any other general Signs." These two points, general ideas and language, made for Locke the "perfect distinction" or "proper difference" between human and animal intelligence.[19] Animals, said David Hartley, partly repeating Locke, do not use "Symbols, such as Words, whereby to denote Objects, Sensations, Ideas, and Combinations of Ideas."[20] The same account of the matter satisfied Dugald Stewart in 1792: animals lack "those intellectual processes" that "imply the use of general terms. Those powers, therefore, which enable us to classify objects, and to employ signs as an instrument of thought, are ... peculiar to the human species."[21]

But David Hume reduced most reasoning to the associating of ideas; the process was the same in humans and animals.[22] As for general ideas, Erasmus Darwin, the learned grandfather of Charles, was delighted to point out in 1794–96 that "these abstracted ideas have been since demonstrated by Bishop Berkeley, and allowed by Mr. Hume, to have no existence, not even in the mind of their inventor [Locke], and we are hence necessitated to look for some other mark of distinction." Darwin located this in the relative incapacity of animals to form ideas of future pleasures and pains or to be motivated by such ideas. Lacking such motivation, Darwin slyly adds, animals do not learn languages, make tools, earn money, or pray "to the Deity, as another *means* to procure happiness."[23] No wonder some persons in the 1790s suspected that, as the *Monthly Review* put it, the superiority claimed for man was "founded on our predilection for a supposed distinction, that flatters our pride, rather than on a careful and accurate examination of the facts."[24]

When the topic was the emotions, the differences that were formerly clear between baleful, lustful, ferocious brutes and human beings evanesced. Similarities in the emotional nature of humans and animals would have seemed especially significant in an age when human merit or greatness was increasingly located in emotional capacities. Literary works habitually attributed human emotions to animals. So also did keepers of pets, of whom the number was increasing mightily. They had backing from scientific and philosophical opinion. David Hartley maintained that many species "have most of the eminent Passions in some imperfect Degree," and "there is, perhaps, no Passion belonging to human Nature, which may not be found in some Brute Creature in a considerable degree."[25] David Hume also perceived a "correspondence of *passions* in men and animals," as well as of the "*causes*, which produce those passions." He noticed that animals are capable of love, fear, anger, and grief, and added that "envy and malice are passions very remarkable in animals. They are perhaps more common than pity; as requiring less effort of thought and imagination."[26] Though no philosopher or scientist, William Wordsworth may be cited as typical of those who went all the way in idealizing animal emotion. He maintained that though animals lack "the faculty of reason," they share with humans "the principle of love."[27]

Partly by means of vivisection, the bodily structures and physiology of higher animals were increasingly found to resemble human ones. As knowledge became more detailed, so did the physical correspondences. Vegetarians seized on these facts to argue that since humans have teeth similar to monkeys, and intestines not very different from orang-utans, they could very well subsist on vegetables, as apes and monkeys do.[28] With so many physical likenesses, the argument for psychological, moral ones became more compelling. Erasmus Darwin summed up:

If we turn our eyes upon the fabric of our fellow animals, we find they are supported with bones, covered with skins, moved by muscles; that they possess the same senses, acknowledge the same appetites, and are nourished by the same aliment with ourselves; and we should hence conclude from the strongest analogy, that their internal faculties were also in some measure similar to our own.[29]

That animals feel pain is regularly urged in arguments for animal rights, and the fact was strongly pressed two hundred years ago, the more strongly, perhaps, because it was still necessary to refute Descartes's opinion to the contrary. The point is said or implied in many of the passages I have quoted.

But if animals do feel pain, it became for some persons a moral duty not wantonly to inflict it. Jeremy Bentham's statement in his *Principles of Morals and Legislation* is the classic, much-quoted one: "The French have already discovered that the blackness of the skin is no reason why a human should be abandoned without redress to the caprice of a tormentor. It may come one day to be recognized, that the number of the legs, the villosity of the skin, or the termination of the *os sacrum*, are reasons equally insufficient for abandoning a sensitive being to the same fate . . . The question is not, can they reason? nor, Can they *talk*, but, Can they *suffer?*"[30] "Why should the law refuse its protection to any sensitive being?" Bentham asks in his *Principles of Penal Law*. "We have begun by attending to the condition of slaves; we shall finish by softening that of all the animals which assist our labours or supply our wants."[31]

Bentham speaks as a Utilitarian, and his philosophy includes two premises that were and still are important in the plea for animal rights. One is simply that pain is an evil. The other is that an ethical act is one that seeks the greatest total happiness of *all* those whose interest is in view. The next step, of course, would be to include the happiness of animals in this calculation. Thomas Young's statement was typical: a "constant and inviolable rule of action" should be that of increasing "the quantity of pleasure in the world, and diminishing that of pain." In carrying this into practice, a person should not "overlook one created thing that is endowed with faculties capable of perceiving pleasure and pain."[32]

Many persons shared or partly shared these premises without being Benthamites. In Humphry Primatt's 1776 discourse on the *Duty of Mercy and Sin of Cruelty to Beasts*, "Pain is pain, whether it be inflicted on man or on beast; and the creature that suffers it, whether man or beast, being sensible of the misery of it while it lasts, suffers *Evil*."[33] George Nicholson, the vegetarian printer of Stourport, echoed Primatt: "Pain is pain, whether inflicted on man or beast; the endurance of it is an evil; and the being who communicates evil is guilty."[34] In Mary Wollstonecraft's *Original Stories* for children, Mrs. Mason asks the girls, "Do you know the meaning of the word Goodness? . . . I will tell you. It is, first, to avoid hurting any thing; and then, to contrive to give as much pleasure as you can."[35] In Percy Shelley's *Prometheus Unbound*, the moment of moral resurrection and apocalypse arrives when the suffering Titan can say, "I wish no living thing to suffer pain."[36]

To Christian minds, cruelty to animals might seem literally devilish, hell being the place where pain is deliberately inflicted. I mentioned that James Granger called England "the Hell of Horses," and so did others also – it was a common saying. Coming from an eighteenth-century clergyman, however, the words have a force of accusation they would lack today. For the Gothic imagination in novels, cruelty to animals might be a trait of the accursed. In Henry Brooke's *The Fool of Quality*, we meet a dying man on whose face was written "all the malignity and horrors of hell." As a child, he "took a heart-felt pleasure in dismembering flies and impaling worms on pins." As a schoolboy, he tortured cats and dogs. "As I grew in stature," he says, quoting Milton's Satan, "Evil became my good." On his walks he "stabbed the cattle of the neighbours in the belly or fundament" with his cane, "and chuckled to see them leap, and kick, and plunge about in their agonies."[37]

What about the moral character of animals? Since moral philosophies had such various premises in England at this time, the answers to this question might be opposite. At one extreme, Mary Wollstonecraft, though strongly in favor of kindness to animals, maintained that their behaviour is merely instinctive: "Every affection, and impulse, which I have observed in them, are like our inferior emotions, which do not depend entirely on our will, but are involuntary; they seem to have been implanted to preserve the species." From this point of view, animals were incapable of morality, which required free will, at least in Wollstonecraft's quite traditional opinion. Animals, she said, could not "do good, or acquire virtue."[38] At an opposite pole, in Hume's analysis, morality more or less became sympathy, feeling with others, which, said Hume, animals abundantly illustrate. Animals at play "most carefully avoid harming their companion, even tho' they have nothing to fear from his resentment; which is an evident proof of the sense brutes have of each other's pain and pleasure. Every one has observ'd how much more dogs are animated when they hunt in a pack, than when they pursue their game apart; and 'tis evident this can proceed from nothing but sympathy."[39] At one point Hume seems to argue that human beings must be capable of "disinterested benevolence" because animals are.[40]

At a more popular level, virtues were habitually attributed to animals. Buffon's great *Histoire Naturelle* was the basis of several natural histories in England: translations by Kenrick and Murdoch in 1775–76 and in seven volumes by William Smellie in 1780; redactions by Oliver Goldsmith in his *History of the Earth and Animated Nature* (1774), by Thomas Pennant in his *History of Quadrupeds* (1781), and by Thomas Bewick's partner, Ralph Beilby, in their *General History of Quadrupeds* (1790). In these works the various creatures were described seriatim, and along with the looks, habits, environment, and so forth of the animal, there was also a characterization, including the moral qualities of the animal. Thus one may learn that the donkey is gentle, patient, and persevering, the stag noble, the dog faithful, and so forth, nor were the moral failings of animals overlooked. The domestic cat, says Buffon, is lazy, cowardly, and dishonest.[41] Among the virtues of horses, John Lawrence listed "fortitude, patience, generosity, obedience, [and] a limited sense of justice."[42] Authors of children's literature acclaimed the moral virtues of animals as examples to their small readers. Sarah Trimmer, for example, pointed out that robins are not gluttons.[43] *Goody Two-shoes* (1766) noted the example set by rooks in rising early.[44] Poets, of course, spoke a similar language. William Hayley's *Ballads Founded on Anecdotes of Animals* (1805), for which William Blake supplied engravings, illustrated surprising virtues in various creatures. We have heard Byron on the virtues of the dog Boatswain. In "Fidelity" Wordsworth celebrated a dog who had stayed alone for three months by the body of his dead master.

> How nourished here through such long time
> He knows who gave that love sublime;
> And gave that strength of feeling, great
> Above all human estimate![45]

That animals have souls was now assumed, in opposition to Descartes, by most people who thought about the question.[46] As the immaterial center of thought and emotion, the spiritual substance that determines action, souls had traditionally been attributed to animals from classical times. The usual commonplaces about souls that were current in the eighteenth century can be reviewed in Samuel Colliber's *Free Thoughts Concerning Souls* (1734), though I warn that this is not a lively book. On animal souls in particular, the longest, most thoughtful discussion was in French: David-Renaud Boullier, *Essai Philosophique sur L'Âme des Bêtes* (1728). As in the passage from Erasmus Darwin that was quoted earlier, new arguments from vivisection could now be applied to traditional questions, and in addition to the usual considerations, Boullier infers "the existence of the soul in animals by the analogy of their bodies with the human body. The admirable structure of their organs can have no other end except to lodge an immaterial soul, and to be for this soul the principle of sensation and the instrument of action."[47]

A soul might not be immortal, but, as we saw in Barbauld's "The Mouse's Petition," the question of animal immortality was discussed. In his *Essay on Man*, Alexander Pope introduced "a poor Indian, whose untutored mind" supposed his dog would follow him to heaven.[48] Pope kept dogs as pets, and might have been the Indian, for he remarked to Spence that dogs must have souls "as imperishable in their nature as ours . . . where would be the harm in allowing them immortality."[49] John Hildrop's 1742 *Free Thoughts upon the Brute Creation*, one of the earliest pleas for animal rights, had been written against Father Bougeant, a French Jesuit, who denied to animals reason and an immortal soul. John Wesley believed animals had a life after death. So did Bishop Joseph Butler, whom Coleridge, though disagreeing on this point, would later describe as one of "the three greatest, nay, only three *great* Metaphysicians which this Country *has* produced."[50] Grieving for a dead spaniel, Robert Southey declared that "there is another world / For all that live and move – a better one!"[51]

For this belief the major arguments, as contrasted with sentimental wishes, referred to the justice of God, His perfect goodness. Rationalizing theology in the eighteenth century could infer the immortality of human souls without biblical revelation, and the same arguments were cogent for animals. William Wollaston, for example, observed that the world bursts with innocent suffering: "how can we acquit the *justice* and *reasonableness* of that Being . . . if there be no *future state* where the proper amends may be made."[52] Wollaston does not mention animals, but others pointed out that their innocent lives may also contain a huge excess of pain over pleasure. Richard Dean, a clergyman, tried to prove animal immortality from the Bible, relying on such passages as Romans 8. 21 and Isaiah 65. 25. But in his *Essay on the Future Life of Brute Creatures* (1768) he also used the rationalist argument: animals suffer in this world; if they are not compensated in the next world, "I know not whether we shall not be obliged to . . . impeach the divine Goodness."[53] This also was Wesley's argument.[54] As late as 1824, in his *Scriptural and Philosophical Arguments . . . that Brutes Have Souls*, Peter Buchan was swayed by this point: a just God must recompense "undeserved pain," and therefore must have appointed "a future state" for animals.[55]

But like other ideas that weakened the distinction between humans and animals, the immortality of animal souls was objectionable on emotional, moral, and religious grounds as well as on practical, economic ones. One danger may be seen in David Hume's "Of the Immortality of the Soul," where the similarities between human and animal souls were deployed in a skeptical sense. "The souls of animals are allowed to be mortal; and these bear so near a resemblance to the souls of men that the analogy from one to the other forms a very strong argument."[56] This is probably why, when Richard Dean's book was mentioned in conversation by a "gentle-man" (presumably Boswell), Samuel Johnson "discouraged this talk" and was "offended at its continuation."[57] Such talk activated doubts always latent in Johnson about the immortality of humans. For Samuel Taylor Coleridge, who maintained that the truth of immortality is known by self-awareness, the possession of this idea helped constitute the humanity in human beings in contradistinction to animals.[58] Even "a common man would startle at hearing talk of the *Souls* of Brutes: for he connects with the word the faculty of Self-consciousness, and (on the strength of this) believes in immortality."[59]

Those who denied animal immortality of course countered the arguments from the justice and goodness of God. Boullier, whom I mentioned earlier, was a Protestant pastor in Amsterdam. He had been active in London for several years, and may have become interested there in the question of animal immortality. His book on animal souls was his first publication, and won him considerable reputation, though he was known chiefly for his later attacks on Voltaire and the *philosophes*. In his book he concedes that the argument for animal immortality has force. Animals suffer, they are innocent, and "what is worse, their soul dies with their body; this is what doubles the difficulty . . . It seems that every hypothesis that attributes feeling to animals strikes at two attributes essential to the Supreme Being, goodness and justice."[60] But God, says Boullier, being free, is not constrained to produce perfect happiness for all existence. "The correct idea of a good God" is that "when he acts, he tends always to the good; it is that there is no creature from his hands who does not win from existence more than it loses from it . . . I am persuaded that whoever could penetrate the interior of animals would find there a compensation of pains . . . that would turn all to the glory of divine Goodness."[61] With this faith Boullier extricates himself from his difficulty. He concludes that animal souls can act only through a body and must perish with it. Some English considerers maintained that in a total and a long view there is an overbalance of happiness over suffering in animal lives, and for them, as for Boullier, this saved the justice of God. Besides, said T. R. Malthus, animal suffering "is but as the dust of the balance in comparison of the happiness that is communicated" to the whole system of creation.[62] Boswell, in the passage I quoted, calls animal immortality a "curious speculation," and no doubt for most people it was merely that. It was not confined to the intelligentsia. E. P. Thompson describes a discussion among the Muggletonians, a Dissenting sect, in which it was concluded that beasts do not "partake in the Last Ascension."[63]

Thus in the advanced thought of the time the bodies, minds, emotions, morals, and even souls of animals might be kin to the human. Should we not, then, apply the golden rule of Matthew 7. 12 to animals? "Our sympathy," said George Nicholson, should "be strongly and zealously exerted in their favour; we should never violate their rights, never make warfare against or injure them, compassionate their sufferings, relieve their wants, cultivate harmony and peace, and exchange good offices with them, as humanity, morality, and Christianity enjoins."[64]

But Nicholson, who was a vegetarian, was more committed and fervent than most animal sympathizers. We shall see again and again that the cause of animals was seldom urged without reservations. For those who were not hunters, cockers, baiters, or horse racers, a strong limiting consideration was what may broadly be called economics. "They pity and they eat the objects of their compassion," Goldsmith's Citizen of the World reported of the English.[65] This dilemma checked enthusiasm for animal rights.

The literature for children that urged sympathy for animals also taught, usually, that their souls do not live hereafter. This was, to repeat, the majority opinion, and, moreover, this literature stressed that in the hereafter the soul would be judged. If animals were incapable of moral choice, how could this be said of them? In *The Life and Perambulation of a Mouse*, Dorothy Kilner wrote that "animals having no souls to survive in another world, may without any crime be put to death, whenever it is necessary either for the food or convenience of man."[66] The well-known publisher of books for children, John Newbery, made the same argument in *The Mosaic Creation* (1749): animals do not have "a Fund of Knowledge to attain; and a Path marked out by the ALMIGHTY to lead them to Eternal Happiness."[67] As editor of *The Guardian of Education*, Sarah Trimmer was in the business of advice for parents, and in her tale of Dicky, Flapsy, and Pecksy, the three young robins, she held the same line: Harriet should not grieve for dead animals, says Mrs. Benson, for "we are taught to think their sufferings end with their lives, as they are not religious beings; and therefore the killing them, even in the most barbarous manner, is not like murdering a human creature, who is perhaps unprepared to give an account of himself at the tribunal of heaven."[68]

Authors such as Trimmer were educating their child readers to live in the society and economy that was, rather than in Utopia. In her *Fabulous Histories* Trimmer has Mrs. Benson conduct her children to an exemplary farm, one that reconciled kindness with economic exploitation. The visit, which goes on for forty pages, was full of instruction in many departments. The bees, for example, furnish useful lessons, as they always have, and Mrs. Benson finds "something very wonderful . . . in the strong attachment these little creatures have to their sovereign, and very instructive too . . . What say you, Frederick, would you fight for your king? Yes, mamma" (p. 165). More to my point, however, is that Farmer Wilson's wife, a curate's daughter, had been taught "the Christian doctrine of universal charity, which she exercised, not only towards the human species, but also to poultry" (p. 156). It turns out that Mrs. Wilson does not kill the chickens herself, but pays someone else to do it; moreover, she does not shut them up to fatten "any longer than I can help," and she uses "no cruel methods of cramming them" (p. 159). There is no more mistreatment on this farm than market forces require.

The plea on behalf of animals was part of a much broader civilizing, educative, and disciplinary effort. Which brings me to some large, familiar themes in intellectual and cultural history. Though much discussed, they cannot be completely omitted here, for they influenced attitudes to animals. In the writing and preaching of the age, a relatively new ideal of humanity emerged. Stern virtues of the past, such as courage and duty, were admired, but intellectuals now also extolled sympathy, compassion, the person who felt with and for others, who was benevolent not only because it is right but because of a sensitive, tender nature. Robert Burns, for example, waxed indignant because a hare, "probably a Parent, perhaps the mother," had been shot: "to leave two little helpless nurslings to perish with hunger amid the pitiless wilds, such an action is not only a sin against the letter of the law, but likewise a deep crime against the *morality of the heart*."[69] He wrote a poem about it. Among the innumerable exemplars in novels, Henry Brooke's *Fool of Quality* may be cited again. As a boy he found one day that his favorite rooster had been carried off to be the target at a cock-throwing. Coming to the rescue, Henry made his way "through the assembly, perceived his cock, at some distance, tied to a short stake, and a lad prepared to throw at him with a stick." Protecting his bird, Henry was himself hit. When asked why he risked himself, he replied, "Why Sir, because he [the bird] loved me."[70]

The new ideal of humanity claimed two endorsements of tremendous ideological power. It was said to be natural and, as the endorsement of history, it was said to be modern. It is natural, wrote Lord Shaftesbury, "to love and to be kind." It is not natural "to delight in the Torture and Pain of other Creatures . . . of our own or of another Species . . . to feed, as it were, on Death, and be entertain'd with dying Agony; this . . . is wholly and absolutely unnatural, as it is horrid and miserable."[71] To claim the endorsement of nature is important at any time, but it was especially so in the Romantic age, when the "natural" became a source and criterion of the good.

Cruelties to animals were said to be not only unnatural but also anachronistic, atavistic, characteristic of an unenlightened past. Hence they were termed savage. But by far the favored term, used almost as a code, was "barbarian." A barbarian was outside the pale of civilization. From the standpoint of civilized modernity, one could feel superior to barbarians even if they were socially upper class, such as the hunting gentry. The word was especially resonant because the precedent of ancient Rome was so much in mind.

II

In a post-Freudian, post-Holocaust age, the arguments from human nature and historical progress have lost much of their force. But the most powerful and usual argument in the Romantic age, now probably the weakest, was drawn from religion, and to it I now attend. Two hundred years ago arguments about animal rights referred habitually to religion. To a present-day reader, this is one of the more striking things about them. By religion I do not mean the churches, for though individual clergymen spoke out, the church and the great majority of the sects did not take a position on animal rights. The most important exception might be found in Methodism; Wesley urged his preachers to be kind to their own animals and to teach kindness to their hearers.[72]

The Bible, for many persons the dictated or inspired word of God, was, of course, the ultimate source of authority for most believers, and it was combed for instruction on how to treat animals. Whoever wishes to know just which passages could be cited can refer to the sermon I mentioned in chapter 1 by James Plumptre, which takes up almost all of them. Undeniably God had given man dominion over the animals (Genesis, 1. 26), but there was nothing to suggest that humans should be harsh or uncaring. After the flood He had made His covenant not only with Noah but with the animals also (Genesis 9. 12), and this surely implied His concern for them. There were regulations in Deuteronomy (22. 4, 6) that enjoined kindness to cattle and to nesting birds; Balaam's ass (Numbers 22. 21–34) had seen the angel when Balaam could not; Job (17. 14) had said "to the worm, Thou art my mother, and my sister"; Christ had ridden an ass into Jerusalem (Mark 11. 1–7) and been born among beasts in a stable. And so forth.

As an example of the earnestness and ingenuity brought to bear in interpreting such passages, we may view William Paley wrestling with the vegetarian question: is it right for humans to eat animals? Meat eating was often numbered among the consequences of Original Sin. God had certainly authorized our feeding on animals (Genesis 9. 3), but this had not been until after the flood, and it was no less certain, as Paley read his Bible, that man in paradise had lived only on vegetables (Genesis 1. 29). Might greens be preferable in God's eyes? Thus Paley was interested in knowing what the antediluvians ate, those persons who had lived between the Fall and the flood, and, so far as the Bible informs, had not yet been given permission to eat animals. "Whether they actually refrained from the flesh of animals, is another question. Abel, we read, was a keeper of sheep; and what purpose he kept them for, but to eat, is hard to say (unless it were sacrifices): might not, however, some of the stricter sects among them [the antediluvians] be scrupulous, as to this point; and might not Noah and his family be of this description; for it is not probable that God would publish a permission to authorise a practice which had never been disputed?"[73] Because its texts and their interpretations were discrepant, the Bible, though continually referred to, could not weigh more on one side than the other in questions of animal rights.

With the rationalizing theology of the age the story is quite different, for this line of thought projected upon God moral ideals of reasonableness and benevolence. "Besides, these creatures, insignificant as they appear in your estimation, were made by God as well as you . . . How then can you expect that God will send his blessing upon you, if instead of endeavouring to imitate him in being merciful to the utmost of your power, you are wantonly cruel to innocent creatures which he designed for happiness?"[74] So, in Sarah Trimmer's *Fabulous Histories* (1786) Mrs. Benson reproves Miss Lucy Jenkins, a visiting ten-year-old who had neglected to feed some young birds – chicks wickedly taken from their nests by her brother. Mrs. Benson's remarks were commonplaces, repeated over and over in treatises, sermons, pamphlets, poems, and literature for children such as Trimmer's very popular book. But in no other age could these ideas have seemed so obvious – for example, that animals are innocent, that God designed them for happiness, and that He will punish cruelty to them.

I do not in the least suggest that the religious views about to be described prevailed in most households. The diversity of religious belief and experience in Great Britain between 1775 and 1820 defies summary. In his fine survey of English social history in the eighteenth century, Roy Porter quotes Defoe: "each man goes his own byway to heaven," although, of course, Porter makes clear that this was not the whole story either.[75] The ideas Mrs. Benson implies about God were held by intellectuals, but by no means all intellectuals; they were derived from some lines among others in the religious thought of the eighteenth century. They were, however, newer, more modern ideas about God and His relation to His creation. They were communicated in sermons, newspapers, poems, and the like. They seeped into the minds of readers and mixed, often illogically, with other beliefs. Whether or not Sarah Trimmer had read John Locke, Samuel

Clark, Matthew Tindal, William Wollaston, the Earl of Shaftesbury, and other shapers of these ideas, I do not know. She would not have needed to. For the intelligentsia and, to some extent, for readers generally, such thoughts were in the air.

Let us, for the moment, assume with Coleridge's Ancient Mariner, that "the dear God who loveth us, / He made and loveth all" (lines 616–17). Why a person might believe this in the Romantic age may be deferred till later. If one believed, what should follow for attitudes and behavior? Thomas Paine, for one, gave the answer in *The Age of Reason* (1793): "the moral duty of man consists in imitating the moral goodness and benefi-cence of God, manifested in the creation toward all his creatures."[76] "Like his great Creator," said James Granger, the righteous man "extends his benevolence to the brute creation."[77] Since the mere "Light of Nature," as Thomas Young held, reveals that "the Creator wills the happiness of these his creatures . . . humanity towards them is agreeable to him, and cruelty the contrary."[78] In *Keeper's Travels in Search of His Master* (1799), a story for children that was much read for almost a century, Edward Augustus Kendall made a further claim: humans should "acknowledge the Rights; instead of bestowing their Compassion upon the creatures, whom, with themselves, God made, and made to be happy."[79]

Thus cruelty to animals could be described as impious. Persons who urged kindness to animals did not typically believe in a God of wrath and vengeance, but He was just. "Man may dismiss compassion from his heart, / But God will never," Cowper wrote in *The Task*, and whoever showed no mercy to animals would himself "seek it, and not find it."[80] Sometimes this rhetoric became alarming. Blake's Thel knew "That God would love a Worm . . . and punish the evil foot / That wilful bruis'd its helpless form," and there is Blake's much quoted couplet in *Auguries of Innocence*: "A Robin Red breast in a Cage / Puts all Heaven in a Rage."[81] We have learned to read Blake's personal associations and symbolism into his words, but should not ignore the literal threat. In the anonymous sermon against the Shrovetide sport of throwing at roosters, it was spelled out that "Had the good Being never revealed his Will [in the Bible], . . . yet plain Reason might have evinced, that wantonly to destroy" animals, "or put them to unnecessary Torment must be displeasing to him . . . Clemency to the inferior Animals is a Duty from us as we are Men, and particularly as we are Christians," and "our Happiness in the future World depends in some Measure on our practice of it."[82] In *The Rights of Animals and Man's Obligation to Treat Them with Humanity* (1838), William Drummond waxed terrorizing: "to injure, to abuse, to maim, torture, or inflict upon them [animals] any pain which can be avoided, is to act in opposition to the will of Heaven, and rise in rebellion against his Maker," the sin of Satan.[83] The same threats were habitually directed to children. Sarah Trimmer: "whoever wantonly destroys" the happiness of animals "acts contrary to the will of his Maker"; Edward Kendall: "none but the wicked would dare to insult any of the creatures of God."[84]

The argument that God intends the happiness of *all* his creatures was, if you believed it, the most compelling one in the Romantic age for kindness to animals. In the boxing terms of the era, the argument might not be a "settler," but it was at least a "facer." It made you pause. It put you on the defensive. If we ask what sort of person typically believed it, no precise answer can be given. Several of the persons quoted in the last couple of paragraphs were political radicals who also harbored radical thoughts on other topics. But Granger, Cowper, and Trimmer were generally of the center, and the latter two were influential shapers of opinion. The argument was repeated over and over in the literature of animal rights.[85]

It presupposed a particular description of God's being and attributes and a set of inferences from this description. The idea of God that is convergingly set forth in the eighteenth century by rationalizing theology, sentimental preference, and the great argument from evidences of design in nature has been the subject of many scholarly studies, and there is no need to rehearse this familiar development at length. Sentimental assumptions and rational arguments could join to show that since God is a perfectly good being, He must wish the happiness of all beings. As Thomas Reid told his students at the University of Edinburgh in 1780, "Goodness, Mercy & forbearance are evidently implied in a perfect moral character, for without it we can conceive no moral character whatever." Therefore, the laws of the universe must be and are "fitted to promote the interest of his creatures & to give all that degree of happiness of which their several natures are capable."[86]

A major development in religious thought was the elaboration, through empirical study of the natural world, of the traditional argument from design. Observation of nature proved the existence of a Creator and at least some of the Creator's attributes. When stated in smug, popular ways, the argument from evidences of design in nature was easy to parody and laugh away. But when carefully stated, even so powerful a logician as Kant found it almost impossible to resist, though Kant believed he had refuted it. Few persons yet thought that species had evolved under the pressure of natural selection. Each species, it seemed, and each organ and instinct of a species, must have originated in a separate act of creation. Hence one

could infer a Creator, and the marvelous intricacy and functional effectiveness of the designs in nature proved His power and intelligence. I quote
Cleanthes in David Hume's *Dialogues Concerning Natural Religion*, which
was first published in 1779, three years after Hume's death: "Look round
the world . . . The curious adapting of means to ends, throughout all nature, resembles exactly, though it much exceeds, the productions of human
contrivance – of human design, thought, wisdom, and intelligence. Since
therefore the effects resemble each other, we are led to infer, by all the rules
of analogy, that the causes also resemble, and that the Author of Nature is
somewhat similar to the mind of man."[87] Whether Hume himself accepted
this argument is uncertain. Perhaps he allowed it to prove the existence,
power, and intelligence of God but not His so-called moral attributes – His
goodness, His benevolence.

However, for more than two hundred years, through William Paley's
Natural Theology (1802), which marks more or less the culmination of this
discourse, the benevolence of God was evidenced by study of nature. The
method of argument was to describe, often with lavish detail, the physical
character and functioning of an organ or bodily part of humans or animals,
to point out the necessity or use of this part for the creature, and hence
to infer God's care for the creature, for its well-being. Paley describes eyes,
ears, joints, and so on for pages. For brevity I quote him on the "oil with
which *birds* preen their feathers . . . On each side of the rump of birds is
observed a small nipple, yielding upon pressure a butter-like substance,
which the bird extracts by pinching the pap with its bill. With this oil or
ointment, thus procured, the bird dresses his coat."[88] In this and the "vast
plurality of instances in which contrivance is perceived," it "is *beneficial*"
to the animal.[89] Lord Erskine more briefly assured Parliament that God
had provided for every creature "organs and feelings for its own enjoyment
and happiness."[90] E. A. Kendall thought that "the colors and stripes upon
seeds" and the "ornaments of flowers" had been created for the convenience
and aesthetic satisfaction of birds and insects.[91]

The argument also called attention to the beauty of the natural creatures
as the work of God. Among the various writers on animal rights, William
H. Drummond especially developed the aesthetic argument. Drummond
dwelt on the intricate structure of animals and on the appeal of their forms
and colors to the senses. His point, of course, is that one does not wantonly
destroy what is so marvelously made.[92] In Coleridge's "Rime of the Ancient
Mariner," the happiness and beauty of the creatures became a motive for
loving and blessing:

O happy living things! no tongue
Their beauty might declare:
A spring of love gushed from my heart,
And I blessed them unaware.

(lines 282–85)

The whole weight of the argument from design lies behind this moment of feeling.

Moreover, God had often made gratuitous provisions for creatures, that is, He had given more than mere existence would require. In Hume's *Dialogues Concerning Natural Religion*, Philo somewhat anticipates the subsequent argument of natural selection: "no form ... can subsist unless it possess those powers and organs requisite for its subsistence; some new order or economy must be tried, and so on, without intermission, till at last some order which can support and maintain itself is fallen upon." To this Cleanthes replies by pointing to the generosity of the "economy": "But according to this hypothesis, whence arise the many conveniences and advantages which men and all animals possess? Two eyes, two ears are not absolutely necessary for the subsistence of the species ... Though the maxims of nature be in general very frugal, yet instances of this kind are far from being rare; and any one of them is a sufficient proof of design – and of a benevolent design – which gave rise to the order and arrangement of the universe."[93] Paley makes the same argument. Capacities that "according to the established course of nature, ... must have been given, if the animal" was to exist at all, do not "prove the goodness of God." But "there is a class of properties which may be said to be superadded from an intention expressly directed to happiness – an intention to give a happy existence ... capacities for pleasure in cases wherein, so far as the conservation of the individual or of the species is concerned, they were not wanted, or wherein the purpose might have been secured by the operation of pain."[94] Paley mentions the pleasures of eating as an example.

Neither Paley nor most others who pursued this line of thought maintained that God's sole purpose in making animals was their happiness. The argument from design did not contradict the traditional belief that at least some animals were created for the use and benefit of man, that is, presumably, so that they could be eaten, be made to pull carriages, and so forth.[95] But as had long since been pointed out, God created many animals of which man can make no use, animals, even, of which we have no knowledge. In *Evenings at Home*, John Aikin and Letitia Barbauld explained to their child readers that "there are vast tracts of the earth where few or no men inhabit, which are yet full of beasts, birds, insects, and all living things. These certainly do not exist for [man's] use alone." Asking why, then, they were made, these authors reply simply that "they are made to be happy."[96]

Thus it was possible to think that God produced animals primarily for His own sake or for theirs. I am touching on what A. O. Lovejoy called "the principle of plenitude," the idea that it belongs to the perfection of God to create all kinds of living things that are possible. Along with its correlate, the great Chain of Being – that is, the hierarchical, continuous scale of beings from the lowest to God – the idea of plenitude had, said Lovejoy, its "widest diffusion" in the eighteenth century.[97] These ideas tended to undermine the supposition that man is the center and purpose of creation, and so, more indirectly, did the idea, as Aikin and Barbauld go on, that "the Creator equally desires the happiness of all his creatures, and looks down with as much benignity upon these flies that are sporting around us, as upon ourselves."[98]

Paley and those who thought as he did were led by their religious reasoning to believe that for individual creatures, on the whole, existence is happy. This estimate was, as I said, a necessary inference from the power and goodness of God, for Paley could not think God's intention is aborted. But if a reasoner took the preponderance of happiness in experience as a fact, as empirically demonstrable, it would prove or, at any rate, support a belief in God's goodness. Paley asserted, as did many another Romantic, that nature or the Creator had attached a feeling of pleasure to the most ordinary sensations and doings of living beings – to seeing, hearing, moving, feeding, sleeping, and, generally, being alive and using capacities. Perhaps Wordsworth had this in mind when he referred to the "pleasure that there is in life itself."[99] To modern readers Wordsworth's "Lines Written in Early Spring" have been a scandal, but in their time they were unusual mainly with respect to plants:

> The birds around me hopped and played,
> Their thoughts I cannot measure:
> But the least motion which they made,
> It seemed a thrill of pleasure.
>
> The budding twigs spread out their fan,
> To catch the breezy air;
> And I must think, do all I can,
> That there was pleasure there.[100]

The sober, rational Paley was hardly less visionary. "It is a happy world after all," he concludes: "Swarms of new born *flies* ... Their sportive motions ... testify their joy ... in their lately discovered faculties. A *bee* among the flowers ... so busy, and so pleased ... fish ... their leaps out of the water, their frolics in it ... show their excess of spirits ... What a sum, collectively, of gratification and pleasure have we here before our view."[101] To all this happiness, gratitude was the right response.

With the argument from design so firmly in mind, to consider any natural thing, from the stars in their courses to the well-adapted, happy aphids on a leaf, might bring the Author of this and all to mind. And, as many a scholarly study has shown, the transition from this quasi-inferential knowledge of God through nature to a more emotional communion with God in nature came quickly, spread widely, and lasted well into the nineteenth century. I quote a few passages in illustration. For Henry Needler, in 1724, every part of the natural world "abounds with manifest Proofs and Instances of the Wisdom, Power, and Goodness of its Maker"; hence when Needler wanders "into the fields," his thoughts "take a Solemn and Religious Turn."[102] The divine is moving into the landscape, and, in the process, is endowing it with the immense appeal and significance that it retained throughout the Romantic age. In nature, wrote James Thomson, taking a further step, "we feel the present Deity,"[103] a feeling that famously culminated, so far as poetic utterance is concerned, in Wordsworth's "Lines Composed a Few Miles above Tintern Abbey": "I have felt / A presence" in the mountains and streams, a "something far more deeply interfused ... a spirit" that "rolls through all things."[104] So far as statement is concerned, Wordsworth was actually more cautious than several earlier poets on this theme. His achievement was to convey, or seem to convey, personal experience rather than doctrine – this and his grandeur of phrasing. In *An Essay on Man* Pope had written that "All are but parts of one stupendous whole, / Whose body Nature is, and God the soul." (Pope admitted privately that this might "at first glance be taken for heathenism," though he denied that it was.)[105] The pious Cowper equally affirmed in *The Task* that "there lives and works / A soul in all things, and that soul is God," and, going further, he added that He "is the life of all that lives."[106] In this context, Blake's "For every thing that lives is Holy" sounds neither unusual nor unorthodox.[107] To find God in "all that lives" places Him in the animals also, whose happiness is thus doubly grounded: in the first place, God designs them to be happy; and, secondly, the happiness of animals is ultimately that of the Divine Life in them.

In a final step, the assumption that animals are happy might be detached from its religious provenance and become a fact or even a supposedly scientific truth about animal nature.

> Birds delight
> Day and Night
> Nightingale
> In the dale
> Lark in Sky
> Merrily. [108]

These lines in Blake's *Songs of Innocence* would now be interpreted as perspectival, as expressing the character of innocence, but innumerable descriptions of animals in Romantic poetry presented them as bundles of gladness, even descriptions by skeptics such as Byron and Keats or by atheists such as Shelley. We are speaking, to emphasize the point, of animals as God intended them to exist, animals living their wild lives in freedom or domestic animals rightly treated. When animals were hunted, driven, imprisoned, or otherwise tormented, their sufferings seemed all the more shocking as a deprivation of their natural endowment or of their endowment from heaven.

The poets we now call Romantic usually interpreted animal flights, frisks, bounds, and sounds as expressions of delight, like Paley with the flies and fish. For example, the happiness of the water snakes, in "The Rime of the Ancient Mariner," was signified in their motions – "they coiled and swam" (line 280). In Cowper's *The Task* the "bounding fawn . . . darts across the glade . . . through mere delight of heart, / And spirits buoyant with excess of glee," and the awkward gambols of cows give "such act and utt'rance as they may / To ecstasy too big to be suppress'd."[109] In Wordsworth's "Resolution and Independence" the hare is "running races" and the poet assumes it is "in her mirth."[110] Similarly in the "Immortality Ode" Wordsworth takes the songs of birds and the leaps of lambs as "joyous." Wordsworth's skylark, like Shelley's, pours forth its "joy divine" in soaring and singing, and "joy awaits" his butterfly when the breeze "calls you forth again." However, an alternative literary topos dwelt on the hunger and other suffering of mice, birds, hares, and other wild animals in winter. Keats alludes to this in the owl and "limping hare" of "The Eve of St. Agnes" (lines 2–3). It became a literary occasion for displays of benevolence, whether by feeding the starving creatures or by at least tolerating their depredations. Burns's "To a Mouse" includes this theme. Thomson mined this vein, and so did William Cowper.[111] In Thomas Day's *History of Sandford and Merton*, Mr. Barlow "took Tommy by the hand, and led him into a field at some distance, which belonged to him, and which had been down with turnips." Innumerable larks rose up from the field, and Mr. Barlow explained that "these little fellows are trespassing upon my turnips in such hosts, that in a short time they will destroy every bit of green." They are hungry, says Mr. Barlow, and "though they do me some mischief, they are welcome to what they can find."[112]

At sight of the water snakes "a spring of love" (line 284) gushed from the ancient mariner's heart, and in literature, at least, this love, this sympathy, yearning, and blessing was a frequent and approved response to happy animals, just as compassion was the right response to suffering ones. The poet longs to share their happiness, as Wordsworth does in the "Immortality Ode," as Shelley does in "To a Skylark," and as Keats does in his ode "To a Nightingale."[113] In Blake's *Milton* the sun becomes a surrogate of the poet observer: the "little throat" of the lark "labours with inspiration; every feather . . . vibrates with the effluence Divine," and the sun

> Stands still upon the Mountain looking on this little Bird
> With eyes of soft humility & wonder, love & awe.[114]

III

Two centuries ago "animal rights" did not have the extended meaning it now has. The phrase was used in stricter analogy to the rights of man. Since these were being much debated, those of animals came up, but rights were not then prominent in the argument for kindness. I notice the scattered statements on animal rights from that time mainly because of the importance the concept has for us.

The first English work in which animals were said to have rights was Thomas Tryon's *The Way to Health, Long Life and Happiness* (1683). Tyron was a Gloucestershire shepherd, Anabaptist, and vegetarian, who believed that "violence or killing either Man or Beasts is as contrary to the Divine Principle as light is to darkness."[115] He attacked hunting by using the common comparison of the hunter to a tyrant, "invading all the rights and privileges of inferior creatures."[116] Here the concept of animal rights is connected with that of English liberty, the rights in law and tradition of the people against arbitrary power of the sovereign. Something like this is implicit in innumerable verses, from Thomson to Shelley and Byron, that also depict the hunter as a Nimrod, a tyrant. In the Preface to his *The Lower World* (1810), Samuel J. Pratt says, "At a time in which the Rights of Man are so vigilantly watched" we should recognize "that brutes have *their* rights, and that there should be some *reform* of the tyrannical and wanton cruelties exercised by *man* upon the animal world."[117] However, animal rights were not usually compared to political ones.

"The meanest creature upon earth," said Humphry Primatt, "has an equal right with himself [man] to enjoy the blessings of life."[118] If this was so, it was "not obvious," said Francis Hutcheson, that humans have a right to enslave and eat animals, though he defended this in his chapter on "Adventitious Rights." But, he added, "Brutes may very justly be said to have a right that no useless pain or misery should be inflicted on them . . . 'Tis true brutes have no notion of rights . . . but infants are in the same case, and yet have rights, which the adults are obliged to maintain."[119] According to William Drummond, a man can no more treat animals just as he likes than he can his wife, children, and servants. There are "reciprocal duties," an implicit contract.[120] The extent to which this was a commonplace is shown by Margaret Cullen's novel, *Mornton* (1814), where it enters into drawing-room conversation: "God has given to the inferior orders of the creation rights and privileges also, which the superior have no right to infringe."[121]

The longest discussion of animal rights in the Romantic age came in the third chapter, "On the Rights of Brutes," in John Lawrence's 1796 volume on horses. In theoretical argument, Lawrence shows himself relatively helpless. But at the practical level he is superb – informed, down to earth, willing to compromise, and yet steadfast to principle – and one sees why Richard Martin consulted him before introducing a Parliamentary bill against cruelty to animals. Lawrence grants the economic interest in exploiting animals harshly, and adds that similar arguments are used to defend slavery: "There are also other short cuts to interest . . . It has been said, that the world could not have either gold, sugar, or coals but at the expense of human liberty."[122]

Two hundred years ago there was something to be gained but also much to be lost in arguing for animal rights. Within the legal system at this time animals were, as I said, regarded as property, as they still are. If you injured another's property, the law could intervene, but you could do what you liked with your own. And though kindness might be described as a moral and religious duty, it was desirable also to erect a quasi-legal protection, partly because the law was a teacher and partly because it was a threat, the only means, Lord Erskine told Parliament, of impressing the brutal and the wretched. A natural right, if it could be established, would logically prepare the way for a legal one.

On the other hand, the argument from natural rights was especially associated at this time with the French *philosophes* and with radical politics. To put it another way, one obtained animal rights by extending rights from human beings downward. You could not grant a right to animals that you denied to subordinate classes of humans. Hence the implication for human politics. Radicals generally supported what we now call "animal rights" among their other causes. Tom Paine, for example, published a poem entitled "Cruelty to Animals Exposed" in the *Pennsylvania Magazine*, and we have seen that Mary Wollstonecraft, Percy Bysshe Shelley, and many other radicals were also polemically active in this cause.[123] But the cause of animals also appealed to a great many persons whose politics were not radical. Their enthusiasm might be dampened by the theory that animals had rights. Sarah Trimmer was typical. Though all for kindness, she rejected "the levelling system, which includes the RIGHTS OF ANIMALS," and was glad the creatures themselves could not be inflamed by such agitation.[124]

3

Keeping pets: William Cowper and his hares

The reform of prison conditions is forever associated with John Howard, whose single-minded, indefatigable investigations led to acts of Parliament in 1774. A few heroic personalities stand out in the abolition of the slave trade, such as William Wilberforce, Granville Sharp, and Thomas Clarkson. In the cause of slaves Clarkson was a "Moral Steam-Engine, or the Giant with one idea," according to Coleridge, and had "listened exclusively to his Conscience, and obeyed its voice at the price of all his Youth & manhood, at the price of his Health, his private Fortune, and the fairest prospects of honorable ambition."[1] The cause of animals did not enlist comparably dedicated persons. It was an effort that one might take up occasionally, episodically, among other projects, paying for a sermon on the subject, giving one, or getting up a petition, or introducing a bill in Parliament. And then, in most cases, you went on to matters that concerned you more.

I

If literature has practical influence, no writer in the eighteenth century had more effect than William Cowper in transforming attitudes to animals and stimulating reform. He was quoted over and over in sermons, pamphlets, and in Parliament, sometimes from memory.[2] He was not the most radical or the most eloquent poet on this subject, far less so than William Blake or Christopher Smart. But Cowper reached and moved opinion much more than they.

His impact depended on a combination of appeals radiating from the poetic image of himself and his way of life. His Christian piety – serious, reflective, deeply sincere – was moving and exemplary for his readers, and Davidoff and Hall report that the "families of bankers, shopkeepers, manufacturers, farmers, tanners, brewers, millers, and clergymen . . . found succour and inspiration in Cowper, whether their politics were radical or conservative. With him Quakers, Independents, Unitarians, Baptists, and Anglicans all found food for thought."³ To this was added the attraction of his domestic life in the countryside, as he pictured it in *The Task*. The Horatian ideal of cultivated retirement in a rural setting had immense appeal in the eighteenth century and was the subject of poem after poem. By Cowper's time, the Romantic idealization of nature also lent its glow to this theme. Cowper presented such a life as his own – not, in other words, as a wish but as lived experience. He wrote with enough realism and detail to substantiate the picture. This way of life corresponded, in an idealized way, to the one many genteel persons were actually obliged to live, and Cowper's strong appreciation of ordinary, everyday pleasures – "Domestic Happiness, thou only bliss / Of Paradise that hast survived the fall!"⁴ – was especially important for readers who, like Cowper himself, had little access to other pleasures. No one conveys more gratefully the satisfactions of gardening, of tea before the fire on a winter night, and of a familiar walk. "In celebrating domesticity," Davidoff and Hall report, "Cowper crossed political, religious, and economic divisions and established himself as the most beloved writer of the period."⁵ The poet-speaker of *The Task* also won his audience by his strenuous moral concern, his patriotism, and his gentle, kindly sympathies. Such was the poetic image. Cowper's great poem, *The Task*, strongly urged compassion for animals, weaving this virtue into his powerful image of the good person and the good life.

But it is possible to go behind this poetic image. We have many of Cowper's letters, bits of diary, and letters and memoirs by his friends. They afford a near view of the feelings, self-conflicts, and motivations of an eighteenth-century animal lover and pet keeper. In his deepest, most personal motivation, Cowper identified with animal terror of human beings, of human nature. The tendency to denounce human nature as cruel has of course been present in the animal protest movement from then to now.

In 1774 Cowper acquired a leveret or young hare about three months old. Its round face, snub nose, and large eyes and ears might have been perceived, consciously or unconsciously, as baby features and evoked protective emotions. Moreover, it was cuddly. Its life, as Cowper knew, had to this point been hard. When it was three days old, the leveret, like all English brown hares, had been placed by its mother in a shallow depression or "form," there to lie alone day and night. Its mother visited it once in twenty-four hours to nurse for three or four minutes. A shepherd's dog discovered it, and the shepherd gave it to the parish clerk, who intended it as a pet for his children. They, however, neglected it, and the compassionate clerk offered it to the poet.

At this time Cowper was emerging, still shattered, from fifteen months of insanity, and he was glad, he tells us, "of any thing that would engage my attention without fatiguing it . . . in the management of such an animal, and in the attempt to tame it, I should find just that sort of employment which my case required."[6] Soon he had two more hares. How the hares felt about being kept and managed, Cowper seems not to have worried. Young hares, as Buffon explained, "are easily tamed, but never acquire that degree of attachment which is requisite to render them domestic," and will "take the first opportunity to escape and fly into the country."[7] Cowper's hares were captives. But Cowper's conscience as a keeper of hares (and wild birds in cages) did not trouble him. He had saved the hares from being hunted:

> Yes – thou mayst eat thy bread, and lick the hand
> That feeds thee; thou may'st frolic on the floor
> At evening, and at night retire secure
> To thy straw-couch, and slumber unalarm'd.
>
> (III, 342–45)

Cowper wrote about his hares in Book III of *The Task*, in the great epitaph for Tiny ("Epitaph on a Hare"), the Latin epitaph for Puss ("Epitaphium Alterum"), a brief prose report in the *Gentleman's Magazine* (June, 1784), and occasionally in his letters. The prose piece was a favorite with children for several generations and with many older persons, Jeremy Bentham among them.[8] It moved an anonymous admirer (actually his cousin Theodora) to present Cowper with "a Snuff-box of tortoise-shell with a beautifull Landschape on the lid of it glazed with chrystal, having the figures of 3 hares in the fore ground."[9] He wrote affectionately about other animals, and composed several elegies or epitaphs for pets of neighbors and friends. While the hares were with him, he also had five rabbits, two guinea pigs, a magpie, a jay, a starling, a linnet, two goldfinches, two canary birds, two dogs, and sixteen pigeons.[10]

A long passage in Book VI of *The Task* decries cruelty to animals. His arguments are the familiar religious ones. He cites passages from the Bible to show that God cares for the creatures. He finds God immanent in the world and hence also in animals. They are happy, unless "cruel man" interferes, and a good person sympathizes with this happiness. Whoever does not is "dead alike / To [human] love and friendship" (VI, 323–24). Parents must guard against cruelty in their children, which is "dev'lish" (VI, 594). Though no law punishes cruelty to animals, heaven takes note, and God will not show mercy to the merciless.

The varying flow of Cowper's poem includes moments of strong emotion. He would not "enter on my list of friends . . . the man / Who needlessly sets foot upon a worm" (vi, 560–63). He grows furious as he thinks of the ox driven "with stripes and yells" to the slaughter house:

> goaded, as he runs,
> To madness; while the savage at his heels
> Laughs at the frantic sufferer's fury.
> (vi, 420–23)

But usually Cowper is more temperate or compromising. His letters refer repeatedly to chickens that his housemate Mrs. Unwin was fattening for the table, perhaps feeding them by hand, as Cowper's friend Lady Throckmorton did her turkey. The letters also mention oysters, lobsters, fish, and game that disappeared down Cowper's throat, and doubtless there were also sheep and steers. That we need animal food is a consequence of Original Sin, Cowper thought – "what a serious business it was in olden times to rob an orchard," as John Lawrence said[11] – but Cowper had no doubt that we are justified in taking what we need (*The Task*, vi, 456–58). His attitude to animals, however sympathetic, was firmly hierarchical. Happy as animals are, the person who sympathizes with animals enjoys "a far superior happiness to their's, / The comfort of a reasonable joy" (vi, 346–47). Of course Cowper thought that animals should be slaughtered with all possible consideration; he deplored, the "inadvertent step" that crushed the snail on the public path (vi, 564); but he approved the destruction of snails in the garden, where they endanger the plants. As for spiders in the house, snakes in the shed, and so forth, tenderness of heart shows in raising the question – is it allowable to kill destructive, noxious, unclean, or otherwise unwelcome small intruders? – but Cowper's answer lies well this side of Buddhism. So also with larger animals, such as turkeys, sheep, oxen, and horses. It is not wrong to use them, but only to cause unnecessary pain by venting on them human aggression and rage. As we consider such passages, we must imagine Cowper being read aloud in households, much as Jane Austen describes in chapter 3 of *Sense and Sensibility*. For this audience, if not for Marianne, Cowper's authority was enhanced because he seemed not to be radical.

His descriptions of animals have, for my feeling, a special moral fineness. Most of us, I imagine, would like both to be understood in a more or less realistic way and also to find ourselves valued – a rare experience. This is the attitude Cowper brings to animals. He avoids the idealization of animals and the mystifications about them that are often present in the poetry of the Romantic tradition. Most of the time Cowper also restrains sentimental gush. He describes animals affectionately and realistically, taking a sympathetic interest in the creatures they naturally are. His "Epitaph on a Hare," on Tiny, is an example:

> His diet was of wheaten bread,
>   And milk, and oats, and straw,
> Thistles, or lettuces instead,
>   With sand to scour his maw.
>
> On twigs of hawthorn he regal'd,
>   On pippins' russet peel;
> And, when his juicy salads fail'd,
>   Slic'd carrot pleas'd him well.[12]

II

Keith Thomas points out that pet keeping was increasingly common in eighteenth-century households. The reasons, he thinks, lie in the tendency to live in small family units, and in the growth of cities, which, for many people, hindered a direct contact with nature. With the Romantic view of nature, to bring a pet into your home was to bring innocence, spontaneity, gladness, and goodness. In turn, the practice of keeping pets enormously influenced attitudes to animals. As Thomas sums up, "it encouraged the middle classes to form optimistic conclusions about animal intelligence; it gave rise to innumerable anecdotes about animal sagacity; it stimulated the notion that animals could have character and individual personality; and it created the psychological foundation for the view that some animals at least were entitled to moral consideration."[13]

Pet keeping promoted views of animals that differed, in some ways, from those suggested by general humanitarian benevolence, by natural theology, and by the Romantic idealization of nature. We perceive our pets as individuals; we have a continuing relation with them; we identify with them; we see them go through their entire life history and so they become, as Joanna Baillie writes in her poem on "The Kitten," an "emblem" of our own course of life;[14] we bestow care as well as affection on them; we imagine that they love us; we view them as belonging to our household or even as family members; and we may feel slightly guilty about confining or disciplining them and about eloigning them from their free, wild being. All this is plainly visible in the very numerous epitaphs on pets composed from 1750 to 1850 almost as a separate genre.[15] It may also be important that taking care of pets especially involves feeding them, and in doing this, we play a parental, maternal role. And then, of course, we transfer to wild animals the ideas that pet keeping produces.

Particularly I call attention to the simple but all-important facts that we give pets a name and recognize them as individuals, each with its unique life history. If they are perceived as individuals, even wild animals may serve the heart as pets, like the prisoner of Chillon's mice and spiders.[16] Stories about individual animals were numerous in the children's literature of the Romantic age: Stephen Jones, *The Life and Adventures of a Fly* (1789); *Memoirs of Dick, The Little Poney* (1800); Elizabeth Helme, *Adventures of a Bullfinch* (1809); and several by E. A. Kendall, of which the best known was *Keeper's Travels in Search of his Master* (1799). The same individualizing view recurred in other genres when pets were the topic, as in Dorothy Wordsworth's story of "Mary Jones and Her Pet Lamb," Robert Southey's pleasant "Memoir of the Cats of Greta Hall," and the greatest of all verses on a pet, Christopher Smart's on his cat Jeoffry in *Jubilate Agno*. As individuals, the animals evoked identification and sympathy.

Even in this sentimental age, it was possible to analyze the motive for keeping pets as love of power. In E. A. Kendall's *The Canary Bird* (1799), about a caged bird who briefly escapes, the canary is instructed by the yellow-hammer, a wild observer of human beings, that "mankind likes nothing that is not dependent upon it . . . You are one of *their* creatures – your cage is a world of *theirs* – they can starve you, and they can surround you with plenty, *therefore* they *love* you. For us, who are totally independent of them, they have little regard."[17] Alexander Pope had alluded to this aspect of pet keeping in his brilliant epigram to be engraved on the collar of the Prince of Wales's dog:

> I am his Highness' dog at *Kew*;
> Pray tell me Sir, whose Dog are you?[18]

Robert Burns wrote three poems on pets. As compared with Cowper, he is less protective and more humorous and companionable. His attitudes bring Cowper's into relief. Two of Burns's poems concern the pet sheep, Mailie: "The Death and Dying Words of Poor Mailie, the Author's only Pet Yowe, An Unco' Mournfu' Tale," and "Poor Mailie's Elegy."[19] In the first of these Mailie is the speaker, and in the other a neighbor tells how Mailie fell into a ditch and drowned. Not every sheep has a name. That Mailie does indicates that she is a pet, and in the poems the fondness of pet and master for each other is both strongly affirmed and humorously exaggerated. The poems have been called a "comic treatment of sentimentalism."[20] More exactly, the poems are idylls of pet keeping, sentimental indulgences that are also self-mocking, so that the reader need not be ashamed of enjoying them.

Despite the comic exaggeration, the details reveal what pet keepers might feel and believe. The neighbor denies, for example, that the master's grief at Mailie's death is for the loss of property; it is for a dear "friend and neebor." In the speech invented for Mailie she affirms that she loves her "Master dear," thus fulfilling a fantasy of pet owners, who commonly wish to be both master and loved. This is the central paradox of living with pets, that we imagine pets to be neighbours, friends, or family members, and yet imagine ourselves as their "owners" or "masters." Not incidentally, similar fantasies were projected into slaves in the so-called "plantation" literature of the South after the Civil War and into colonialized people in the popular literature of the British Empire.

The owner profits materially from the pet if it is a sheep, and Mailie is shrewd enough to recognize the bond of interest on both sides – lambs and wool for him, hay and grain for her. Whichever her motive, love or food, she always wanted to be near her master:

> Thro' a' the town she trotted by him;
> A lang half-mile she could descry him;
> Wi' kindly bleat, when she did spy him,
>   She ran wi' speed:
> A friend mair faithfu' ne'er came nigh him,
> Than Mailie dead.
>   ("Poor Mailie's Elegy," lines 12–18)

For Romantic writers such signs were true expressions of love, and they understood perfectly how the greeting rituals melted the pet-keeping heart. Thus in "The Little Dog: A Fable," one of the pieces in John Aikin's and Letitia Barbauld's *Evenings at Home*, Fido, wanting to show his love for his master, "ran to him, licked his feet, gamboled before him, and every now and then stopped, wagging his tail, and looking up to his master with expressions of the most humble and affectionate attachment." These behaviors had their effect, for "the master observed him. Ha! Little Fido, said he, you are an honest, good-natured little fellow," and ever after Fido was cherished as a companion. I regret to add that this story also has a tail: "*Moral.* The poorest man may repay his obligations to the richest and greatest by faithful and affectionate service."[21]

Remarkably but typically, the acts of Mailie are judged by the moral code. Just as hunting dogs in the eighteenth century were punished for "lying" if they gave tongue without scenting the quarry, Mailie would have been "thievish" if she had broken through a fence to get at food. This absurd language is typical of us pet owners; we call animals "good" when we mean "docile" and wax morally indignant at inconvenient natural behavior. Mailie has completely internalized this morality – a triumph of training! – and herself condemns "vile" pets that "steal" peas or kale (lines 36–37).

Since sheep are slaughtered for food, a poem on a pet sheep required no little dexterity to be both plausible and acceptable to readers. Through a hundred and fourteen lines of verse, Burns allows no suggestion that Mailie might be mutton. Presumably she would have born lambs and wool for her grateful master until she died of old age. But as Mailie thinks of her lambs, a glimpse of farm realities opens, for she hopes the master may save them "Frae dogs an' tods [foxes], an' butchers' knives" (line 30). Thus the master, who is also the poet, is pictured in flattering terms as the rescuer rather than the butcher, and the knives become not a doom but merely a possible mischance in life's course, a peril like dogs and foxes.

Mailie speaks, and her thoughts are human. She was imported from beyond the Tweed and is snobbish about her high breeding. She scorns, she says, common sheep that roam about the moors; she would not mingle with them, and hopes her offspring will be similarly fastidious. A snobbish sheep is of course a joke on snobbery, but Mailie is a sympathetic figure.

To imagine Mailie as quasi-human is typical of pet owners and becomes, in this poem, excessive, as in Disney films. But it at least precludes endowing Mailie with the mystery, otherness, unity of being, and sublimity that Romantic poets often bestowed on animals. This perspective is generally not plausible in poems on pets, farm animals, or any animals that human beings live with. Moreover, with her shrewdness, assertiveness, and volubility, Mailie is hardly the innocent, gentle sheep of pastoral fictions. Neither can Mailie be associated with biblical and Christian figurations of sheep. To pluck away stock associations was part of the humor in these poems. Nor is Mailie a sentimentally pampered pet, as sometimes happened in this age, when dogs might receive doctor's visits and go to the theater. Napoleon was one of many husbands who reluctantly shared his wife's bed with her dog, which nipped his toes. Amid all these alternative possibilities in a poem on sheep, the attitudes Burns projects seem somewhat down to earth and mature. Mailie is an individual creature, an animal person, and is imagined as a friend.

This relation to domestic animals is pictured more convincingly in Burns's "The Auld Farmer's New-year-morning Salutation to his Auld

Mare, Maggie," a poem that Robert Frost might have envied for its raciness
and voice. The old farmer's character is caught from his opening lines:

> A Guid New-year I wish thee, Maggie!
> Hae, there's a ripp to thy auld baggie.[22]

(A "ripp" is a handful of grain.) As the farmer monologues, we learn that
the mare Maggie has shared his life and work from his early manhood.
To the farmer Maggie is an individual. For reasons of long association,
appreciation, and gratitude, the farmer is fond of his mare. Together they
have grown old and tottery, but the mare will still be kept and fed. This
implies an impressive measure of sentiment; the worn-out mare might have
been sold for dog food. The perspective of the speaker is elegiac. Both he
and his horse were "skiegh" (mettlesome and fiery) in youth; a bit of grain
worked in the horse like a dram in the farmer. Both are now "crazy" (infirm)
with age. Thus there is with Burns not the least feeling in the poem that
animals are happier or more wretched than human beings, that they are
morally or metaphysically higher as nature or lower as brutes, or even that
their emotions and life experience are essentially different.

III

I come now to the finest poetry on a pet from this time, Christopher
Smart's verses on his cat Jeoffry in *Jubilate Agno*.[23] The poem was composed
between 1758 and 1763, in years when Smart was confined in institutions
for the mentally ill. According to Samuel Johnson, Smart was brought to
the madhouse by his religious eccentricity. He would fall on his knees in
prayer at any time and place, and he insisted that others pray with him. The
treatment of the insane was changing as Bedlam horrors gradually gave way
to enlightened benevolence, and Smart was lucky in his keepers. Probably
he was not subjected to chains, whippings, and dungeons, but he was a
prisoner. Smart observes that one in seven mice escapes from Jeoffry as he
toys with them. Thus we feel the hours going slowly as he counts the mice
that get away.

The form and meaning of *Jubilate Agno* is complex, difficult, and controversial. My comments pertain only to the lines on Jeoffry. The general
intention of the whole poem is to show all things turning to God in love and
worship. The most ordinary and familiar behavior of a cat is interpreted in
this sense:

For at the first glance of the glory of God in the East he worships
  in his way.
For this is done by wreathing his body seven times round with
  elegant quickness.

(v. 697–98)

Thus Smart's attitude to animals intertwined with his strong religious con-
victions. The opening line, "For I will consider my Cat Jeoffry" (v. 695),
means, I will consider how Jeoffry stands in relation to God. Perhaps Smart
would not have gone so far as Blake's "every thing that lives is Holy."[24] Nevertheless, the poetry of Smart's madness records seriatim how God blesses
the creatures or how they worship God. To envision them as worshipers
transvalues them.

Just such a redescription takes place in his lines on Jeoffry. Smart speaks
all the good he can of his cat. Moreover, though he feels why cats might
be thought malicious and dangerous, he struggles to suppress these ideas.
"For he is of the tribe of Tiger" (v. 722), writes Smart. Then as now, cats
were said to incarnate wild nature. As Joanna Baillie put it, the "charm" of
this pet may be that

> While we at ease, secure from ill,
> The chimney corner snugly fill,

we can observe

> A lion darting on his prey,
> A tiger at his ruthless play.[25]

A large chunk of cultural history lies behind the wish to bring wild, even
ferocious nature into your home. But this was not Smart's wish, for he
deprives the tribe of its wildness. "The Cherub Cat is a term of the Angel
Tiger" (v. 723). Cats are feared because they slash with sharp claws, but
Smart tunes this into praise: "For the dexterity of his defence is an instance
of the love of God to him" (v. 733).

In the folk mind, cats were familiar spirits of witches, uncanny and demonic, their eyes glowing with hellfire. These associations troubled Smart.
Jeoffry hisses, and Smart thinks of the serpent, the beast into which Satan
crept, the biblical archetype of evil. "For he has the subtlety and hissing
of a serpent, which in goodness he suppresses" (v. 724). The cat has "elec-
trical skin" – its fur sparks when rubbed – and "glaring eyes"; but Smart
redescribes these as illuminations by which Jeoffry "counteracts the powers
of darkness" (v. 719). Though a nocturnal creature, Jeoffry is not of the

devil's party but a guard posted against him: "For he keeps the Lord's watch in the night against the adversary" (v. 718). "He counteracts the Devil, who is death, by brisking about the life" (v. 720). Perhaps this verse especially suggests how much Jeoffry meant to Smart in his depressed states of mind.

This redescription of the cat expresses love, obviously, and some lines fall into sentimental nonsense. For example, Jeoffry dallies with a mouse in order "to give it a chance" (v. 715). Other lines go beyond the normal madness of us pet owners to Smart's special one. He writes that Jeoffry "knows that God is his Saviour" (v. 737). I like better the more balanced utterances in which Jeoffry appears merely as "compleat cat" affectionately regarded. "For he will not do destruction, if he is well-fed, neither will he spit without provocation" (v. 725). No doubt a part of Smart wanted to leave out the "well-fed" qualification, but a better part of him put it in. "For God has blessed him in the variety of his movements" (v. 763) holds because it is followed by noting a limitation: "For, tho he cannot fly, he is an excellent clamberer" (v. 764), and,

> For he can swim for life.
> For he can creep.
> (v. 767–68)

Better is the sequence of verses (740 and 741) in which Jeoffry becomes one of the "Lord's poor," a creature whose poverty confers religious merit.

For he is of the Lord's poor and so indeed is he called by benevolence perpetually – Poor Jeoffry! Poor Jeoffry! the rat has bit thy throat.

For I bless the name of the Lord Jesus that Jeoffry is better.

Best of all is,

> For the divine spirit comes about his body to sustain it in compleat cat.
> (v. 742)

IV

With Cowper we encounter a different set of attitudes toward pets. Much modern research suggests that keeping pets is medically and psychologically beneficial to human beings. Pets amuse by their play, valuably distract us by their demands, and offer companionship. They like us, seek physical contact, are not judgmental, and enhance our self-respect. They reduce stress, lower blood pressure, and make us live longer. The difference they can make seems to be particularly important for people who feel lonely, alienated, or rejected: the handicapped, the imprisoned, the convalescent, the elderly, the insane – in fact, anyone who, for whatever reason, finds it difficult to form close relationships with other people. Pets help us to socialize not only with themselves but with our own kind. All this seems intensely relevant to Cowper, who charmed people and had a few intimate friends, but was pathologically shy, retreative, and anxious in ordinary social life. Hares are said to be friendly with persons they know and frantically nervous with strangers, and Cowper was no different. He was insane at times, and even when apparently sane, he was trying hard not again to become insane. His sense of self-worth cannot have been high, since he felt that God had rejected him. During all his pet-keeping years, moreover, Cowper lived in a childless household. Since, presumably, he had normal paternal instincts, the popular and scientific belief that pets are child substitutes would also be relevant to his case.

Cowper knew that the care of pets helped him manage his own insanity, but generally their therapeutic value for the insane was not yet understood. The first deliberate use of pets for such purposes did not come until the end of the eighteenth century at the Friends' Retreat, near York. This institution was founded in 1796 under the leadership of William Tuke, a merchant of that city, who solicited money for the project from Quakers all over England. The main building had courts for men and for women "to which, the respective patients have free access in the day-time. In these courts are kept a number of rabbits, and other domesticated animals" for "the afflicted objects of the Institution's care."[26] Another report mentions rabbits, sea-gulls, hawks, and poultry: "These creatures are generally very familiar with the patients; and it is believed they are not only the means of innocent pleasure, but that the intercourse with them sometimes tends to awaken the social and benevolent feelings."[27]

Various features of hares could conceivably have strengthened Cowper's identification with them. Unlike rabbits, hares do not have bolt holes, but rely for survival on concealment and speed. They live more or less in the open, and though the folk belief that they never close their eyes is wrong, they are unusually anxious animals. "Fearful of every danger," explained Ralph Beilby in the *General History of Quadrupeds* (1790) he produced with Thomas Bewick, "and attentive to every alarm, the Hare is continually upon the watch."[28] "Timorous" was the stock epithet. Their behavior often seems irrational, so much so that Edward Topsell, in his *Historie of Four-footed Beastes* (1607), described them as "melancholy":

If they heare the Dogges, they raise themselves on their legges and runne from them, but if fearefull imagination oppresse them, as they oftentimes are very sad and melancholy, supposing to heare the noise of Dogges where there are none such sturring, then doe they runne too and fro, fearing and trembling, as if they were fallen mad.[29]

Particularly in breeding season the behavior of males or bucks has given rise to the proverb "mad as a March hare." Hares are hard to keep in zoos. A sudden fright may cause them to leap against the wire with sufficient force to kill themselves.[30] Cowper's first mental collapse was precipitated when, in order to obtain a sinecure, he was required to present himself for a *pro forma* examination, and with this and similar memories, he might readily have sympathized with the hare's readiness to panic. In extreme danger hares shriek with the sound of a terrified baby.[31]

Pet keeping was not, in itself, coded as masculine or feminine, but Cowper's attitudes to pets were not traditionally appropriate for a man. The correct male attitude to a dog combined friendship with mastery, not the protective tenderness of Cowper that he himself thought feminine. Finding in James Hurdis an animal lover like himself, Cowper wrote him, in a letter, that "I seemed to have need of somebody to keep me in countenance . . . in my attention and attachment to animals . . . it is well . . . that here and there a man should be found a little womanish, or perhaps a little childish in . . . kissing and coaxing, and laying them [animals] in one's bosom."[32]

In folk belief it was thought that male hares as well as females give birth to young. Hares change sex every year, it was said, or are hermaphrodite. There is no male hare, Edward Topsell summed up, "that is not also female."[33] Cowper doubtless knew better, since the science of his time did. Buffon explained that with hares the "gland of the clitoris is prominent and almost as large as the sexual distinction of the male . . . It is these circumstances which have given rise to the opinions that there are many hermaphrodites among these animals, that the males sometimes bring forth, and that some are alternately males and females and perform the office of the other sex."[34] However, even male hares were (and are) referred to by feminine pronouns, though no one knows the reason for this. Cowper named his male hares Tiny, Puss, and Bess.

Cowper's sexuality is largely a mystery. He flirted a bit, in cautious, conventional ways, with some of his women friends. He lived as a housemate with Mrs. Unwin, but they seem to have had no sexual relations. Suggestions that he marry Mrs. Unwin helped to precipitate Cowper's second episode of insanity, presumably by arousing intense anxieties. Their relation,

Cowper said, was maternal/filial: "Mrs. Unwin has almost a maternal Affection for me, and I have something very like a filial one for her, and her Son and I are Brothers."[35] Unconsciously, perhaps, she replaced the mother he had lost at the age of six; perhaps there were other causes of anxiety. If women did not enflame Cowper, nothing suggests that males did either. It seems unlikely that Cowper was at all sexually active or even interested after his breakdown in 1763, at the age of thirty-two, for he was struggling to relieve his mind of depression and terror. There are even rumours of what his most intelligent biographer, David Cecil, calls an "intimate deformity." Cecil has in mind a statement by John Newton, in a letter that has since been lost. Newton said that Cowper once confided to Newton that he was a hermaphrodite. Most modern scholarship assumes that if Cowper said this, he did so in a fit of madness, and that the statement had no basis in fact.[36] His character and way of life may suggest a more than ordinary degree of feminine identification, but, on the other hand, he performed masculine roles within the household. For example, he gardened and did carpentry, but he did not supervise the kitchen, and while Mrs. Unwin and Lady Austen knitted, he read the newspaper aloud to them. If his unaggressive, unambitious, domestically sheltered lifestyle could seem somewhat androgynous as he described it in *The Task*, it nevertheless (or all the more) appealed to many readers. Whatever seemed androgynous about Cowper fitted in with the sentimental culture of his moment in history and was not incompatible with some tendencies in its religious life. The sentimental man, represented as an ideal in much of the literature of the age, blended supposedly feminine qualities of character, such as gentleness, sensitivity, and emotional susceptibility, with supposedly masculine qualities. What we may call the Evangelical man had attitudes and practices, such as "fervent singing, praying, and weeping" in public, that could seem feminine to persons outside his circle. Davidoff and Hall, whom I just quoted, explain that for readers who shared Cowper's type of religiosity, "manliness and sweetness could go together, tenderness was a truly Christian *and* male attribute."[37]

Whatever else hares may have represented or been associated with, the main thing, for Cowper as for everyone else, was that they were hunted – they were "the common game of hunters," as Johnson's Dictionary says. Poets were usually sympathetic to them. I have in mind, among other items, Robert Burns's "On Seeing a Wounded Hare Limp By Me, which a Fellow Had Just Shot At," and James Thomson's *The Seasons*, "Winter" (1726), lines 257–61:

The Hare,
Tho' timorous of Heart, and hard beset
By Death in various Forms, dark Snares, and Dogs,
And more unpitying Men, the Garden seeks,
Urg'd on by fearless Want.[38]

When Thomson narrates the hunting of a hare, he tells it from the hare's point of view.[39] John Gay's "The Hare and Many Friends" (in *Fables*, 1727) was a favorite with Cowper as a child. John King notes the similarities in plot between this poem and "The Castaway"; when Gay's hare is hunted, its friends abandon it, being powerless to help. King adds that "one of Cowper's last efforts as a poet . . . was to translate three of Gay's fables, including 'The Hare,' into Latin."[40]

In Cowper's epitaph on Tiny, the association of hares with hunting comes immediately to the fore. The poem begins,

Here lies, whom hound did ne'er pursue,
    Nor swifter greyhound follow,
Whose foot ne'er tainted morning dew,
    Nor ear heard huntsman's hallo.

Cowper is congratulating himself on having saved Tiny from the common fate of hares. That Tiny's "foot ne'er tainted morning dew" may suggest the pathos of captivity, but taint, in this context, means to leave a scent, to become vulnerable to the pursuing dogs. A creature leaves more scent on dewy mornings than on dry ones. Cowper perhaps remembered Alexander Pope's brilliant scene in *Windsor Forest*, where the spaniel picks up the scent on the breeze:

But when the tainted gales the game betray,
Crouch'd close he lies, and meditates the prey.[41]

Cowper's distinction of hound and greyhound refers to two modes of hunting. The keen noses of hounds could not easily be thrown off the trace, but these dogs were not fast enough to overtake a hare. In fact, they were bred for slowness, so that the hunt would last longer, and they persisted on the trail until the hare was exhausted and could run no further. Greyhounds, on the other hand, hunted by sight and were bred for speed. On level ground they could overtake a hare, as John Gay describes in "Rural Sports" (1713):

She turns, he winds, and soon regains the way,
Then tears with goary mouth the screaming prey.[42]

Sometimes greyhounds were trained not to bite the hare but to toss it with their noses. Starting again to its feet, the hare would furnish longer sport.

Cowper deplored hunting. "Detested sport," he calls it,

> That owes its pleasures to another's pain;
> That feeds upon the sobs and dying shrieks
> Of harmless nature, dumb, but yet endu'd
> With eloquence, that agonies inspire,
> Of silent tears and heart-distending sighs!
>
> (III, 326–31)

In attacking hunting, Cowper at times writes in a quasi-Wordsworthian way of a calm, innocent nature into which the hunter intrudes, violating and defiling by the noise he makes and the blood he spills (III, 298–307). He also uses the argument from snobbery, picturing hunters as boorish and uncivilized. In "The Progress of Error" a hunter who dies leaping a fence will be missed only by his dogs and his groom. In "Conversation" a hunter is smelly and noisy, fit company only for his horse and (again) his groom, neither of whom desire his company. Like most animal lovers, Cowper harbored inconsistent attitudes. At times beasts were innocent, but at other times hunters might be compared to beasts. In a letter describing a fox hunt, Cowper calls the huntsman a hound and also a fiend.[43] When Cowper's pet hare, Puss, escaped, it was chased through the town "by a most numerous Hunt, Consisting of Men, Women, Children, and Dogs," trying to recapture it. Cowper wanted this hunt to succeed, yet feels, as he describes it, a slight distaste for the mob uproar, which he treats as comic.[44] In a passage of *The Task* (III, 307) to which I have already referred, he speaks of hunting as filling the scene with "riot." The hunters come into nature like a lower-class mob.

It seems likely that Cowper was peculiarly sensitive to ideas of cruelty. Though he was horrified by the slave trade and wrote against it in Book II of *The Task* and in a few other poems, he was reluctant to read accounts of the sufferings of slaves, fearing that they would be hurtful to him. We know very little about the nightmares and fantasies that tormented him, sometimes night after night, for he thought them indecent and did not describe them. According to his cousin John Johnson, Cowper classified his dreams as "dreams of contempt and horror – some of shame – and some were dreams of ignominy and torture" – for example, he was tortured on the rack and he "was to be let down to the bottom of the sea with ropes and drawn up again."[45] In the most lurid instance of which we have a record, he dreamed he was taking leave of his home

on the Evening before my Execution. I felt the tenderest regret at the separation, and look'd about for something durable to carry with me as a memorial. The iron hasp of the garden-door presenting itself, I was on the point of taking that, but recollecting that the heat of the fire in which I was going to be tormented would fuse the metal, and that it would therefore only serve to increase my insupportable misery, I left it. – I then awoke in all the horror with which the reality of such circumstances would fill me.[46]

It seems at least possible that certain grim passages in his poetry echo such horrors in a displaced form. I have in mind, for example, the long passages in *The Task* on the prisoner in the Bastille (v, 379–445) and on the woe of the man who revolts from God (v, 581–610). But in such passages the personal cannot be separated with any certitude from the conventional. Whether in his madness Cowper imagined himself as the torturer as well as the victim cannot be known. At times, Cowper dared to think that God had treated him cruelly. As a victim, he could strongly identify with the whipped, goaded, hunted animals. This, indeed, is the burden of his famous self-description:

> I was a stricken deer, that left the herd
> Long since: with many an arrow deep infixt
> My panting side was charg'd.   (III, 108–10)

Animals that are not hunted or otherwise victimized by man were thought, as we noticed, to possess an immense natural happiness. We sympathize, says Cowper, with their happiness and thus "augment" our own (VI, 132). Sympathy may mean identification, empathy, a natural response in human beings. By an imaginative reflex, we recreate in ourselves the emotions of the creatures around us. Or sympathy may mean benevolence, good will, a desire that creatures should be happy. In the latter case, sympathy may be a product of socialization. In either case, the happiness of animals is a cause of happiness in us.

Cowper's argument might have been naturalistic: animals suffer; we suffer; therefore we can sympathize with animals and strive not to increase their suffering. We saw that Burns took this line, and Hardy and many others did a century later. But Cowper, like most Romantics, dwells very little on the natural suffering of animals.[47] The main exception is the powerful description in *The Task* (v, 84–95) of hungry birds in winter. In Cowper's perspective, the suffering even of wild animals is largely due to man. Without man the world would be – and was intended by God to be – a place of happiness. He delights in Eden-like scenes, reminders of the world as it was before the Fall, when humans obeyed "the law of universal love" (*The Task*, VI, 360) and the happy animals had no fear of them. In such scenes no human being is present or there is only Cowper, a harmless man to whom the animals are used. On his familiar walk,

> The tim'rous [wild] hare,
> Grown so familiar with her frequent guest,
> Scarce shuns me; and the stock-dove unalarm'd
> Sits cooing in the pine-tree, nor suspends
> Her long love-ditty for my near approach.
>
> (VI, 305–09)

Or there is a dream reported in a letter: "a beautiful Red-breast, while I sat in the open air, flew to me and perch'd on my knee. Then it stood quietly awhile to be strok'd, and then crept into my bosom. I never in my waking hours felt a tenderer love for any thing than I felt for the little animal in my sleep."[48] In psychoanalytic interpretation, the dream would throw light on Cowper's sexual feelings. But he interpreted it as an idyl of human interaction with an animal. With his pet hares, dogs, kittens, and pigeons, Cowper was restoring, in his own garden, the innocent, trusting, and kindly relations that once existed between man and animal.

Cowper rarely mentioned animal predation, though he was perfectly aware of it. He hated wolves, tigers, and all such animals; in fact, like many persons, he demonized some animals and bestowed virtue and innocence on others, and thus, with respect to animals, his imagination inhabited a world that was morally less ambiguous than the real one. Predatory animals were both dangerous to Cowper's imaginative world and superfluous within it. They were dangerous if their existence suggested that aggression and cruelty might also be natural. They were superfluous, because everything Cowper deplored in predatory animals, everything that wolves and tigers might represent to his imagination, was more terribly present in human beings, the real objects of Cowper's fear. In fact, he liked to suggest that mankind was responsible for cruelty in animals as well as to them – for example, in the selective breeding of mastiffs.

At the age of six, in his first boarding school, Cowper was so brutally and continually bullied that he had to be removed from the school. In "Adelphi," his narrative of his conversion, he says that he was

singled out from all the children in the school by a lad about fifteen years of age as a proper subject upon whom he might let loose the cruelty of his temper. I choose to conceal a particular recital of the many acts of barbarity with which he made it his business continually to persecute me. It will be sufficient to say that he had by his savage treatment of me imprinted such a dread of his very figure upon my mind that I well remember being afraid to lift my eyes upon him higher than his knees.[49]

In the light of present-day theories, Cowper's reported statement that he was a "hermaphrodite" raises the possibility that the bullying involved sexual abuse. The term could mean a homosexual or catamite in the eighteenth century just as it can now. Whatever happened in school, it seems likely that this experience was one source of his later attitude to dominance, aggression, and cruelty, and his identification with victims. But since our quarrels are mostly with ourselves, it is also likely that the qualities he feared were strongly represented in himself and that his suppressive energies were directed against himself as well as against others. However this may have been, his poetry – and much of *The Task* especially – represents an attempt to reprove and repress the berserk potentialities of human nature. Indeed, the whole sentimentalist movement in culture can be seen as such a disciplinary effort. The rhetorical strategy of sentimental literature was partly to erect ideals of human nature and life that would supplant the older, more combative ones. But also this literature dwelt on victims, emphasizing their helplessness, innocence, and goodness and displaying their wounds in a strong light. Thus human heartlessness was brought before the court of conscience and condemned, though of course the descriptions of victims also titillated the sadism they were supposed to dispel.

We may ask ourselves why Cowper focused on animals rather than on human victims that were featured in the protest literature of the age. One explanation lies, I believe, in a whirl of feelings I mentioned earlier, that has played a large and growing role in cultural life since Cowper's time. Once man is taken as the antithesis of nature, he can be represented as the aggressor, intruder, polluter, or destroyer of it. Sympathy with nature may be motivated by hatred of man, or hatred of man by sympathy with nature, but once this circle is in being, each emotion intensifies the other. Man views himself with horror, and even the victims among humankind may arouse less compassion simply because they are human. In the case of Cowper, I believe, the fear of man's aggressive cruelty is fundamental. From this he flies to a protected and protective, domestic, perhaps androgenous lifestyle, and he describes this as a countercultural ideal. Edenic relations with animals are one element of this larger complex. His shame from fantasies of indecency and victimization, permeating his inner life, motivated the more strongly the counter-fantasies of innocence and lovingness that he projected on animals. But one might alternatively begin with Cowper's sympathetic identification with animals as victims, and use this to explain his hatred of human masterfulness, dominance, and brutality.

Finally, there is the question of how far Cowper blamed God, saw himself as a victim of divine power unjustly and cruelly exercised. The atrocities inflicted on slaves, he confessed to Newton, almost made him doubt God's benevolence.[50] What about his own sufferings? Most modern biographers assume that Cowper imagined himself as God's victim. The paranoia that led him to hear threatening voices and imagine persecutions – for example, that Mrs. Unwin was poisoning him – might certainly color his interpretation of the dealings of God with him. Moreover, the few pages of his intimate diary that have survived from June and July, 1795, offer a horrifying glimpse into Cowper's mind during a time of insanity and may represent his ordinary though secret communings with himself from 1763 on. In order to understand these jottings one must recollect that Cowper believed God had ordered him to commit suicide. This command had come as a test of his faith, and he had failed. Henceforth he had been irrevocably sentenced to damnation. He asks,

can any sin committed in so terrible and tempestuous a moment deserve what I must suffer? . . . Judgment was infinitely disproportion'd to Mercy . . . Coulds't thou see me entangled as I was, and see me so entangled with such a dreadful moment approaching as must necessarily decide my fate for ever, and would most probably, nay, almost to a certainty, decide it against me, coulds't thou see and foresee all this and be merciful? Vanquist before I fell, what could I do but fall? . . . What sort of Mercy is that which a poor forlorn creature reduced to childish imbecillity through infinite distress may forfeit for ever in a moment? . . . O cruel decree! that connected such terrible consequences with the lapse of a moment.[51]

"It is I who have been the hunted hare," Cowper writes, "and He who turn'd me out to be hunted has" – at this point the sentence breaks off.[52]

In a touching protest against such cruelties, Cowper depicted his parlor as a scene of innocent affection in which the animals play a leading role as both loved and loving creatures. The larger world is so dangerous, so beset with snares and hunters, that the cage figures, paradoxically, as a symbol of protective care. In his household Eden, Cowper reports in a letter to Lady Hesketh, "Beau [the spaniel] is well as are the two cats and the 3 birds, whose cages I am going to clean, and all send their love to you."[53]

4

Barbarian pleasures: against hunting

It was in the eighteenth century that "field sports" first encountered the
strong ideological antagonism that has dogged them, so to speak, ever since.
By 1838 William Howitt, surveying *The Rural Life of England*, could write
that the "charge of cruelty" is "perpetually directed" against hunters.[1] I do
not suggest that the attacks on hunting were similar in content to those
now, though much that was written then is still relevant and moving. The
polemic was different because so also were the cultural contexts, social
meanings, participants, and technologies of hunting.

I

To take game was then an exclusive privilege of the gentry. What was
considered to be game varied with time and place, but deer, grouse, and
pheasants were on the list and so usually were foxes by the early nineteenth century. Game could be hunted only by persons who owned land
worth at least £100 a year and others of equivalent social standing.[2] The
rest of mankind could not take game legally even on their own land, if
they had any, and even if the animals were destroying their crops. No one
was allowed to market it. At a hundred or two hundred guineas, hunting
horses cost about four times more than ordinary ones.[3] According to John
Lawrence, in 1829 it cost about £60 a year to keep a hunting horse.[4] If
one were Master of Hounds, the expenses for hounds, terriers, horses, and
four servants – a huntsman, groom, whipper-in, and dog keeper – were
reckoned at approximately £245 per year in 1765.[5] Riding habits added to
the expense. (All this explains, incidentally, why game was desirable on the
socially competitive menu. Since it could be obtained legally only by hunting or as a gift, it might suggest at the dinner table that one had friends in
the hunting class, though also it might not, for in fact most game was pur-
chased illegally.) The attack on hunting was also on a sociological group, a
circumstance that enormously energized and complicated the war of words.

Even more than is now the case, hunting was imagined as warlike. At this time Peter Beckford was, as John Lawrence put it, "deservedly our Oracle on the Subject" of fox hunting.[6] A Master of Hounds with a Jamaica sugar fortune, Beckford wrote his *Thoughts upon Hunting* in 1779 while recovering from a fall. "Fox-hunting is a kind of warfare," Beckford enthused; "its uncertainties, its fatigues, its difficulties, and its dangers, render it interesting above all other diversions."[7] It was the "Image of war," as William Somerville put it in *The Chase* (1735), though he added that hunting was without war's guilt.[8] The traditional argument in favor of hunting had been its social value in schooling a military aristocracy, a point that had been doing service since Xenophon's *Cyropaedia*. Peter Beckford quotes *Don Quixote* to make this argument. When Sancho wonders "what pleasure can you find . . . in killing a poor beast that never meant any harm," the Duke replies, "you are mistaken, Sancho . . . hunting wild beasts is the most proper exercise for knights and princes; for in the chase of a stout noble beast, may be represented the whole art of war."[9] Members of Parliament still said the same thing, and the idea received quasi-scientific authority from Buffon and his English redactors. In his article on the stag Buffon explained that "to be acquainted with the management of horses and arms are talents equally common to the warrior and the hunter. A familiarity with address, bodily exercise and fatigue, so necessary to support courage, are found in the chace, and carried into the field of battle."[10] Much cultural work, including poetry, had gone into endowing the hunted animals with the strength, cunning, valor, and general nobility that would make them worthy antagonists.

A hunting woman (there were some) seemed anomalous, and though many parsons galloped in the field, this too was thought questionable in a blood-bedabbled sport akin to war. Gradually as the Victorian age loomed, a new emphasis sifted into the traditional defense of hunting. One might still urge with the Duke in *Don Quixote* that hunting instills warlike skills and knowledge, but now one might also stress that hunting valuably hardens the future soldier to violence, prepares him to kill. Repugnance from hunting might in the early 1800s be termed "effeminate." It was even said that without hunting English manhood would become degenerate and imbued with foreign vices. Such remarks were made polemically and without analytic weight, but they have some historical interest as the expressions of hunters, some of whom already, it seems, viewed their sport as a display of maleness. Field sports and attitudes to them had at this time a role in defining both gender differences and different ideals of masculinity – the sympathetic, compassionate one extolled in sentimental literature, as we have seen it represented in Cowper and Burns, and the more aggressive, warrior one that expressed itself in passages now to be quoted.

Already in 1776 Francis Mundy dismissed critics of hunting as fops, pedants, and cowards in his poem on *Needwood Forest*.[11] In 1802 James Yorke explained in a letter to the Countess de Grey that fox hunting "prevents our young men from growing quite effeminate" and contributes to the success "of the English horse abroad, which are perhaps the only cavalry that ever won whole battles against a very superior force of horse and foot."[12] John Cook, a Master of Foxhounds from 1800 to 1813, supposed that without this sport, the "breed" of English manhood would deteriorate: "instead of the hardy, open-hearted, liberal-minded Briton, you would see nothing but an effeminate race" capable of shooting only "a tame pheasant."[13] A writer in the *Sporting Magazine*, 67 (January, 1826), thought that without hunting "gentlemen would turn into a degenerate race of *petits-maitres*, deeply imbued with the vices of foreign countries or with a squeamish hypocritical morality."[14] Such opinions were repeated throughout the nineteenth century. John Henry Walsh, for example, writing as Stonehenge, thought in 1855 that the advantages of field sports had been "exemplified in a very remarkable manner [at] Alma, Inkermann, Balaklava, and Sebastopol."[15]

It seems likely, in fact, that enthusiasm for hunting intensified and pervaded more widely in England as the nineteenth century wore on, while the attacks on it also became more numerous and committed. To give this point focus and particularity, I cite the work of John M. MacKenzie, *The Empire of Nature: Hunting, Conservation and British Imperialism* (1988). MacKenzie's book deals chiefly with the nineteenth-century slaughter of wildlife in parts of Africa and in India, but he notes in the homeland the development of the *battue*, the keeping of records of kills, the passion for trophies, the enmeshing of this with the study of natural history, the liking for scientific classification as a mode of domination and the creation of museums as a display of this. To this he adds the popularity of African hunting narratives in Victorian England. For all this MacKenzie suggests several explanations, and he especially notes the emotions and ideologies of Victorian imperialism. "Willingness to take life was an important part of this ethos, and hunting was seen as a necessary preparation and training for European expansion" – naturally so, for it was still seen as a training for war.[16] The slaughter of wild beasts in Africa and India belonged to the process of conquering, dominating, and taming the colonial lands and signified this process in its less tangible or, perhaps, less discussable aspects.

In this connection I notice a curious piece by John Aikin and Letitia Barbauld in their *Evenings at Home* (1792–96), a book for children. Entitled "The Council of Quadrupeds," it views the colonializing process from the point of view of the wild animals. In it Romantic regret at human violation of the natural world intertwines with anti-colonial sentiments, reinforcing them. "In the interior of the Cape of Good-Hope, the beasts of the forest had for ages lived in comparative peace."[17] Now, however, they encounter for the first time Europeans with guns, and as "the new settlers increased in number, the wild beasts sensibly diminished" (p. 332). The lion and the elephant call a council of the animals for the purpose of organizing resistance. Each animal recommends actions in accordance with its nature, some wanting to attack by night, some by day, some by stealth, some by headlong charge. Heated by their disagreements, they threaten each other, until the lion restores order and calls upon the most sagacious of them all, the elephant, for advice. In a long speech the elephant argues that resistance is hopeless. He has seen the "whites" destroying the native Africans with appalling brutality and treachery. "Such, I am afraid, would be our fate were we to brave their power," and his "advice . . . is, to retire from their settlements," to go "far beyond their reach" (pp. 336–37). This speech merely kindles further angry disagreement, however, and as the council breaks up, the predators once again pursue their prey. Many of the "evenings at home" have a moral, and the intended one of this piece seems to be "the folly of attempting to subdue their common foe while they were at variance with each other" (p. 337), a moral that might have seemed timely during the wars with France. The pathos, however, attaches to the animals and the Africans, whose resistance is hopeless against technology, superior social cohesion, numbers, and ruthlessness. Thus Aikin and Barbauld also make the shooting of African animals their vehicle for speaking of white racial dominance and imperialist conquest, but, opposing colonialism, they evoke sympathy for the hunted animals and peoples.

Perhaps the most formidable argument in defense of hunting was that it, like war, is natural. Animals are themselves hunters. From this point of view, persons who conflate the natural with the moral, as many intellectuals did in the Romantic era, are self-contradictory if they condemn hunting. As John Lawrence put it, there is a "natural inclination of the human mind to the sports of pursuit, which may be deemed analogous to the instincts of beasts of the chase." Since "nature herself" is "alone responsible" for cruelties that are "necessarily attendant" on hunting, "we may rationally and safely quiet our conscience."[18]

Critics of hunting were obliged to justify this activity in animals without doing so in humans. One solution was to ignore or minimize the
amount of predation in the natural world. Another was to compare human
motives for hunting with those of animals: modern humans do it for amusement, animals for survival. In Thomas Day's *Sandford and Merton*, the sage
Mr. Barlow explains to the child Harry that unless lions, tigers, wolves, and
so forth are hungry, "they seldom meddle with anything, or do unnecessary
mischief; therefore they are much less cruel than . . . many children, who
plague and torment animals without any reasons whatsoever."[19] Moreover,
animals act by instinct without moral consciousness:

TOMMY I protest, Sir, it is a large worm. And now he has swallowed it! I should
     never have suspected such a pretty bird could be so cruel.
MR. BARLOW Do you imagine that the bird is conscious of all that is suffered by
     the reptile?
TOMMY No, sir.
MR. BARLOW In him, then, it is not the same cruelty which it would be in you,
     who are endowed with reason and reflection. (p. 159)

The trouble with this argument was that it reinstated the essential, hierarchical difference between humans and animals that an animal lover might
wish to weaken.

In Day's book, for we continue to follow Day amid his perplexities, the
child hero, the exemplary Harry, is astonishingly kind to animals. Among
other items, he "would step out of the way for fear of hurting a worm . . . He
used to pat and stroke the horses as they were at work, and fill his pock-
ets with acorns for the pigs . . . gather green boughs for the sheep . . . go
supperless to bed, that he might feed the robin-redbreasts. Even toads,
frogs, and spiders . . . which most people destroy wherever they find them,
were perfectly safe with Harry: he used to say, they had a right to live as
well as we" (pp. 13–14). Harry rescues a wounded chicken and nurses it
back to health (pp. 27, 87), and beats the beater of a donkey (pp. 48–51).
When the squire is out with his dogs after a hare, Harry refuses to tell
which way the hare has gone, and the squire beats him (pp. 56–59).
Mr. Barlow tells the boys stories of animal gratitude, such as "Androcles
and the Lion" (pp. 44–49), and explains that if animals were not hunted,
they would be friendly. Animals are "wild only because they are afraid of
being hurt, and . . . run away only from the fear of danger" (p. 88). "I think
it is a great shame," says Harry, for humans "ever to be cruel to brute animals, when those creatures are so affectionate and loving toward them"
(p. 94).

But what about dangerous animals? When it comes to them, Day's sympathies are with humans. The vegetarian shepherd Sophron, in an inserted story of the ancient world, defends his sheep against wild predators in a "warfare, which was equally just and honorable" (p. 358). Day shows a tolerant understanding of some sailors who might have been accused of cruelty, for they had wantonly shot the cubs of a polar bear. Mr. Barlow explains that they "had often seen themselves in danger of being devoured," and fear made them "more unpitying than they would otherwise have been" (pp. 147–48).

What about peoples who hunt for survival, such as Eskimos, Amerindians, Africans, and the like? Hunting "has something cruel in the practice," says the Highland soldier who has served in North America: "it is a species of war which we wage with brute animals for their spoils; but if ever it can be considered as excusable, it is in these savage nations [Amerindians], who have recourse to it for their subsistence" (p. 420).

In fact, Day manifests an illogical enthusiasm for practices abroad that he would strongly have condemned at home. The reason is partly, I think, that he denounced colonialism and racism, and wished to extol the virtues of indigenous peoples, partly that he sympathized less with large, dangerous, and unfamiliar animals, and partly that exotic feats of courage thrilled his imagination. Harry tells Tommy about lion hunting in Africa with some enthusiasm, though certainly this animal was not wanted for food. Later in the novel, an African repeats this report, delighting in both the pride and courage of the animal and the skill and valor of the hunters, who are armed only with javelins (pp. 57, 492–93). There are similar descriptions of Eskimos hunting seals and whales (pp. 252–57) and Africans fighting crocodiles (pp. 128–29).

Day would certainly have denounced Arab practices in training camels were Englishmen employing them in the home country. But doings in Arabia he describes with complacency, for Arabs are "in many respects the most admirable [people], of all that inhabit this globe" (pp. 367–70). There is a similarly uncritical report of methods used in India for capturing and training wild elephants (p. 93). There is even a description of a sport in Argentina, where, with "admirable courage and address," bulls are lassoed, thrown, ridden, and knifed (pp. 479–84) – praise that sits uneasily in a novel that condemns English bullbaiting so strongly. Day's dislike, one suspects, was as much to his countrymen as to cruelty to animals.

Even though the main argumentative defense of hunting was its training for war, its pleasures were analyzed in quite other terms. Usually they were not said to be the exhilarations of aggression and killing. Though it dates from 1838, the statement by William Howitt, to quote him again, is typical of the previous fifty years. The appeal lies "in the pursuit of an object, and the art and activity by which a wild creature is captured, and in all those concomitants of pleasant scenery and pleasant seasons that enter into the enjoyment of rural sports."[20] Good health and sociability were usually also listed among the agreeables. The point of such analysis is that the killing of an animal, much less the infliction of suffering, is not the aim in hunting, not the source of its pleasure, but is merely an adjunct, which, says Howitt, "you would spare to your victim if you could." But you could not spare the victim, for unless hounds killed, they would not be keen on the trail.[21]

The polemic against hunting focused on its cruelty. Defenders could deny this altogether or maintain that the cruelties were inevitable, natural, slight, and outweighed by the usefulness of hunting. An article of the 1780s in the *Memoirs of the Manchester Literary and Philosophical Society* is typical of such defenses. The author does not cling to the opinion of Descartes that animals are mere machines and cannot feel. But, he says, death is not a "positive evil" to animals because they have no "gift of foresight," and "therefore . . . in terminating their existence, they only suffer a privation of pleasure." Moreover, since animals do not support each other in old age, the quick death of a hunted animal is painless compared to that "brought on by disease, or the decay of nature . . . compared therewith, the fate of the partridge from the gun of the fowler, or of the trout by the rod of the angler, is mild and enviable."[22]

However, for those persons who believed animals feel pain much as we do, the fact might tell against hunting. They regretted both the suffering of the animals and the human readiness to inflict it. Dislike of this was heightened by considerations dwelt on in earlier chapters, such as the idealization of nature, the ethic of sympathy, and the perception of pet keepers that animals are individuals, each with a unique life history and experience. Critics of hunting also seized whatever ancillary objections could be found against it. They dwelt on its rustic boorishness. Field sports were said to form a harsh, insensitive, unsympathetic, unsocial character, though sportsmen of course denied this. The rough hunter, dying without a friend, appears in many literary representations. In the last chapter I mentioned two poems of Cowper on this figure. Lord Chesterfield, intent on polishing the manners of his son, warned the boy not to associate with "our English Bumpkin Country Gentlemen" and their "illiberal sports of guns, dogs, and horses."[23] Critics also pointed out that a hunting aristocracy was an anachronism. The term "barbarian," the stock epithet for cruelty, could seem especially apt in application to hunters, since it implied coarse pleasures, crude manners, bloodthirstiness, and historical belatedness. Immense piles of dead grouse substantiated these impressions, and so did gruesome rituals that attended the killing of a fox or stag.

Hunting was criticized as economically wasteful. The land that was used to preserve game might better be exploited in growing crops. For example, Cranborne Chase, in Dorset, still had herds of wild deer in 1800, and "the new farming methods . . . could not be harmonized with the law of vert and venison. Landowners wishing to clear-fell woodland and extend their arable acreage within deer-proof enclosures were forbidden to do so by the lord of the Chase, defending his legitimate rights."[24] When fox hunters claimed that they kept down beasts that would otherwise raid chicken coops and sheep folds, their opponents replied that the gentry actually protected the coverts in which foxes bred. There were more foxes in the countryside than ever. And then there was the ruin to crops and fences as the field swept over them, and the strife with poachers as the game laws were enforced.

A few quotations will convey these opinions and sentiments. "The world may be divided," according to William Shenstone, "into people that read, people that write, people that think, and fox-hunters."[25] Being asked his opinion of hunting, Samuel Johnson said it "was the labour of the savages of North America, but the amusement of the gentlemen of England."[26] On other occasions Johnson was more charitable and reflective: "It is very strange, and very melancholy, that the paucity of human pleasures should persuade us ever to call hunting one of them."[27] Percy Shelley attacked the game laws, which protect "a barbarous and bloody sport, from which every enlightened and aimiable mind shrinks in abhorrence and disgust." "Persons of great property nurture animals on their estates . . . that they may kill and torture living beings for their sport."[28] Shelley also objected that "this amusement of shooting familiarizes people with the society of inferiours & the gross and harsh habits belonging to those sort of pursuits."[29] In *Don Juan* Byron quoted one of Lord Chesterfield's several sneers against hunters, and he told his sister, in a letter, "I hate all field sports."[30] (Byron was a reformed character in this respect. He had been a fox hunter in his youth, and he was twenty-six when he resolved to shoot no more birds.)[31] Since the critics of hunting were mostly intellectuals of what we would now call the middle class, hunters were socially superior to them. But in the hierarchies of intellect, manners, and sensibility, the critics felt themselves to be superior. "Men of refined understanding are never addicted to this vice," wrote George Nicholson, "and women who delight in the butchery of the chase, should unsex themselves, and be regarded as monsters."[32]

Three Dialogues on the Amusements of Clergymen, an anonymous publication of 1797, asks whether field sports are proper for clerics, a controversial question. Dean Stillingfleet, the authoritative speaker, raises the objections to hunting just cited, and adds also "the riotous uproar of the chase, so opposite to the mild serenity, which should characterize the clergyman – and the noisy, intemperate evening, to which it often leads." Considering this "accumulation of mischief . . . I should be sorry any clergyman should give his countenance to it." When a young clergyman who enjoys the chase suggests that hunting is a "manly exercise," the Dean replies, "If the *manliness* of the action lie in the risk you run of breaking your neck, for *no end*, it would be still greater manliness to jump down a precipice."[33]

In another anonymous pamphlet, *The Hare* (1799), the criticism is from the standpoint of nature, that is, of the calm groves and fields. In a striking, quasi-Wordsworthian reversal of the real case, hunters are depicted as city dwellers, that is, they bring the passions of city life destructively into the natural world, transferring "the turbulence of their spirits from the croud [of cities] to the retirement [of countryside]; and, when they are wearied of engaging in conflict with their fellow creatures, they turn the tide of their ferocity upon the brute creation."[34]

The Reverend Legh Richmond, rector of Turvey, wrote moral stories of village life that reached a very wide audience. His readers were so devoted that he and his opinions became objects of interest. After he died, a friend collected and published his sayings. Generally he was Evangelical and very antagonistic to dancing, card-playing, the theater, and other "flesh-pots of Egypt." Richmond viewed hunting as sinful because it deliberately inflicted suffering. "The man who should whip a beast to death or cut him up alive, like an Abyssinian savage, would be deemed a monster; yet the same man may hunt to death, and halloo, and exult with satisfaction, while his dogs are tearing to pieces a defenseless animal, and yet be considered a gentleman and a Christian."[35]

When Peter Beckford published his 1781 *Thoughts Upon Hunting*, the *Monthly Review* pounced on it. Quoting Beckford on the coursing of hares, the reviewer pointed out, correctly, that the hunters' intention was "not to put a speedy end to the sufferings of this little timorous animal; but to prolong its terror, until it has tried all the efforts agonized nature can dictate, and until the utmost exertions of its feeble strength are painfully exhausted." (According to the medieval *Master of Game*, "a hare shall last

well four miles or more or less, if she be an old male hare.")[36] After citing
a number of items, the reviewer calls "upon the feelings of any man who
does not avowedly disclaim all tender feelings, to attend to the treatment
of animals as represented in the work before us, and then to lay his hand on
his heart, and declare how far they agree with those sentiments we dignify
by the term humanity."[37]

The cruelties that might be decried were not only to grouse, pheasants,
hares, otters, foxes, and deer – the quarry in the pursuit. The training
and running of dogs involved habitual flogging. John Cook, the master of
hounds quoted earlier, advised that it is almost impossible to train hounds
without flogging them.[38] The hearty William Somerville seems not sadistic,
exactly, but without reluctance to inflict pain. He writes in *The Chase* that
the whip, the huntsman's "brisk assistant," should "bite to the quick."[39]
In the first chapter I described methods that might be used to train fox
hounds not to annoy sheep and not to to turn aside at the scent of a hare.
During a hunt, dogs and horses might be forced to exhaustion. Somerville,
to quote him again, has a long passage on a foundered horse in a fox hunt:

> In vain the impatient rider frets and swears,
> With falling spurs harrows his mangled sides;
> He can no more: his stiff unpliant limbs
> Rooted in earth, unmoved and fixed he stands,
> For every cruel curse returns a groan,
> And sobs, and faints, and dies.[40]

Servants might be in hardly better case. For though the gentry of course
rode, the servants might keep up on foot, like Wordsworth's Simon Lee,
the old huntsman, who in his youth "all the country could outrun,/ Could
leave both man and horse behind."[41]

Given these considerations, many persons tried to ease conscience with
a compromise: we must hunt with all possible kindness to dogs, horses,
and foxes. To represent this position, I cite John Lawrence in his book on
British Field Sports. He is uncertain about the ethics of hunting. He tells us
he never hunted himself, but I do not know the reason. He distinguishes
between the hunting of deer and hares, on the one hand, and foxes on the
other. He was influenced, he says, by reading James Thomson to believe
that timorous, inoffensive animals should be left in peace (p. 296). Foxes,
however, are themselves cruel predators, and it is right and useful to destroy
them. Yet that the chase involved the ancillary sufferings I mentioned of
dogs and horses gave Lawrence pause. And he was appalled at the bloody
rituals that concluded a hunt, when with a howl of "tear him" the corpse of

the fox was thrown to the dogs. Thus divided, he argued that field sports must be conducted in harmony with "the moral sense and the feelings of humanity" (p. 15), and, ever practical, Lawrence described at length kindlier methods of training horses and dogs for the hunt and more compassionate management of them during it. (One of the problems was of course that the dogs and horses might need no whipping or spurring to run themselves to death, might seem as ardent in pursuit as their masters.) The foxes were to be dispatched quickly and painlessly. Still uneasy, Lawrence relieved his qualms in passionate, unequivocal remarks on the baiting of animals: he condemns "every infamy which comes under the foul and disgraceful name of BAITING, OR BINDING TO THE STAKE, for the base and unnatural purpose of worrying out animal life by protracted suffering" (p. 7). As I noticed before, you could relieve a bad conscience about the sport you favored by declaring another worse.

The polemic against hunting, though often fierce, was inhibited in comparison with that to which I come in the next chapter, against abuse of animals by the lower orders. It was checked by the social prestige of hunters. See, for example, the anonymous member of the Manchester Literary and Philosophical Society I quoted earlier: that hunting is enjoyed by many persons who are "at once the ornament and the Blessings of society" proves that it cannot be a cruel diversion.[42] The political power of hunters also inhibited criticism. Without the support of the squires, there was no hope of legislation to protect animals from the myriad other abuses to which they were exposed. It should also be remembered that many clergymen were dependent on the gentry for their livings. Perhaps such considerations led James Granger and many others to assure their congregations that the charge of cruelty "is only applicable to the most stupid, ignorant, and uncivilized part of our countrymen. Those of higher rank and knowledge are far more humane and benevolent."[43]

II

Poetry played an important part in forming opinion, but poets did not speak with one voice. As Sir Walter Scott described a hunt in "The stag at eve . . . ," the first Canto of *The Lady of the Lake* (1810), he still performed the traditional cultural work of ennobling the quarry. The "noble stag" is compared to a "leader," a "Chief," and a "monarch," like the hunter, who turns out to be King James incognito. The hounds are "foes," the hunt a battle or "silvan war," and both monarchs win glory. But even in Scott the chase is presented, at the start, from the stag's point of view and the stag escapes at the end. To this extent Scott's poem concedes to the modern feelings of his readers.

Poetry is a traditional art, learned from predecessors and governed in varying degree by conventions. It does not easily shed the cultural traditions of the past, in fact, as they become more remote, a Romantic poet may cling to them nostalgically. The hunting song flourished most incongruously at this time. It was written not only by poets such as Scott ("Waken, lords, and ladies gay") but by Burns, although, as we noticed, Burns attacked hunters in his letters and in other poems.[44] Burns's lilting "My heart's in the Highlands . . . a chasing the deer," was composed with perfect insincerity except in its desire for escape and freedom. The most unexpected of all poets in the genre of the hunting song were John Clare and Robert Bloomfield. Both presented themselves as peasant poets and nature lovers and yet composed stock celebrations of this aristocratic pursuit: Robert Bloomfield in his "Hunting Song" in *The Farmer's Boy*; John Clare in "Sports of the Field," "To Day the Fox Must Die," "Milton Hunt," and "Hunting Song" –

> Then mount on your saddle in doublet of scarlet
> & bring in the hounds to the field.[45]

Field sports were repudiated in verse by Thomson, Goldsmith, Burns, Cowper, Beattie, Wordsworth, Byron, and Shelley, not to mention poets of lesser fame or influence. Women poets are not on this list because for them the subject was impossible. A representative poem on hunting is Robert Burns's "On Seeing a Wounded Hare limp by me . . . " It begins in rage at cruelty – "Inhuman man! Curse on thy barb'rous art" – and ends in elegy:

> Oft as by winding Nith I, musing, wait
> The sober eve, or hail the chearful dawn,
> I'll miss thee sporting o'er the dewy lawn,
> And curse the ruffian's aim, and mourn thy hapless fate.[46]

The repudiation of hunting is associated in this poem with a certain notion of the poetic character. The speaker is a reflective, sensitive, lonely haunter of landscape, romantic and a bit mysterious. His loneliness suggests some hurt in past life. He seems to sympathize more with nature than with mankind; at least, the only companion we hear of was the hare.

In the last chapter I mentioned the attraction for eighteenth-century readers of the Horatian ideal of life, the cultivated, country retirement that Cowper represented as his own. Evoking such a life in *The Seasons* (1726–30), James Thomson found, like Cowper, an enormous response among readers. The necessary material elements, in Thomson's analysis, are rural quiet, leisure, books, a few friends, and a bit of income, what Thomson, sounding like Jane Austen, calls "an elegant Sufficiency."[47] On the moral and spiritual side there would be content, a clear conscience, sympathy, aesthetic appreciation, and religious communion. So lived, the seemingly empty round of days is filled with perceptions, discriminations, and pleasures that others might not obtain, with an attention to nature that is motivated partly by the sense of beauty, partly by imaginative sympathy, and ultimately by religious feeling, for God is in everything.[48] And so, as we noticed, Thomson suffers with the worm on the hook, with the fly in the web, with the fish on the line, with the birds that, he writes, deprive themselves of food to feed their offspring, and with the stockdove whose mate has been shot. But let us note well that the way of feeling depends on the elegant sufficiency. It is a mark of economic as well as cultural status. Romantic sympathy with nature presupposed at least a modest income.

Of course this attitude and way of life were incompatible with hunting. Thomson describes the netting and shooting of birds, the coursing of a hare, the chase of a stag, and a fox hunt, repudiating all. He narrates the chase from the point of view of the stag and foregrounds its suffering, which is mental as well as physical. It tries with increasing desperation to escape the rout behind; "sobbing," it makes for its familiar glades; it tries to cool its "burning sides" in the brook; and finally, in "despair," it stands at bay:

> And big round Tears run down his dappled Face;
> He groans in Anguish; while the growling Pack,
> Blood-happy, hang at his fair jutting Chest,
> And mark his beauteous chequer'd Sides with Gore.[49]

Thomson had famous poetic precedent for these lines in John Denham's *Cooper's Hill* (1642), where a splendid description of a stag hunt tells how the tired, forsaken animal resolves to stand, and then to fly, and finally plunges in despair into the stream, but is pursued even there:

> But fearless they pursue, nor can the floud
> Quench their dire thirst; alas, they thirst for blood.[50]

Deer parks had been destroyed during the civil wars of the seventeenth century. By 1800, stags could be found only in Scotland and in a few of the wilder, more remote parts of England, such as Exmoor. Writing in 1790, Thomas Bewick's partner Ralph Beilby said that "the Stag is almost unknown in its wild state."[51] Foxes had formerly been regarded as mere vermin, but as stags became rare, foxes became the passionately pursued quarry. They were then upgraded in character; in other words, the courage, cunning, and so forth formerly attributed to the "monarch of the forest" and its pursuers were transferred to the fox and its hunters. (Around 1800 there were roughly ten thousand of the latter.) Thomson glances ironically at the cultural promotion of the fox by narrating the pursuit of it as mock epic, a style which describes low things in high, bombastic terms. The exaggeration parodies how fox hunters themselves felt and spoke about their doings:

> Him, from his craggy winding Haunts unearth'd,
> Let all the Thunder of the Chace pursue.
> Throw the broad Ditch behind you; o'er the Hedge
> High bound, resistless.[52]

After the hunt there is a night of revelry. As Thomson describes this, he most reveals his repugnance. The ancient manor is gloomy, its "drear walls" hung with dead game, "antique figures fierce." Manners are as crude and medieval as the manor. With "desperate knife" the diners plunge into an immense sirloin and pasty. Then comes a carouse, with staggering, puking, and passing out. Squirearchical loutishness was a common theme of Enlightened, middle-class, Whig ideology, and Thomson mobilizes this theme in his assault on hunting.[53]

In the period that is my subject the most original, ambivalent, and subtle of the poems on hunting was Wordsworth's "Hart-Leap Well." The relation between its two parts confuses many readers, since the parts seem to express different attitudes. But just so Wordsworth confronts his own self-division and recreates it in the reader, who must identify successively with the hunter and with the stag. Ortega y Gasset speaks of the "orgiastic element . . . the dionysiac, which flows and boils in the depths of all hunting."[54] Many hunters never touch such depths, but for those hunters who find their sport the most enjoyable of all occupations, who are absorbed by it and peculiarly alive while engaged in it, Ortega is surely right, at least in the sense that the hunter's state of mind cannot be explained merely by the delights of outdoors and the feeling of prowess. Looking into himself, Wordsworth understood this and created the heroic, appalling hunter of "Hart-Leap Well."

In writing about the chase of a stag, Wordsworth focused on the hunting that was most saturated with Romantic associations, with baronial pageantry and far-heard horns. The reality was, of course, rather different: a male deer of about five years old was rousted out of a covert and pursued by a yelling crowd of men and dogs until, exhausted, it could run no more.

It was then torn to death by the dogs or shot. Nevertheless, stags were the largest and fastest of the quarry that could be pursued in England, they had the most stamina, and they could be dangerous, at least to the dogs. Whatever virtues of courage and endurance may be exhibited in hunting might most be seen in the chase of stags. Hence this of all hunts was most readily susceptible to an idealizing representation. Moreover, among the field sports, stag hunting was the least concern of animal sympathizers, for, as I said, by 1798–99, when the poem was composed, few stags still ran wild in England.

Wordsworth might have seen stag hunting occasionally in the Lake District and on Exmoor in 1797–98, when he was living in Alfoxden. Simon Lee, the "running huntsman merry" of Wordsworth's poem, was based on a neighbor who had formerly been huntsman to the Alfoxden squires. Probably Simon had pursued foxes, perhaps also hares and stags; the poem shows that Wordsworth was familiar with practices of hunting. The impoverished and secluded vale of Grasmere did not ring with tallyho! in Wordsworth's time, although John Peel, the fox-hunting squire of the famous song, was at Caldbeck, about twenty miles north of Keswick on the other side of Skiddaw. So far as I know, Wordsworth himself never hunted, unless we count snaring woodcocks as a boy. But hunting had a special meaning for his imagination. The famous skating scene in *The Prelude* pictures exhilarated vitality and associates it with hunting: on the ice the children imitated

> the chase
> And woodland pleasures, – the resounding horn,
> The pack loud chiming, and the hunted hare.[55]

The boy was "Proud and exulting like an untired horse / That cares not for his home" (lines 432–33).

Five years after "Hart-Leap Well" was composed, we find William and Dorothy Wordsworth on a hillside above Martindale. Amid the peaceful breathing of nature they were not perfectly contented. They liked "the quiet everyday sounds, the lowing of cattle, bleating of sheep, and the very gentle murmuring of the valley stream," yet "could not but think what a grand effect the sound of the bugle-horn would have among these mountains": the tumultuous, warlike stag hunt with horses, horns, and hounds. They were glad that the bugle "is still heard once a year at the chace," though they felt sorry for "the poor deer."[56]

Wordsworth famously believed that "the human mind is capable of being excited without the application of gross and violent stimulants"; moreover, "one being is elevated above another, in proportion as he possesses this capability."[57] Wordsworth's momentary sigh for the "grand effect" of the bugle-horn represents a not uncharacteristic falling away from this ideal. If it is not a "craving" for "gross and violent stimulants," it is at least a slight dereliction from "the calm existence that is mine when I / Am worthy of myself."[58]

In a passage of *Home at Grasmere* (MS B) that is closely connected with "Hart-Leap Well," Wordsworth puts forward his own version of the Enlightenment plot of history as the moral progress of mankind. He says that when he and Dorothy were actually at Hart-Leap Well they foresaw in trance or vision a future era when love and knowledge will bring "blessedness... To all the Vales of earth and all mankind."[59] He inserts their way of life into this historical vision by hoping that in their quiet Grasmere nook they may be forerunners. In other words, the sensitivity, imaginativeness, and reflectiveness to which they owe their happiness may one day be general human possessions. Both in this passage and in "Hart-Leap Well," the hunting of the stag functions as a reminder and symbol – a summary, as it were – of the old world that must and will be left behind.

Yet the old world strongly persisted in Wordsworth, and not only in transient nostalgias for hunting horns. He thrilled to stories of warlike prowess and glory. He was capable of an almost beserk battle-joy, at least in imagination. Even in the peaceful *Home at Grasmere* he confesses that

> I cannot at this moment read a tale
> Of two brave Vessels matched in deadly fight
> And fighting to the death, but I am pleased
> More than a wise Man ought to be; I wish,
> I burn, I struggle, and in soul am there.
>
> (MS B lines 929–33)

This is the side of Wordsworth that enabled him, as narrator, to sympathize with the emotions of the hunter, Sir Walter, in the first section of "Hart-Leap Well." No one has seen this identification more clearly than Don H. Bialostosky, and I quote from his analysis: the narrator's

references to "that glorious day," "this glorious act," "a joyful case," and "that darling place" assume his hero's attitudes toward the events of the hunt without explicitly distinguishing them from his own... he sympathizes with and in part resembles the Sir Walter he invents... Only if we have seen that the narrator's character and sympathies are as evident in the first part of this poem as in the last will we recognize this motive in his moral and appreciate the need he has to utter it.[60]

In the plot of "Hart-Leap Well" a medieval stag hunt lasts so long that all but one of the hunters are left behind, the dogs fall away or die of exhaustion, and Sir Walter is using up his third horse when the stag, after three prodigious bounds from the top of a hill, expires in a dell next to a spring. To commemorate this chase Sir Walter erects three stone pillars marking the final leaps. He provides a stone basin for the spring or well and builds nearby "a pleasure-house" and "a small arbor" (lines 57–58). In the second part of the poem, situated in Wordsworth's time, the pleasure-house has vanished and the arbor remains only as four lifeless stumps of trees. The narrator, a passer-by, sees the stones and hears from a shepherd the story associated with them. The well groans occasionally, the shepherd adds, and from this and other signs he concludes that the spot is accursed. Though some say a murder was committed, the shepherd traces the curse to the suffering, which the landscape deplores, of "that unhappy Hart" (line 140). The shepherd is sure that the curse will last till nature has effaced all of the memorials that Sir Walter erected – "Till trees, and stones, and fountain, all are gone" (line 160). The narrator – there is no reason not to call him Wordsworth – then adds eloquent reflections on the Being that loves nature's creatures:

> The Being that is in the clouds and air,
> That is in the green leaves among the groves,
> Maintains a deep and reverential care
> For the unoffending creatures whom he loves.
>   . . .
> One lesson, Shepherd, let us two divide,
> Taught both by what she [Nature] shows, and what conceals;
> Never to blend our pleasure or our pride
> With sorrow of the meanest thing that feels.
>   (lines 165–68, 177–80)

Commentaries on this poem in books and articles show that if the poem seeks to instill compassion for animals, it was written in vain. In "Hart-Leap Well," as I read it, the chase, its practices, and the emotions it evokes in hunters are exhibited and ultimately criticized. More broadly, the poem pleads for sympathy with animals. And animals themselves are a figure in the poem for nature in general – as is still the case in discourses today – so that the widest issue the poem raises is that of human relations to the natural world, whether mankind is necessarily egoistically closed and predatory. The commentators generally do not share the poet's feeling for animals. According to John Jones, that the suffering creature is an animal rather than a human being allows Wordsworth to evade the problem of evil or, more exactly, to resolve it in an unsatisfactory way, "banging the big Pantheistic drum."[61] "A wronged human being would be another matter," Bialostosky agrees.[62] Because the "victim is an animal," says James H. Averill, "we do not identify with it." Averill thinks that "the main issue is not the morality of hunting but the morality of pathos" in literary fictions.[63] For Geoffrey Hartman the poem is about modes of imagination; he sees a progression "from one type of animism to another: from the martial type of the Knight, to the pastoral type of the Shepherd, and finally to that of the Poet . . . from primitive to sophisticated kinds of visionariness."[64] The subtle argument of John Hodgson enmeshes the poem in the development of Wordsworth's religious feelings.[65] For John Turner the poem represents the "democratic advance" from feudalism to the present moment when the poet and shepherd can talk "in genuine interchange, for all their difference in class."[66] Had "Hart-Leap Well," like other poems of Wordsworth, been about vulnerable humans – children, women, the mad, the poor, the elderly – interpreters would less reduce or ignore the creaturely desperation it describes.[67]

As the mighty hunter, Sir Walter represents what by Wordsworth's time most poets condemned. But despite the precedents that had piled up in other poems, the first part of "Hart-Leap Well" does not foreground the suffering of the stag or overtly protest against it, but dwells on the tenacity, elation, and triumph of Sir Walter. A contemporary reviewer of the *Lyrical Ballads* remarked that "Hart-Leap Well" represents successively the passions of "exultation and pity."[68] Like many readers in his time, the reviewer was ready to enjoy each emotion as it is presented, without undue striving for consistency. Had he said that the reader is made to share Sir Walter's exultation in order to be involved in his guilt, when pity makes the guilt apparent, he would have been still closer to Wordsworth's intention.

However, for reflective readers, even Part 1 of the poem represents Sir Walter's emotions as morally questionable, most especially when he "gazed upon the spoil" – the dead stag – "with silent joy" (line 36). The meanings of "spoil" connect war, plunder, and hunting, and the word also suggests, in this context, that something has been spoiled. The "silent joy" of Sir Walter irresistibly brings to mind the emotion of the boy in "Nutting," "Breathing with such suppression of the heart / As joy delights in" – a sadistic joy before a helpless victim.[69] Obviously a representation of sadistic feelings, if they are what Wordsworth depicts, would tell against hunting. That the joy is "silent" suggests a psychological tension, which Sir Walter discharges by resolving to build his pleasure house. Like Wordsworth himself on many occasions, Sir Walter desires to memorialize a spot of landscape with which his emotion is strongly connected, to make the place express his feelings.[70]

A pleasure-house seems a surprising way to commemorate a hunt and is the more improbable on a bleak, lonely moor. The improbability of the story might almost tempt one to believe, as Mary Moorman does in her biography of Wordsworth, that he actually heard from a shepherd the story of the hunt and pleasure house.[71] However, in Wordsworth's long letter to Coleridge, December 24–27, 1799, describing the winter journey in which this meeting with a shepherd supposedly took place, Wordsworth does not mention Hart-Leap Well at all. In the "Home at Grasmere" passage that alludes to a "trance" at Hart-Leap Well, he says only that a hunted beast had died there. In his later note to Isabella Fenwick he says that an old shepherd "told us the story so far as concerned the name of the well, and the hart, and pointed out the stones."[72] Thus only the poem tells of a pleasure-house, and the description of it in the poem is unsettled, as though Wordsworth had not imagined it clearly. Sir Walter calls it a pleasure-house, shed, cot, and mansion. The shepherd calls it a mansion, a palace, and a great lodge.

The truth of Wordsworth's story has sometimes been an issue in responses to the poem. For readers who take lyric poetry as fiction, as invention, the question has little importance. But in the nineteenth century, most readers followed a different convention in reading: except when a lyric was obviously spoken in an assumed voice, as in Blake's "The Little Black Boy," it uttered the personal feelings of the author. And the event that occasioned these feelings was supposed to be just as authentic, to have been experienced by the author more or less as it was represented in the poem. Wordsworth's ancillary remarks about the poem supported this way of reading, and readers naturally attempted to locate on the ground a spring to which the poem might refer. These matters have lately been investigated by David Chandler, who credits Wordsworth's story and thinks my "scepticism . . . quite unwarrented."[73] Wordsworth's introductory note to the poem located the well "about five miles from Richmond in Yorkshire, and near the side of the road that leads from Richmond to Askrigg." No guide book, local history, or map before 1854 referred to a Hart-Leap Well in this vicinity, but there was a "Bowes Well," and it seems likely that the name of this candidate was altered to conform with Wordsworth's poem, though other explanations are possible. Seekers could not find the stones described in the poem, but a local antiquarian remembered in 1854 that they had once been visible and had been lost in making a wall. In fact, one person, studying the wall, observed that it incorporated a large standing stone. All this is set forth by David Chandler (pp. 20–22), who also cites what seems to me a more probable source for the standing stones than visible things around the well. "Within thirty miles of Sockburn-on-Tees where the Wordsworths had been living for several months" before taking the road and meeting the old shepherd (p. 21), are still to be seen some stones described by George Young in *A History of Whitby, and Streoneshalh Abbey*: "two stones, each 2ft. high, placed at the distance of 42ft., and on one of them are the words HART LEAP; the stones being erected to commemorate" the leap of a hunted stag.[74] Had there once been a pleasure-house on this site, as the poem claims, its ruins might still have been available to the poet's contemplation, but the narrator does not mention them in the poem and neither did Wordsworth in his notes and statements about it. David Chandler is equally silent about the pleasure-house. The massive 1823 *History of Richmondshire* by Thomas Dunham Whitaker has no reference to a Hart-Leap Well and locates no former mansion, palace, lodge, or pleasure-house at or near the site. Whether Wordsworth ever saw the stones, or met the shepherd, I do not know, but the pleasure-house was surely an invention.

As such, it is interesting. Wordsworth may have had in mind, as do many readers, the pleasure-dome in Coleridge's "Kubla Khan." Any building – a hunting lodge, a tower – might have commemorated the hunt, but only a pleasure-house would have associated it with erotic feelings. A common meaning of "pleasure-house" suggests this, of course, and Sir Walter underscores the suggestion. His pleasure-house is a "place of love for damsels that are coy" (line 60): he will "make merry" in it with his "Paramour" (lines 70–72). To this day the pursuit and killing of deer is represented as a quasi-sexual experience, by both defenders and antagonists of hunting, and the association of woman and deer is age-old in western culture.[75] The first part of the poem is lavish with erotically suggestive imagery, such as the stone pillars and the basin or cup that receives the "living well." When Sir Walter, "too happy for repose or rest . . . gazed and gazed upon that darling spot" (lines 45–48), the spot is literally where the deer lies dead, but no reader can ignore the connotations.

As he hunts the stag and then gazes at its corpse, Sir Walter enjoys emotions of prowess, power, dominance, pride, and grandiosity – in fact, he experiences so enhanced a sense of self that he feels invulnerable and immortal. He expresses the latter feelings by transferring them to the pleasure-house, which will last "Till the foundations of the mountain fail" (line 73). Thus the description of the hunt, in Part I of the poem, expresses and evokes morally conflicting responses. Sir Walter is a figure of vitality, joyousness, courage, tenacity, cruelty, lust, egoism, and megalomania. The suggestions of solipsistic egoism are reinforced by the falling away, repeatedly emphasized, of Sir Walter's retinue (lines 15, 25–28, 34), which leaves a "doleful silence" (line 12) in the air. The situation of Sir Walter somewhat resembles that of Coleridge's Ancient Mariner – "Alone, alone, all, all alone" (line 232). In both poems egoistic self-assertion expresses itself in killing an animal and is figured as solitude.

At moments in the narrative Sir Walter is compared to features of landscape – to a cloud (line 2) and a wind (line 17). He also is swift as a falcon (line 11), and his horse shares his joyous excitement (lines 9–10). These comparisons would be puzzling if the poem were structured on a simple dualism of man versus nature, pleasure-house (architecture, minstrelsy, dance) versus landscape, for the comparisons suggest that Sir Walter's motions and feelings also are natural. This simple dualism is mediated, however, by another, that of past versus future (and present). The suggestion is that hunting and the emotions that accompany it were natural in the past but will not be in the future. Like "Tintern Abbey," the *Prelude*, and many other poems by Wordsworth, "Hart-Leap Well" presents a development of, or into, a state of higher moral sensitivity. The difference is that "Hart-Leap Well" locates this development not in the maturing individual but in mankind through history.

If Sir Walter represents the mentality of the middle ages, he is contrasted to the narrator, a modern poet. This person is fully able to include Sir Walter, that is, to understand and sympathize with Sir Walter's hunting passions. Yet the modern poet, more reflective, sensitive, and aware than Sir Walter, has no wish to hunt, because his insight and feeling connect him more sympathetically with nature and with nature in a deeper sense – with the "Being that is in the clouds and air / That is in the green leaves" (lines 165–66). This Being was always opposed to hunting, as we see in the refusal or inability of the landscape to flourish where the stag was killed. But mankind must develop sensitivity over time. If we applied the language of personal development from "Tintern Abbey," we might say that Sir Walter embodies the "coarser pleasures of my boyish days" and the modern poet intuits and loves the life that "rolls through all things" (lines 73, 102). Sir Walter is "proud and exulting," like the child skater in the *Prelude*. In a word, Sir Walter is boyish.

Wordsworth's two poems "To a Butterfly" offer a useful gloss. In "Stay near me – do not take thy flight!" the speaker recalls that he and his sister would chase butterflies in their childhood. He was the hunter: "A very hunter did I rush / Upon the prey." He was also a soldier, for in a conversation with Dorothy, William recalled that "they used to kill all the white ones [butterflies] when he went to school because they were Frenchmen."[76] Dorothy, on the other hand, "feared to brush / The dust from off its wings." "God love her!" the speaker interjects, thus indicating that he now warmly shares her tender, loving attitude. In the other poem "To a Butterfly" ("I've watched you now . . .") the orchard belonging to himself and his sister, now adults, has become a "sanctuary" where butterflies are protected, so much has he changed since the "sweet childish days" when he was a hunter. The child-hunter is not in the least condemned in these poems, is, in fact, indulgently remembered. But thanks in part to his sister's example and companionship, he has developed into a person who appreciates the beauty of the insects and sympathizes with their naturally happy existence.

As the second part of "Hart-Leap Well" begins, the narrator, this modern, reflective poet, says that his subject matter is not of the adventurous kind just presented in Part 1. Though Wordsworth avoids identifying this poet with the artifice of pastoral, it is fully appropriate that he should meet a shepherd and engage him in dialogue. The pastoral care of shepherds for their flock is about to be extended as a "deep and reverential care" for all animals.

As the shepherd tells the story of Sir Walter's chase, the narrative is governed by sentiments and strategies that were typical of contemporary discourse against hunting. The focus is on the stag, not Sir Walter. The suffering of the animal is emphasized, and is psychological as well as bodily – "What thoughts must through the creature's brain have past!" (line 141). The shepherd endows the deer with an individual life history, with a story that makes it interesting. The shepherd credits the stag with quasi-human, wholly sympathetic emotions. For example, the shepherd suggests that the stag returned to die at this particular spring because "he" loved the place (line 147). The stag might have been born nearby:

> This water was perhaps the first he drank
> When he had wandered from his mother's side.
>
> (lines 151–52)

Tear-jerking details fill two stanzas, rousing pity and indignation, so that the reader identifies with the deer and finds the hunter deplorable.

Negative judgments on the hunter are laid one over the other, and some of them are attributed to supernatural powers. Some persons, the shepherd reports, believe that the waters of the spring groan because a murder took place there. Literally the locals are wrong, but the suggestion is planted that the hunt is a murder. The poet, in his final stanzas, adds the weight of his deliberate criticism, and also attributes his own sentiments to the Being in nature. Meanwhile, the site has long since made itself waste, "doleful," and if the interpretations of the shepherd are correct, the landscape has thus signified its disapproval of the hunt. It may be noticed, however, that unlike Cowper and Thomson, Wordsworth maintains a sad, steady reflectiveness without anger against the hunter. This is appropriate to the poem because, unlike other critics of hunting, this poet is not frustrated and hopeless. The dell now looks like perpetual winter (line 115), but a "milder day" is coming (line 175), when nature will again "put on her beauty and her bloom" (line 172) at this spot. Sir Walter's monuments "shall all be overgrown" (line 176), and hunting will be no more.

Thus "Hart-Leap Well" may be read as another of the many poems by Wordsworth which begin in excited, maybe desirous emotion and end in reflective calm. In such poems the intense initial state usually involves troubling cross-currents of anxiety, egoistic self-assertion, lust, fear, or guilt. The final calm is linked to a widened perspective, a more sympathetic, receptive state of mind, a deeper communion with the spirit of the universe. This is the plot of "There Was a Boy," of "Nutting," and of the episodes of bird-snaring and boat-stealing in the first book of the *Prelude*. In "Tintern Abbey" and the *Prelude* Wordsworth imposes this plot on his life history as a whole, and in the poems "To a Butterfly," and many others, he constructs the same story in a fragmentary way. The moment of headlong, passionate arousal lies in youth, needless to say. "Simon Lee" keeps the basic structure in which intense, transient vitality – Simon's days of hunting – end in deeper awareness. But in "Simon Lee" reflective insight is not granted to the aged huntsman but to the narrator, who hopes to find and foster it also in the reader.

What is problematic in many of these poems, and certainly in "Hart-Leap Well," is the acceptance of tranquility, as Wordsworth represents it, as the more desirable state. For, as has long been recognized, the tranquility seems, at times, to imply unfeelingness or lifelessness, and is occasionally compared to death. If the subject is human history, I suggest, final tranquility – the "milder day" (line 175) of "Hart-Leap Well" – involves the vanishing of mankind from the face of the earth.

In commentary on the poem the meaning of the "milder day" is usually determined by reference to MS B of "Home at Grasmere," which uses the phrase and refers to the death of the stag at Hart-Leap Well. Here the "milder day" is unambiguously a future time when, as we noted, "all mankind" will share the "blessedness" that the poet and his sister now know in Grasmere. In this state of mind one would not be a hunter, and when, in "Home at Grasmere," it seems that a shepherd may have shot one of the wild swans, the idea is rejected as impossible. Whoever lives in this vale must feel an "overflowing love"

> for all
> Which is around them, love for every thing
> Which in this happy Valley we behold![77]

In the "milder day" of the future, the relations of human beings with animals will presumably be like those in Eden.

Using this passage in "Home at Grasmere" to gloss "Hart-Leap Well," a reader might infer that in the "milder day" of the latter poem, mankind will have learnt a "reverential care / For the unoffending creatures." The vanishing of Sir Walter, of his pleasure-house, and finally of all trace of him might be a figure for the transformation of historical humanity, of "what we are, and have been" (line 174), into a utopian humanity in the future. The sympathetic personalities of the shepherd and especially of the poet might be taken as evidence of man's spiritual progress since the days of Sir Walter and as proleptic of humanity in the future.

On the other hand, nothing in "Hart-Leap Well" requires or even strongly suggests this interpretation. Tremendous emphasis is given to the effacing of Sir Walter, his fellow hunters, and his monuments. "Horse and man" of his retinue "are vanished, one and all" (line 15); "Where is the throng, the tumult of the race? / The bugles that so joyfully were blown" (lines 25–26); "Till the foundations of the mountains fail," Sir Walter boasts, "My mansion with its arbor shall endure" (lines 73–74) – the obvious irony imparts the opposite thought to the reader; "The Knight, Sir Walter, died in course of time"; "the pleasure-house is dust" (line 169); "These monuments shall all be overgrown" (line 176). Since these "monuments" represent "what we are, and have been," it is natural to understand their evanescence as a figure for that of mankind.

The poet says that Nature

> leaves these objects to a slow decay,
> That what we are, and have been, may be known.
> (lines 173–74)

In other words, these reminders of Sir Walter are also reminders of the character, moral being, or spirit of human kind: Sir Walter is us. Nature, it seems, wishes to keep this reminder present, for since she leaves the objects to a "slow decay," there is an implication that she could efface them more quickly. Her intention, the poet says, is to make us known, but to whom?

and why? are not declared. Ordinarily when monuments are preserved and memories kept alive, it is because there is an elegiac feeling of regret for what has been lost. One wonders, then, whether nature can be suspected of a pious respect for "what we have been" – all that vitality of Sir Walter. Or does nature preserve these memorials of hunting and all that it represents as admonitions, wishing to keep before us our need to change? And, of course, whatever nature is thought to intend as a memorialist, Wordsworth's poem actually carries out.

After "what we are, and have been," one might have expected a reference to what we will be. Instead, the stanza continues:

> But at the coming of the milder day
> These monuments shall all be overgrown.
> (lines 175–76)

Thus nothing is directly promised in the poem about what *we* will be or even that we will be. The promise is only that there will be no trace of what we are and have been, and that nature will itself persist and revive:

> But Nature, in due course of time, once more
> Shall here put on her beauty and her bloom.
> (lines 171–72)

A reader might infer, then, that the "milder day" will be when humanity itself and all memorials of its existence have gone from the face of the earth. With this reading the poem expresses misanthropy – a typically Wordsworthian emotion, as many critics have emphasized. It is very difficult for a lover of nature also to be a lover of man, most especially when man, "what we are," is a hunter.

5

Savage amusements of the poor:
John Clare's badger sonnets

I

Among the "sports" and diversions of Romantic England were gladiatorial battles between animals. While intellectuals and poets urged their ethos of loving communion with nature, a more numerous sociological group hugely enjoyed cockfights, dogfights, and the baiting of bulls and badgers. Occasionally bears, lions, leopards, apes, otters, polecats, foxes, or donkeys were used, though these victims were less common by 1800 than they had been earlier. These events were completely legal. They might be officially sponsored by town or city governments or carried on spontaneously in backyards and village streets. A London advertisement of 1729 and 1730 indicates what a grand entertainment might then have offered: "A mad bull to be dressed up with fireworks and turned loose in the game place, a dog to be dressed up with fireworks over him, a bear to be let loose at the same time, and a cat to be tied to the bull's tail, a mad bull dressed up with fireworks to be baited."[1]

Just what went on in bullbaiting can be read in Thomas Day's *History of Sandford and Merton*. The boys see in the distance "a prodigious crowd of people, all moving forward in the same direction." This attracted their curiosity, and,

on inquiry, they found that a bull-baiting was on the point of taking place . . . A bull of the largest size and greatest beauty was led across the plain, adorned with ribands of various colors . . . he was fastened to an iron ring, which had been strongly let into the ground . . . An innumerable crowd of men, of women, of children, then surrounded the place . . . Presently, a dog of the largest size and most ferocious courage was let loose; who, as soon as he beheld the bull, uttered a savage yell, and rushed upon him . . . just as the dog was springing up to seize him, [the bull] rushed forward to meet his foe, and, putting his head to the ground, canted him into the air several yards . . . The same fate attended another, and another dog, which were let loose successively; the one was killed upon the spot, while the other, who had a leg broken in the fall, crawled howling and limping away . . . [then] three fierce dogs rushed upon the bull at once, and by their joint attacks rendered him almost mad . . . he roared with pain and fury . . . He hurried around the stake with incessant toil and rage, first aiming at one, then at another, of the persecuting dogs, that harassed him on every side, growling and baying incessantly, and biting him in every part.[2]

By 1790 bullbaiting was less pursued than it had formerly been. Thomas Bewick and Ralph Beilby said that it "had been almost entirely laid aside in the North of England."[3] But it had not yet been prohibited.

Badger baiting continued in 1800 as in the past. In fact, an authority writing in 1948 says that the sport is still pursued "in the larger towns and cities as well as in the remoter country districts."[4] I quote a description of badger baiting from Thomas Bewick's and Ralph Beilby's *General History of Quadrupeds* (1790): the badger

is frequently baited with Dogs trained for that purpose. This inhuman diversion is chiefly confined to the indolent and the vicious, who take a cruel pleasure in seeing the harmless animal surrounded by its enemies, and defending itself from their attack, which it does with astonishing agility and success. Its motions are so quick, that a Dog is frequently desperately wounded in the first moment of an assault, and obliged to fly . . . this singular creature is able to resist repeated attacks both of men and dogs, from all quarters, till, being overpowered with numbers, and enfeebled by so many desperate wounds, it is at last obliged to submit.[5]

In the 1820s Bewick remembered badger baiting from his childhood in the 1760s, when he rather enjoyed it; "for in the fierce conflicts between them & the Dogs, there was, something like an exchange of retaliation . . . and I have with pleasure seen that wonderfully courageous Animal [the badger] . . . (with fair play) beat all the Dogs, of a whole Neighbourhood (one after another) completely off."[6] The qualification "with fair play" may be annotated: Bewick means that the dogs should be set on one by one, not all together, and he perhaps also means that certain ancient practices should not be followed. For example, the chain might be passed *through* the badger's tail; sometimes its teeth were broken to make it less dangerous or the lower half of its jaw was cut off. The latter was recommended in *The Gentleman's Recreation*, which was used as a handbook on hunting for generations: "cut away the nether Jaw, but meddle not with the other, leaving the upper to shew the fury of the Beast, although it can do no harm therewith."[7] No wonder, then, that as an adult Bewick viewed badger baiting as an "inhuman diversion." Sometimes a badger was spared to provide fun another day. During these battles the owners of the dogs experienced glory if their champion were successful or even brave, rage and humiliation if it cowered or ran.

Though the sufferers were animals, baiting must have afforded some of the same satisfactions as human combats in the arena of Rome. Daniel Defoe made the comparison in reference to cockfights: "the very model of an amphitheatre of the ancients . . . It is wonderful to see the courage of these little creatures, who always hold fighting on till one of them drops, and dies on the spot." The combat of Hector and Achilles resembles a cockfight in that it is an encounter of single, trained champions, each representing a side, with the death of one as its inevitable outcome. I mention Hector and Achilles to suggest the age-old fascination of all such occasions. With an impulse of modernization (to which I return), Defoe goes on to repudiate cockfighting as "a remnant of the barbarous customs of this island, and too cruel for my entertainment."[8]

Baiting presumably appealed to spectators by its cruelty; by fear, ferocity, and courage vicariously experienced; and by the doubtfulness and suspense of its events. It was safely warlike, allowing spectators to indulge emotions of violence without danger to themselves. It satisfied whatever in the psyche makes it pleasurable for human beings to gang up on a victim. Perhaps for some spectators it activated the psychology of tragic catharsis. For others the bull was an incarnation of ferocity and lust, and a baiting was a scapegoating. The power of the spectacle to grip emotion was exponentially heightened by the reality of death in it. A doomed struggle against death, the fact of inevitable defeat is an obvious symbolism of baiting as it was usually conducted. However valiant and resourceful the animal might be, the end was always that, in John Clare's words, it

leaves his hold and cackles groans and dies.[9]

Both baitings and cockfights had been extremely popular, so much so that to provide the bull was thought a public benefaction. Writing in 1818 in Dorset, William Chafin remembered that "cock-fighting also, in the last century, was a favourite diversion, greatly delighted in by persons of all ranks; and there was a Nobleman, Lord Albemarle Bertie, who was so fond of the amusement, that he attended cock-pits when he was totally blind. And there were but few gentlemen in the country who did not keep and breed Game Cocks, and were very anxious and careful in the breeding of them. Frequent matches were made, and there were cock-pits in almost every village . . . But in our days of refinement, this amusement of Cock-fighting hath been exploded, and in a great measure abandoned, being deemed to be barbarous and cruel."[10] In both bullbaitings and cockfights there was much assessing of champions, much cheering on, betting, and celebrating in a holiday mood. I mentioned in the Preface objections to them because they attracted unruly crowds. That the protest intensified in the wake of the French Revolution was not happenstance. The poor were now more feared, particularly in crowds.

The cruelty of baitings and cockfights was also assailed. Obviously in baiting the victims were not only the animals who were attacked but also the dogs who tore at them and might themselves be injured or killed. In cock-fights the birds dealt appalling wounds and fought on till one or both died. George Crabbe gives a vivid, accusatory description in the *Parish Register*:

> Here his poor bird th'inhuman Cocker brings,
> Arms his hard heel and clips his golden wings;
> With spicy food th'impatient spirit feeds,
> And shouts and curses as the battle bleeds.
> Struck through the brain, deprived of both his eyes,
> The vanquish'd bird must combat till he dies;
> Must faintly peck at his victorious foe,
> And reel and stagger at each feeble blow:
> When fallen, the savage grasps his dabbled plumes,
> His blood-stain'd arms, for other deaths assumes;
> And damns the craven-fowl, that lost his stake,
> And only bled and perish'd for his sake.[11]

In calling the cocker a "savage," Crabbe uses an alternative term to "barbarian"; it was commonly applied to low-class abusers of animals. The pre-fight mutilations Crabbe mentions were routine. In preparation for combat, part of the wing feathers was removed, the beak was scraped smooth and sharpened, and the comb and wattles were cut off so that the opponent could not take hold of them. William Blake alluded to these operations in "Auguries of Innocence":

> The Game Cock clip'd & arm'd for fight
> Does the Rising Sun affright.[12]

(With its orange-red colors the rising sun appears in these lines as a cock who sees a rival cock about to do battle.) James Plumptre represents a typical opinion of moralists and clerics in his time: instead of

endeavouring to make animals dwell in 'harmony and family accord,' they are generally set against each other, and man delights to see them worry and tear, rather than 'lie down together' in love and happiness.

In this view of the subject, it deserves our consideration, how far those *amusements* may be lawful, which consist in making animals pursue, and worry, and destroy one another. None of them can be followed without a mixture of *cruelty* . . . Are they, then, proper for those . . . whose ruling principle is commanded to be LOVE?[13]

On the defensive side of the argument, the satire of Windham and Canning was widely echoed. As I mentioned in an earlier chapter, these ministers of state described the bill against baiting as a hypocritical attempt of the rich to interfere with the pleasures of the poor. The charge of hypocrisy was repeated over and over. For example, an author in the journal, *Medusa*, in 1820, was disgusted by the attempts of the Society for the Suppression of Vice to control "the amusements of our fellow countrymen" under the pretense of preventing cruelty to animals. The author describes fishing, fox hunting, brawning of pigs, and crimping of cod as "high-life cruelties":

they cannot think of punishing these. O no! the real thing which calls forth their sympathy, and harrows up their souls, is, to see a number of artizans, by a relaxation of their labour, baiting a bull or a bear, while a man with ten thousand a year may worry a hare, a stag, or a fox, as much as he pleases! Any cruelty may be practised to gorge the stomach of the rich, but none to enliven the leisure hours of the poor.[14]

Broad social reform rarely takes place without a great deal of hypocrisy among its supporters. It was also claimed, though not by the journalist just quoted, that cocks found their natural fulfillment in fighting and even that bulls enjoyed being baited. Otherwise, much the same arguments were advanced as in favor of hunting: baitings and cockfights fostered Britain's military prowess by inuring to combat, violence, and wounds; they inspired with the spectacle of courage; to enjoy animal combats was manly.

The polemic against cockfights and baiting criticized a traditional model of manhood. Hunters, soldiers, and empire builders sometimes associated this modernity with sexual deficiency. I quote a late, embittered blast from Herbert Atkinson: "We have traveled fast on that road ever since, until the present age, when corporal punishment, physical pain, and all things combative, are looked on with horror. Moreover, the men of England are unable to manage their own womenkind, and effeminacy, sentimentality, and sham humanitarianism are the features of the present time."[15] Though Atkinson was writing after the 1849 law against cockfighting, his sentiments could be shared in 1800.

The spectators at baitings and cockfights gradually became sociologically different. In Elizabethan times persons of all classes enjoyed both entertainments, just as later they did horse races and boxing matches. In due course this also became an objection to them: they were a saturnalia in which "are to be found my Lord in dispute with a butcher, and his Grace with a farrier, all hail fellow well met."[16] Nevertheless, the gentry, especially in the country, continued to patronize cockfights and bullbaitings until they were outlawed in the nineteenth century. However, the respectable middle classes increasingly stayed away. As they withdrew, the majority of spectators could be described as idle and drunken poor, and, in a circular process, such characterizations increased exponentially the reluctance of the respectable to attend or to countenance the baiting of animals.

Just how contemptuous one might be of the crowd at such spectacles is clear in a casual insertion of Joseph Strutt, who remarks in his 1801 history of English sports, "Bull and bear-baiting is not encouraged by persons of rank and opulence in the present day; and when practised, which rarely happens, it is attended only by the lowest and most despicable part of the people."[17] In 1822 *The Sporting Magazine*, a journal that generally favored every so-called "sport," denounced the "horrible cruelties" of bullbaiting and went on to describe the spectators: "These meetings are frequented by the most abandoned and profligate of the human race, the refuse and offscourings of this vast city – pick-pockets and thieves of every description, with the idle, dissolute, and infamous of every class and service – low gamblers, and some, to their ineffable shame, of a higher description and education; jack-ass drivers, drovers, the scum and dregs of Smithfield, nackers or horse-boilers . . . Whole troops of this *canaille*."[18]

When we combine the departure of the respectable from baitings with the fact that most work with animals, and hence most abuse of them in driving, coaching, and so forth, was performed by persons of the lower class, we have the basis in social fact for a widely accepted belief. The lower classes, it was said, are especially prone to cruelty to animals. Hunters affirmed this. So did persons of the "middling sort" who had caged birds in their parlors. We have seen that writers might dwell satirically on the cruelties inflicted by the wealthy, but no one could actually deny that the poor willy-nilly inflicted the greater part of the suffering. "The most fruitful source of misery to Horses," said John Lawrence, "is, that they are committed . . . to the absolute discretion, in all respects, of their drivers; a majority of whom are the least enlightened, the most hardened and profligate of all the lower people."[19] To proceed from facts of economic life to a moral condemnation was typical in the rhetoric of animal rights at this time, as one sees, for example, in Lord Erskine's 1809 Parliamentary speech: "these unmanly and disgusting outrages are most frequently perpetrated by the basest and most worthless; incapable, for the most part, of any reproof which can reach the mind, and who know no more of the law, than that it suffers them to indulge their savage dispositions with impunity."[20] Just such a person was depicted by Wordsworth in his poem of *Peter Bell*, the poor, ignorant potter who beats his donkey. Though the poet was still politically liberal, more or less, when he composed the poem in 1798, he seems to have associated the abuse of animals with the poor. In *Keeper's Travels in Search of His Master*, a story for children, E. A. Kendall gives a usual explanation for wanton cruelty of the poor to animals. As it wanders the roads, the lost dog is lashed by "waggoners and coachmen, unprovoked and without other motives than that the men had whips in their hands . . . Such temptations to the exercise of power are seldom neglected by the low and the ignorant." Kendall was modestly radical in politics, and added that "There are those in every rank of life."[21] But clearly he supposed, as did most middle-class persons, that the poor compensated against animals for their own social inferiority and powerlessness. As Mary Wollstonecraft put it, persons who are "trodden under foot by the rich" revenge on animals "the insults that they are obliged to bear from their superiors."[22] The argument implies that cruelty to animals is exacerbated in a hierarchical society and would be less in an egalitarian one.

It was not supposed, by most commentators, that the poor were inherently more hard-hearted than the well-off, as though they were a different species of human being. If, to repeat the telling quote from James Granger, the charge of cruelty "is only applicable to the most stupid, ignorant, and uncivilized part of our countrymen," while those "of higher rank and knowledge are far more humane and benevolent," the reason was, precisely, the ignorance of the poor, their lack of education, of civilization. The distinction between moral and social superiority was less likely to be drawn in 1800 than it is now, but so far as it would be drawn, kindness to animals went with social standing and was the more valued for that reason. The lower orders were "savages." "The ignorant and brutal mind," said John Lawrence, "is too prone to tyranny and measures of barbarous and savage coercion."[23] Most eighteenth-century intellectuals would have agreed with Henry Crowe, in *Zoophilos* (1819), that "humanity" is "a quality wholly acquired, and derived from mental, or rather moral culture. Hence savages, and uninstructed children scarcely know it; and for the same reason the lower classes are often lamentably deficient therein."[24]

II

Few poems mentioned baiting at all. The closest approximation I know of is Byron's description of a bullfight in *Childe Harold*, 1, in which the narrator goes through a gamut of emotions – heroic admiration, suspense, sorrowful triumph – that could be activated at baitings. But even Byron's report would have been less acceptable to middle-class readers if the narrator, while hugely enjoying himself, had not also condemned Spanish cruelty.[25] Baiting was a disagreeable subject.

But John Clare wrote a remarkable series of sonnets on the baiting of a badger. Clare grew up in a country village and lived in it as a member of the community. Socially he belonged to the rural poor. He thought of himself and was presented by his publisher as a "peasant poet," one whose horizon of experience was interestingly special and limited to the rural life he knew.[26] Clare also thought of himself in the Romantic role of a "nature poet," a close, loving observer of plants, trees, animals, and landscape appearances. This role distinguished him from most other human beings who view nature with less sensitivity, tenderness, and delight, or perhaps with none. Other poets, such as Wordsworth, might exhibit the social group to which Clare belonged as natural in contrast to the artifices of urban humanity, but when Clare represents human beings who are indifferent to nature, they must be persons within his own horizon. In his poetry they are either wealthy enclosers of the land or they are rustics. The latter are exactly the group that Wordsworth and other poets idealized – shepherds, ploughmen, milkmaids, hedgers, horseboys. Clare called them louts and clowns.

As many critics have elaborated, Clare's situation as a "peasant poet" placed him between the literary culture of his time, which he had internalized and for which he wrote, and the rural, village culture that he had also internalized in growing up.[27] His intimate knowledge of country life was one of the things he could offer to readers of literature, yet he was, as a poet, out of sympathy with many aspects of the life he described. At the same time, he was, as a peasant, out of sympathy with many feelings of the audience for which he wrote. Given the complexities of his situation, it is not surprising that Clare could in different poems be sentimental, humorous, participatory, realistic, or satiric about the village. He could even include different attitudes in the same poem, as I think he does in the "Badger" sonnets, by shifting from one attitude to another. But he could not synthesize these attitudes. The more the "Badger" sonnets are read as poems of pity for the animal, the more they must also be perceived as hostile, perhaps satiric descriptions of rural village life.

Whatever his private views about baiting, Clare had to condemn it in poetry if he touched upon it at all. Given the feelings of readers, no other attitude was now possible if Clare wished to achieve fame, status, and cash through his poetry. Clare's poems have many passages, now painful to his admirers, in which he voices attitudes of the respectable classes with regard to property and poaching. Whether these were "really" his attitudes cannot be known. Similarly with badger baiting. Had he felt what his fellow villagers did, he would have enjoyed the noise, confusion, and fighting much as he shows them doing.

Clare's "The Village Minstrel" thematizes the impossibility of badger baiting as a subject of poetry. The poem describes a country lad, Lubin, who was endowed with poetic sensibility. He looked with "wild enthusiasm" at natural scenes while the "other louts gaumd [gaped] heedless bye."[28] Among the amusements of his village were badger baiting and cockfighting, but "sports too barbarous these for lubins strains" (line 862). This gesture of avoidance tells that Lubin was too sensitive to compose on these themes and also that the narrator has the same sensitivity; the long description of village sports makes no further reference to baitings. However, a stanza describes the "monstrous fun" in the village with a greased pig, a sport that Clare evidently did not consider barbarous. In such events a soaped and larded pig ran about the streets while pursuers tried to grab it. If we ask who was having the fun, it was not the pig. Possibly it was the "louts" who were after it. But chiefly it was the spectators, such as the narrator, who were entertained by the tumult, including the sights of old and young tumbled down and "bedaubd wi muck" (lines 852, 860).

"The Badger" was not published in Clare's lifetime. It was later quarried as a group of sonnets from Peterborough MS B9, where it is found without any title or indication that it constitutes a separate group. We cannot know how Clare might have revised and arranged these sonnets for publication, or whether he would have published any or all of them. In several modern editions only sonnets two, three, and four are printed, since these make a more coherent sequence.

According to Eric Robinson, Clare's chief modern editor, Clare identified in these sonnets with the animal as a victim. Clare was "estranged, in Northborough, from his neighbours, his wife, and himself"; he was a "failure as a smallholder and therefore as a provider for his wife and seven children, wearied with the delays of publishers and disappointed with the income provided by his writing." His mood alternated between "apathy and anger" and his tragic insanity was coming on. Occasionally he was delusional. He composed at this time a number of sonnets on "hunted animals."[29] Robinson does not develop this interpretation of "The Badger," but if he did so, he might suggest that Clare saw himself as an innocent, well disposed creature (line 65) arbitrarily persecuted, a loner set upon by many.

Alan Porter, who was, I believe, the first person to view the poems written in Northborough as a separate group, also interprets the "Badger" sonnets as personal poems expressing Clare's appalling state of mind at this time.

For Porter the poems report "cruelty of the most brutal kind . . . with utter impartiality." Their attitude, Porter says, is utterly unlike that in Clare's earlier poems, for these were wont to "irradiate Nature with love," but in the "Badger," "The Marten," and similar poems of Northborough, the poet might be "suspected of enjoying the cruelty for its own sake . . . These are, I think, the most gruesome poems in the English language."³⁰

The "Badger" sonnets tell how at night, when the animal would be abroad, a sack is placed just inside its hole. As the badger returns, a dog is released, and the badger, incautiously bolting, entangles itself in the sack. After a furious and noisy struggle, the animal is pinned with a forked stick and carried to the village, where it is baited. The sonnets allude to two styles of baiting. In one the badger runs about the streets, pursued by boys and men. Stones are thrown at it, dogs are set on it, and if the relatively slow animal tries to escape into the woods, it is turned by sticks and cudgels. The dogs are put on individually and then all at once. This goes on until the badger dies. Alternatively, in the last sonnet, the badger is semi-tamed until it will bite only dogs, not humans. It is then baited either by chaining it and setting dogs on it or by placing it in a barrel and trying whether the dogs can drag it out.³¹ By this method it could be baited repeatedly on different days and become a source of income for its keeper, since challengers would pay to try their dogs against it. This sort of baiting might be scheduled in advance for appropriate days and accompanied by drinking and betting.

Much in Clare's sonnets is compatible with the polemics against baiting that I noticed at the start. Undoubtedly we see cruelty, and the sonnets emphasize that it goes on "for hours" (line 36), "all the day" (line 25), and make this duration felt by repetitive detail. Furthermore, Clare remarks that the badger, if tamed, becomes faithful ("follows like the dog," line 56) and gentle – "licks the patting hand and trys to play" (line 65). These details activate feelings of the pet keeper, and make the cruelties that are described seem all the more heartless.

Obviously, also, the sonnets present people of low social class, and the villagers may resemble the sorts of persons who were, by this time, described as the participants at baitings. They are a mob, a "crowd" (lines 41, 45, and 52), "a host of dogs and men" (line 15). The latter phrase recurs (lines 8, 15, 51), linking dogs and men (or boys) and suggesting human brutishness. One notes that the "boys and men" go on kicking the badger after they think it is dead. The scene includes swearing and drunkenness (line 42), and the speaker makes a specifically moral distinction between the women who take away the boys and the "blackguard" who "laughs and hurrys on the fray" (line 44). The village is disorderly in the extreme. There is much imagery of disagreeable noise – screaming, firing, grunting, hooting, hallooing, shouting, beating. The baiting is confused, with much running, turning, reeling, and falling. Hogs also are scampering in the streets.

Thus to a middle-class reader of Clare's time the sonnets would picture a riot of cruelty and loutishness. Such a reader could have no sympathy with these villagers, no imaginative participation or indulgence in their pleasures. In 1835, approximately when the poems were written, Parliament made badger baiting a misdemeanour, along with cockfighting and bullbaiting, and the poems might seem to have been composed to assist this legislative effort.

Was this Clare's attitude? Not completely, for at least the last six lines of the first sonnet and two middle lines of the second sonnet must have been intended as humor. Nothing is duller than jokes explained, especially if they are poor jokes, and I apologize for the next few sentences. The laughter at the end of the first sonnet is at the expense of the woodman. He goes out at night to do a chore that generally preceded fox hunts, that is, he stops up the fox holes so the foxes cannot bolt into them in the morning, when the hunt will be after them. In the darkness and hurry, the woodman falls up to his chin into badger holes. The humor seems somewhat broad, but the speaker of these sonnets is rooted in the village life he describes. For example, he says "Some keep a baited badger tame as hog" (line 55), a comparison for tameness that would not occur to a genteel poet. A rustic speaker may plausibly enjoy rustic humor.

The other jokes, in the second sonnet, depend on knowing that the badger's cry is loud and blood-curdling. "The noise of the badger," Clare wrote, "is absolutely frightful its yells are like those of a woman under the agonys of murder & in fact it is believd to be the noise of a spirit that has been murderd."[32] When the badger is captured in a sack, its terrible cries alarm night prowlers in the woods, so that the fox lets go the goose it has captured and the poacher misses his aim. The theme of humorous panic continues through the sonnets, in the frightened hogs that scamper about the streets, in the badger running from the swarm of bees at the end of the fifth sonnet, and possibly in the men and boys driven by the badger. But though the woodman, the fox, and the poacher are frustrated in Disney style, they are hunters and the hare is wounded.

I do not find other passages of humor in the sonnets, though I think it possible Clare did. And I am not gripped by the combat, but the speaker seems to be. He dwells on the badger's formidable battle skills, how it beats bigger dogs, never relaxes its hold, plays dead and suddenly "starts and grins," resuming the fight. He wonders at its courage: though "dimute and small," it drives men and dogs before it. The words *bite*, *beat*, and *drive* recur, emphasizing the badger's aggressive triumphs: "He runs along and bites . . . drives . . . The badger turns and drives . . . He fights with dogs . . . and beats . . . He drive[s] the crowd . . . And bites . . . He turns again and drives the noisey crowd / And beats the many dogs . . . He drives away and beats them . . . drives the crowd." (But *bite* and *beat* recall *bait*, and the badger lies *beaten out* in the end.) In sonnets three and four the battle turns and turns, from hope (from the point of view of the badger) to defeat, to victory, to anxiety, uncertainty, defeat ("He falls as dead"), sudden revival, and final death. Such were the vicissitudes of emotion that animal combats afforded their aficionados, much as in the bullfight of *Childe Harold*. A poet who excites these emotions is not completely repelled by the sport.

It is time to think further about the formal qualities of these sonnets in couplets. As with all successful works of art, the effect of the sonnets results from a unique combination. To me the most effective elements are the powerfully moving subject matter; the objective, impersonal report of it; the extreme clarity and speed of the presentation, which the direct, simple diction and syntax enables; and the strict metrical regularity and closure.

The couplets are formally firm to the nth degree:

> The bull dog knows his match and waxes cold
> The badger grins and never leaves his hold.
>
> (lines 39–40)

The clauses are short, and the terminations of sense coincide with the half-line, line, or couplet, creating a strict closure. Semantically, however, the poetry is open. The progression of thought jumps and surprises:

> He comes and hears they let the strongest loose
> The old fox hears the noise and drops the goose.
>
> (lines 19–20)

Most lines are monosyllables with one word of two syllables, and the mono-syllables are colloquial:

> Till kicked and torn and beaten out he lies.
>
> (line 53)

Despite the monosyllabic diction, the rhythm of the lines is emphatic and regular. If we accept the convention that a syllable becomes long in English when its vowel is followed by two consonants or is itself long, an unusually high proportion of Clare's verse accents coincide with long syllables:

He fights with dogs for hours and beats them all.

(line 36)

Hence there is seldom uncertainty as to which syllables are accented and which are not, and there is relatively little variation from strict iambic pentameter. Most lines have a caesura somewhere between the fourth and the sixth position. A high proportion of the rhyming syllables are long. The formula for such verse was given by Clare's friend George Darley:

ease is not music, gracefulness is not music, smoothness – nay suavity, is not music. To ensure music, lines must be full of sound, or *soundingness*, which results from . . . single endings [masculine endings], even pauses [pauses after even syllables], sonorous terminative words, sustained tone, and regular cadence or tread of the numbers.[33]

Clare's style in the "Badger" sonnets (and many other poems) suggests to me that chaotic emotions have summoned a firmly governing technique. Clare could not completely sort out what he felt. The last four lines of the fifth sonnet express a stronger or more overt sympathy for the badger than earlier verses, but the final couplet forgets about baiting and releases the subject of the badger into openness. There is no conclusion. The sonnets adopt varying and incompatible attitudes towards their subject matter. Their objective, impersonal method of report makes Clare's attitudes the more difficult to perceive and interpret. Hence readers are free to project into Clare their own pity for the badger.

Having read many Romantic poems of compassion for animals, I am struck that Clare, if he sympathizes with the badger, does not idealize or sentimentalize it. The badger's appealing qualities are its fighting prowess (a doubtful virtue by the morality of animal protest) and its goodness of heart (lines 65–66). It is not credited with innocence, as robins and lambs were in the literature of Clare's time, or happiness, like Shelley's lark or Wordsworth's linnet, or infantile helplessness (hares, mice, worms). It is not noble like the stag or handsome and proud like the cock. It grunts and roots like a hog (lines 1, 3, 18); it is shaggy (line 2) and awkward (lines 5, 45); it is captured in a sack. When it dies, it groans, as any animal might, but before that, it *cackles* (line 54). The word is wonderfully fresh, homely, and descriptively realistic, but "poetically" it is grotesque in a death scene. In short, there is something rude about the badger, uncouth, like the village and its populace. In the "Badger" sonnets Clare viewed the baited animal with a somewhat affectionate realism and the villagers with a somewhat humorous distaste. His strongest desire, it seems, was to keep both at an emotional distance.

APPENDIX

The badger grunting on his woodland track
With shaggy hide and sharp nose scrowed with black
Roots in the bushes and the woods and makes
A great huge burrow in the ferns and brakes
With nose on ground he runs a awkard pace
and anything will beat him in the race
The shepherds dog will run him to his den
Followed and hooted by the dogs and men
The woodman when the hunting comes about
Go round at night to stop the foxes out
and hurrying through the bushes ferns and brakes
Nor sees the many hol[e]s the badger makes
And often through the bushes to the chin
Breaks the old holes and tumbles headlong in

When midnight comes a host of dogs and men
Go out and track the badger to his den
And put a sack within the hole and lye
Till the old grunting badger passes bye
He comes and hears they let the strongest loose
The old fox hears the noise and drops the goose
The poacher shoots and hurrys from the cry
And the old hare half wounded buzzes bye
They get a forked stick to bear him down
And clapt the dogs and bore him to the town
And bait him all the day with many dogs
And laugh and shout and fright the scampering hogs
He runs along and bites at all he meets
They shout and hollo down the noisey streets

He turns about to face the loud uproar
And drives the rebels to their very doors
The frequent stone is hurled where ere they go
When badgers fight and every ones a foe
The dogs are clapt and urged to join the fray
The badger turns and drives them all away
Though scar[c]ely half as big dimute and small
He fights with dogs for hours and beats them all
The heavy mastiff savage in the fray
Lies down and licks his feet and turns away
The bull dog knows his match and waxes cold
The badger grins and never leaves his hold
He drive[s] the crowd and follows at their heels
And bites them through the drunkard swears and reels

The frighted women takes the boys away
The blackguard laughs and hurrys on the fray
He trys to reach the woods a awkard race
But sticks and cudgels quickly stop the chace
He turns agen and drives the noisey crowd
And beats the many dogs in noises loud
He drives away and beats them every one
And then they loose them all and set them on
He falls as dead and kicked by boys and men
Then starts and grins and drives the crowd agen
Till kicked and torn and beaten out he lies
And leaves his hold and cackles groans and dies

Some keep a baited badger tame as hog
And tame him till he follows like the dog
They urge him on like dogs and show fair play
He beats and scarcely wounded goes away
Lapt up as if asleep he scorns to fly
And siezes any dog that ventures nigh
Clapt like a dog he never bites the men
But worrys dogs and hurrys to his den
They let him out and turn a barrow down
And there he fights the pack of all the town
He licks the patting hand and trys to play
And never trys to bite or run away
And runs away from noise in hollow tree[s]
Burnt by the boys to get a swarm of bees

6

Work animals, slaves, servants: Coleridge's young ass

I

To this point my theme has been the controversies around hunting, cock-fighting, baiting, and similar amusements. In the view of their critics, such things could be dispensed with. A better world would go on without them. Moreover, animal sympathizers were usually not engaged in these, not complicit. I come now to exploitations of animals for work and for food. These involved almost everyone and could not be abolished. Economic life in 1800 was still enormously dependent on animals. They were the cars and trucks, transporting people and goods; the tractors, laboring in the fields; the engines turning wheels that powered machines. And, of course, animals provided or were themselves food, and processes of raising, transporting to market, fattening, and slaughtering animals might evoke compassion. Riders, passengers, mule drivers, hauliers, carters, coachmen, and agricultural laborers, among many others, used work animals – at least two thirds of the population. Households, even urban ones, kept their own poultry and sometimes a pig or cow. With work and food animals, the literature of animal rights could criticize only abuses, unnecessary cruelties, not the thing itself.

Bit, spur, whip, bridle, harness, yoke, and goad now serve most people only as metaphors, but in real life, so to speak, they compel because they constrain or hurt. They hurt more in 1800 than they do now, for designs have improved. Moreover, the treatment of work animals two hundred years ago was probably harsher than it now usually is. In the first chapter I cited some then ordinary practices that now seem cruel. And I noticed earlier that the management of animals was generally the work of persons whom the genteel thought "savages." Many animals belonged to people who could barely feed themselves. They had to beat the utmost possible amount of work from their hungry animals. Donkeys especially were likely to be the work animals of the poor, and the ordinary life of the animal might be day after day of semi-starvation, beatings, cumbersome and galling rigs, excessively heavy loads, and accumulating sores and injuries. Giovanni Verga's short "Story of the Saint Joseph's Ass" can be read on this subject. Although its location is nineteenth-century Sicily, this did not much differ for a donkey from eighteenth-century England.

The literature of animal rights criticized excessive beating and whipping and excessively heavy loads. Coach horses most aroused compassion and protest, particularly horses in the stage coaches and the mails. Of these there were a great many. For example, around 1800 some fifty coaches a day departed from London for Manchester, forty for Brighton, thirty for Edinburgh, and twenty for York. Each coach would have four horses, and the team would be changed at intervals along the route. The drivers or coachmen were under pressure to maintain their schedules, the horses were anonymous to them, and the whip was used as we use an accelerator. For the most part, wear and tear of the animals was due less to speed, for the coach went an average of ten miles an hour, than to overloading. Merchandise was profitable cargo and was piled on. Sometimes a passenger would bribe the coachman to hurry, though galloping was dangerous; sometimes the horses had insufficient rest between stages. The horses might be driven to the point of exhaustion, until the whip had no more power. When their bodies began to show the effects of accumulating hard use, they were used at night, so that the public would not be shocked by seeing them. The life of a post horse was about three years.[1] A great many novels, memoirs, and travel books of the eighteenth and nineteenth centuries include scenes of travel by coach. Usual topics are the appearance of the coach, its comfort or discomfort, the coachman, fellow travelers, sights and adventures along the way, and inns. The horses are sometimes mentioned but their sufferings almost never. They were invisible to most passengers or, perhaps, the novelist considered them irrelevant to the theme of the novel.

For an example of writing on this subject, I quote verses in Robert Bloomfield's *The Farmer's Boy* in which the speaker addresses the farm horse, Dobbin, and tells him how much he is better off.

> Thy chains were freedom, and thy toils repose,
> Could the poor *post-horse* tell thee all his woes;
> Show thee his bleeding shoulders, and unfold
> The dreadful anguish he endures for gold.
>
> . . .
>
> Ah, well for him if here [at the inn] his suff'rings ceas'd,
> And ample hours of rest his pains appeas'd!

But rous'd again, and sternly bade to rise,

. . .

Come forth he must, tho' limping, maim'd, and sore;
He hears the whip; the chaise is at the door: . . .
The collar tightens, and again he feels
His half-heal'd wounds inflam'd; again the wheels
With tiresome sameness in his ears resound,
O'er blinding dust, or miles of flinty ground.[2]

Those who felt sympathy and tenderness for work animals often compared them to slaves. Jeremy Bentham used this analogy, as we saw in chapter 2, and so did John Stuart Mill, who described work animals as "slaves and victims of the most brutal part of mankind."[3] Slavery was then under attack in the great, public campaign that finally ended it in England, and persons who pleaded on behalf of animals could appeal to anti-slavery sentiment. Thus Humphry Primatt: just as "the white man . . . can have no right, by virtue of his colour, to enslave and tyrannise over a black man, . . . a man can have no natural right to abuse and torment a beast."[4] But the analogy broke down, for the "black man" was to be set free; the animal only not abused and tormented. It would still be forced to work. Nothing else was practicable or even conceivable.

In an age-old trope, animals were also analogous to servants. In the Early Modern Period, says Keith Thomas, "human rule over the lower creatures provided the mental analogue on which many political and social arrangements were based . . . The 'dominion' which God gave Adam over the animals, explained a Jacobean commentator, meant 'such a prevailing and possessing as a master hath over servants.' "[5] The habitual associative linking of domestic and work animals with servants persisted well into the Romantic epoch and beyond.[6]

To cite some examples: at the close of his 1772 sermon, *An Apology for the Brute Creation*, James Granger moves with associative inevitability from "the beasts to whose labour we owe so much in cultivating the earth" to "our poor [human] servants and labourers." He prays that "in these times of dearth and scarcity" we may show even greater kindness to them than we do to dogs and horses.[7] The same analogy runs through Sarah Trimmer's *Fabulous Histories* for children. On a visit to Farmer Wilson's the children are told by this estimable person, "I have always considered every beast that works for me as my servant."[8] Even if it was not overtly stated, an analogy to the lower classes could always be read into the discourse of animal rights. Animals also supplied a figure of speech for other socially subordinated human beings, for classes of persons who supposedly were more like animals, such as women, children, and subjected races in the expanding empire. I quote George Nicholson, for example, to illustrate how repudiation of tyranny, of racism, of imperialism, and of slavery might interweave in the rhetoric on behalf of animals: "imperious man looks down with silent contempt on certain animals which he deems inferior and meaner objects. Sovereign despot of the world, Lord of the life and death of every creature, with the slaves of his tyranny he disclaims the ties of kindred."[9]

Let us briefly sketch the political agendas that could be served in representations of animals. In idyllic and sentimental writings, such as Cowper's Edenic visions in *The Task*, Blake's "The Shepherd" and "The Lamb," and Wordsworth's "The Sparrow's Nest" and "To a Butterfly," animals are loved and protected by humans and may reciprocate love. A slightly weaker version of this Utopia offers what might be called the Georgic model, in which work animals and human beings labor cooperatively together to make the earth fruitful, and the shared effort creates a bond. Burns's "The Auld Farmer's New-year-morning Salutation to his Auld Mare, Maggie" is such a poem, and similar visions may be found in Robert Bloomfield.[10] At the end of Wordsworth's "Peter Bell" the faithful ass obtains both love and shrubs, and, in return, helps with its labor to "maintain / The Widow and her family."[11] The appropriate site for the Georgic model would be the small farm. Utopian and Georgic poems are "beautiful idealisms of moral excellence," in Shelley's phrase, and have the impact Shelley assigns to such art, that is, they intensify both disgust with the world as it is and desire for the good they portray.[12] This is an important political function, but it is vague, and the poems themselves seem generally to lack specific political intention. Or poets might describe ungrateful and abusive treatment of work animals and thus glance at similar injustice to human laborers, as takes place in several of John Clare's poems on horses – "Rural Morning," "A Hunt for Dobbin or the Force of Love," and "The Death of Dobbin." In polemics against hunting and baiting, the plea for animals might be or be understood as a covert appeal for equality and justice between the orders of human society. But in most of the great Romantic poems on animals, the ones everyone knows and loves, the political implications of the relation to animals are very indirect and secondary if they are present at all. The reason for this is that, as I discuss later, poems such as Keats's "Ode to a Nightingale," Wordsworth's "The Green Linnet," and Shelley's "To a Skylark," endow animals with qualities that they do not have and that human beings also lack but long to have: joy, immortality, unity of being, transcendent knowledge, immediacy to God. Such poems involve a reversal of hierarchy, placing the animal above human limitations, where it can no longer represent any group within the social structure.

For most writers, the analogy between animals and the lower orders still supplied an argument, as traditionally it had, for social hierarchy. I quote the eighteenth-century moral philosopher, Francis Hutcheson, as he attempts to justify the use of work animals. He makes no specific application to the working poor, but we shall see the same argument deployed with respect to them.

It tends to the good of the whole system that as great a part as possible of the severer labours useful to the whole be cast upon that part of the system . . . which is incapable of higher offices requiring art and reason: while the higher part, relieved from such toil, gains leisure for nobler offices and enjoyments of which it alone is capable; and can give the necessary support and defence to the inferior.[13]

Of course Hutcheson believed that animal servants should be treated kindly, just as human ones should be.

In the wars of figuration, the cause of animals was an embarrassment to radical politics and deeply comforting to conservatives. For except in utopian vision, human relations with animals could not model any form of society that harmonized with radical ideals. Animals could not be equals, much less could they be treated as brothers, and the analogy of animals to subordinate social groups suggested that inequality was natural, gave the sanction of God or of nature to a social system radicals deplored. For an example we may return to Sarah Trimmer, who was no radical, as she describes instances of right and wrong behavior to "inferior creatures" (p. 206). The wealthy Mrs. Addis, who lifted animals from their proper station and cosseted them, merely makes them unhappy (p. 102). In the exemplary establishment of Farmer Wilson, however, animals are well treated and are more productive as a result. We should give an animal its "proper food, and keep it in its proper place" (p. 208).

II

The only utterance I know of that attempts to imagine approaching an animal with the slogans of the French Revolution, *liberté, égalité, fraternité,* is Coleridge's poem "To a Young Ass," and it is significant that this radical attempt breaks down. In the autumn of 1794 Coleridge befriended a young ass that grazed the grass of Jesus College.[14] He would pet it and feed it bread, and when he appeared the little creature would move toward him "askingly" (line 23). In the poem Coleridge wrote about it, he addressed the donkey as "Poor little Foal of an oppressed race" (line 1). At this time Coleridge was writing and lecturing against the slave trade. For him and for any reader the most obvious and appalling instance of an oppressed race was the Africans.

In his 1795 "Lecture on the Slave Trade" Coleridge denounced the mass of "anguish which we have wantonly heaped" on the African slaves, who are, he says, "our Brethren."[15] A year before, in his poem "To a Young Ass," he famously addressed the oppressed animal, "I hail thee *Brother*" (line 26). Though inflammatory in its time, the assertion of brotherhood with slaves now seems splendid. The same statement to the ass has met a different fate. Most commentators still think it ridiculous. Of all Romantic expressions of sympathy with animals, this has been thought the most extreme.[16] Coleridge's contemporaries also laughed at it. Byron satirized "The bard who soars to elegize an ass."[17] Even Coleridge himself, I shall argue, was partly clowning when he wrote the verse. Nevertheless, just as the ass represents, among other things, the English poor, the word "Brother" conveys, as I said, a political intention that goes much beyond the plea for animals. It encodes the Revolutionary ideal – *liberté, égalité, fraternité.*

When Coleridge wrote the poem, he was planning to found a utopian community or Pantisocracy in Pennsylvania. The ass's mother illustrates his protest against the unequal distribution of wealth in England. A prisoner tethered to a log, she has eaten all the grass she can reach while plenty waves just beyond her chain. Because asses were the work animals of the poor and shared their misery, it was reasonable for Coleridge to fear that the ass's master also lived "Half famish'd in a land of Luxury!" (line 22). As Ralph Beilby put it, in Thomas Bewick's *History of Quadrupeds*, "the services of this useful creature are too often repaid by hard fare and cruel usage; and being generally the property of the poor, it partakes of their wants and distresses."[18]

The revolutionary term "brother" replaced, as a salutation, the society of politeness and hierarchy with one of warmly equal mutuality. A Mr. and Mrs. Scott extended their compliments to Coleridge. "*Compliments!*" cried Coleridge, "Cold aristocratic Inanities! – I abjure their nothingness. If there be any whom I deem worthy of remembrance – I am their Brother. I call even my Cat Sister in the Fraternity of the universal Nature."[19]

Thus sympathy with animals and radical politics were intertwined in Coleridge's mind. One might argue that Coleridge's political enthusiasm overflowed into a metaphysical intuition or religious sentiment of the unity of all life, "the Fraternity of the universal Nature." Or, starting with the latter belief, we might say that it entailed social leveling, the Revolutionary equality and fraternity among human beings. As Coleridge wrote in "The Eolian Harp" (though not until after 1796), the feeling of "one Life within us and abroad" makes it "impossible / Not to love all things" (lines 26, 30–31).

To choose an ass as the object of sympathy was far-out, defiant, a provocation. Doubtless Coleridge was moved, at least subliminally, by stories in high and popular culture that made the ass an emblem of spiritual merit, of a patience, humility, lowliness, and suffering that find favor in heaven.[20] Part of this cultural accretion derives from the association of donkeys with poor persons. The spiritual virtues exemplified in asses are those the ruling class would wish in servants and laborers. But a nexus of negative qualities was also ascribed to this animal – foolishness, stubbornness, whatever is implied by asinine. Its looks were grotesque and its cry loud and unmusical. It would eat anything. It could seem impervious to beatings. In these respects as well as in its association with the poor, the donkey was a theme for humor, not for serious pathos or political protest. In 1821 Parliament accepted a Bill to regulate the ill treatment of horses, but when, during the debate, Alderman C. Smith "suggested that protection should be given to asses, there were such howls of laughter that *The Times* reporter could hear little of what was said."[21]

With a similar defiance, Wordsworth chose an ass as the instrument to redeem his Peter Bell. He was well aware of Coleridge's poem when he did so, and he conceived that "Peter Bell" was a counterpoint to Coleridge's "Rime of the Ancient Mariner." In contrast to the Mariner, Peter was to experience a change of heart through events and psychological processes that were natural rather than supernatural. Peter is, as I remarked, exactly the sort of ignorant, lower-class person to whom cruelty to animals was commonly ascribed. He cudgels the donkey unmercifully – I haven't read a longer, more detailed description of the beating of an animal. The donkey, moreover, shows the meekness under suffering that made this species a Christian emblem, and it also manifests a fidelity to its dead master that Wordsworth, like everyone else, generally located in dogs. Against such virtues Peter's cruelty is the more shocking. Yet though Wordsworth thus assembles usual materials for a protest on behalf of abused animals, the poem does not take this direction. Neither does it instill the "Fraternity of the universal Nature" as strongly as the "Rime of the Ancient Mariner" is generally said to do. If the guilt that works redemptively in Peter had been for beating the donkey, the beating might be thought analogous to the shooting of the albatross in Coleridge's poem. Certainly it confirms to the reader how hard-hearted Peter is, but Peter's guilt, as he feels it, lies less in abusing the donkey than in stealing it. He offends against a law of man more than of the universe, and he is redeemed into social probity rather than into love for all – he becomes "a good and honest man" (line 1135).

Wordsworth's provocation to readers was both more and less than Coleridge's in "To a Young Ass." It was less because, though he evoked sympathy for the donkey, Wordsworth did not call it Brother. It was greater because he made the lowly, conventionally comic animal sublime. The motionlessness of the ass, as Peter pulls and cudgels it, is eerie. Its few, slow gestures are made to seem mysterious and portentous. Its bray echoes among the "winding crags" and "mountains far away" (lines 476–77). When the prone donkey at last gets on its legs, it is compared to a "tempest- shattered" ship on the brink of a wave (line 556). Of course all this conveys how the ass appears to Peter's imagination as it is activated by guilt. But if the poem is to succeed, the reader must share Peter's feelings and perceptions. That Wordsworth chose to write thus about a donkey tells much about him.

To call an ass "brother" may be offensive to many people and particularly to your own brothers. Such aggressions may have been one motive for Coleridge's gesture. The fraternity of universal nature may imply, on its dark side, misanthropy. Perhaps we should keep in mind that when he wrote the poem to the young ass, Coleridge was in a peculiar state of feeling with respect to his brothers George, James, and Luke. The previous Spring they had rescued him from service in the dragoons, in which he had despairingly enlisted, having got into trouble. Since then, he had been more closely supervised by George and had lavished upon his brothers utterances of repentance and promises of amendment. He was humiliated. Moreover, George now opposed with all his power Coleridge's plans for Pantisocracy, and Coleridge resented this. If, in a thought experiment, we imagine that both brothers, George and the ass, were starving, would Coleridge have divided his carrots equally between them? Of course not! But the silly question may remind that in the theater of the subconscious, to call an ass "brother" may be a way of calling your real brother an ass.

The poem also resonates to a recent quarrel with Southey. If we ask what the ass would do in the dell of Pantisocracy, the poem mentions "Toil" as a means to "Health" for all Pantisocrats. More specifically we are told only that the ass will "toss thy heels in gamesome play / And frisk about, as lamb or kitten gay" (lines 31–32). No work. Perhaps the light schedule is a concession to the youth of the donkey, but perhaps it reflects embarrassment in Coleridge over the kind of work that might be assigned. Behind the ass may have lurked, in Coleridge's mind, the figure of Shadrach Weeks. Shad, as he was called, was a footman of Southey's aunt, about Southey's age, and had been Southey's boyhood companion. Southey wanted to take him along to Pennsylvania. Fine! said Coleridge when this was proposed in September, 1794: "SHAD GOES WITH US. HE IS MY BROTHER!"[22] But then it appeared that, in Southey's scheme of Pantisocracy, Shad would do the work of a servant while the higher class intellectuals followed their appropriate occupations – books, light household chores, and gardening. Coleridge balked at introducing this inequality into Utopia, and Southey justified it by the analogy of animals. Beasts could not do the work of their masters and would in Pantisocracy carry out the tasks for which they were fitted. Coleridge rejected Southey's arguments but yielded to his wishes. Shad was to join the ideal community as a servant. Thus an ass at work in Pantisocracy would have symbolized for Coleridge, at least in one implication, an inequality not only between man and animals but between human beings. To call the ass "brother" suggested that it should not work as an ass.

Against this background, we may ask, as we did with Cowper, why Coleridge foregrounded the helpless ass rather than its impoverished master. The answers are rather different in the case of Coleridge. I do not question the sincerity, intensity, or goodness of Coleridge's pity for animals. If his expression of this feeling was sentimental, it contributed all the more to a campaign that continues to the present moment and that I support. One cannot denounce all the world's wrongs in one poem, and there is no reason why "To a Young Ass" ought instead to have been Edwin Markham's "The Man with the Hoe." Nevertheless, we may notice that the latter subject might have been personally dangerous in 1794, and it would additionally have offended many readers. Coleridge was a nervously insecure, self-divided poet, with splendid antennae, and he sought sympathy and love.

Then as now, most readers were disposed to like someone who likes animals. In "To a Young Ass," Coleridge exposed himself to laughter and ridicule, as the speaker is perfectly aware – "spite of the fool's scorn" (line 26). But he was also a dear, like Sterne's Uncle Toby with the fly. Presenting himself as a democrat and a republican, and in these respects a Jacobite, he was, nevertheless, not the least bit threatening. Neither was the half-famished owner of the donkey if his animals were figures for him. The mother ass was chained to a log, the young one innocent and helpless. It acknowledged its subordinate position by begging, and evoked a virtuous pity. Such an emotion makes one feel morally good about oneself, a rare pleasure to which one is doubtfully entitled. In a letter to Southey, Coleridge described a little girl begging for food at an inn. "It is *wrong*, Southey!"

said Coleridge, that such things should be.[23] But I think for most of his readers a hungry little ass would have evoked a stronger or, at least, a less conflicted emotion than a hungry little girl, precisely because the suffering ass less challenged existing structures of society.

One could look at Coleridge's choice of subject in different ways. Viewed as rhetorical strategy, the young ass serves as a screen through which Coleridge can allude to social oppression and attack the existing order. The appeal of the ass hurries the reader to an emotional assent, and this assent may embrace the indignation of the speaker at human poverty. As a screen, in other words, the ass deflects criticism and resistance; it is a safer, softer subject through which Coleridge can also implicate a more explosive one.

Alternatively, however, one might argue that Coleridge shared more or less the state of mind I have supposed in many respectable readers: decent, conscientious people, troubled by the sufferings of the poor, and yet fearful of social upheaval and therefore of incendiary words. For such persons, the cause of animals could serve as a sop to conscience; it was a partial measure, a resting place for those unwilling to go all the way in social criticism, a protest that did not activate fears of revolution.

The latter alternative more resembles Coleridge's state of mind when he wrote "To a Young Ass." The poem asks not to be taken seriously. The choice of an ass as subject was, as I said, defiant, an extreme gesture of literary and social leveling. But the gesture was also a bit of clowning. The poem laughs apologetically at its own silliness. To include a donkey in Utopia explodes the utopian project and mood. It is time to consider the different endings of the early versions.

When Coleridge sent the poem in a letter to Southey on December 17, 1794, the final lines went:

> I hail thee Brother, spite of the Fool's Scorn!
> And fain I'd take thee with me in the Dell
> Of high-soul'd Pantisocracy to dwell;
> Where Toil shall call the charmer Health his Bride,
> And Laughter tickle Plenty's *ribless* side!
> How thou would'st toss thy Heels in gamesome Play,
> And frisk about, as Lamb or Kitten, gay –
> Yea – and more musically sweet to me
> Thy dissonant harsh Bray of Joy would be
> Than *Banti's* warbled airs, that sooth to rest
> The Tumult of a scoundrel Monarch's Breast![24]

This is the most politically threatening version of the poem; the sting comes at the tail, in the phrase "scoundrel Monarch." Coleridge kept this wording in early printings of 1794 and 1796, though eventually the last line dwindled into "The aching of pale Fashion's vacant breast."

The earliest manuscript of the poem, dated October 24, 1794, included additional lines.

> I hail thee Brother – spite of the fool's scorn;
> And fain I'd take thee with me, to the Dell
> Where high-soul'd Pantisocracy shall dwell!
> Where Mirth shall tickle Plenty's ribless side
> And smiles from Beauty's Lip on sun-beams glide,*
> Where Toil shall wed young Health that charming Lass!
> And use his sleek cows for a looking-glass –
> Where Rats shall mess with Terriers hand-in-glove,
> And Mice with Pussy's Whiskers sport in Love!
> How thou wouldst toss thy heels in gamesome play,
> And frisk about, as lamb or kitten gay;
> Yea – and more musically sweet to me
> Thy dissonant harsh Bray of joy would be,
> Than Handel's softest airs that soothe to rest
> The tumult of a scoundrel Monarch's Breast![25]

To the line "And smiles . . . glide," Coleridge's footnote is: "This is a truly poetical line of which the author has assured us that he did not *mean* it to have any *meaning*." Since the meaning is clear and inoffensive, I cannot say why Coleridge apologized for it. But I think that the feeling that he was writing nonsense dogged Coleridge in the whole passage and, in fact, in the whole poem. The personifications of Toil, Health, Laughter, and Plenty were easy poetic convention in 1794; they convey little conviction. But the cancelled lines – where "Mice with Pussy's Whiskers sport in Love," and so forth – convey even less. They describe cloud cuckoo land, Cockaigne. Coleridge was right to cancel these lines, but that he originally wrote them testifies to his divided state of mind. He had the gravest doubts about the practicality of the Pantisocratic community. He mocked it as a dream, though in a kindly way, and thus teased by implication all revolutionary utopias. He was a republican and democrat so fervent that he included an ass in the social fraternity, and by this exaggeration, or clowning, deliberately exposed democratic sentiment to mockery. Even for the ass he envisions no hope except escape to a place that will never exist, a poetic vision. Coleridge's poem foregrounded the ass rather than its master because, as a beneficiary of social reform, the ass would less activate opposition – his own inner misgivings about revolutionary zeal and those of his readers. These tensions are not peculiar to Coleridge's poem, but inherent in the campaign for humanity to animals. If the question was, "why do you attack what is done to animals rather than oppressions and cruelties to human beings?" the true answer, never of course actually confessed, might often have been: "I take up the sufferings of animals as a conscience-appeasing substitute. I don't dwell on those of women, slaves, prisoners, prostitutes, foundlings, paupers, and the lower orders generally because I profit from them, because I have material and ideological investments in them."[26] In a letter written about this time, Coleridge assured his brother George that he was not a democrat.[27] The letter was a self-serving lie, of course, but perhaps with a kernel of truth. As a democrat Coleridge was not completely convinced and wholehearted.

7

The slaughterhouse and the kitchen: Charles Lamb's "Dissertation upon Roast Pig"

I

To eat an animal can be seen as an ultimate exploitation. It was and is a cause of bad conscience in many persons. But few animal sympathizers were vegetarians, though we shall hear from them, and enormous economic interests were involved. Most pleaders on behalf of animals neither hoped nor wished to abolish the eating of meat, but sought to reform processes by which animals were reared, brought to market, fattened, and slaughtered. There was much they could deplore. Sheep, cattle, turkeys, and geese were driven from far to feed the city of London. Cattle came from Scotland, 500 miles away, and even from the Hebrides; sheep from Lincoln, Norfolk, Somerset, and Devon; turkey and geese walked as much as eighty miles, their feet in little cloth shoes.[1] Perhaps a million animals were driven to London each year. The same thing happened on a smaller scale with provincial cities. For the animals, these were journeys of woe. They arrived emaciated. Once they were fattened outside London, they were driven to sale in Smithfield market and then to the slaughterhouses. Hogarth's "Stages of Cruelty" shows sheep being beaten through the city streets, an ordinary sight. John Lawrence describes all this. He also tells how in London calves on their way to slaughter were piled on wagons in living pyramids of confused bodies. Once arrived at Smithfield, they were thrown from the wagons to the cobblestones. A crowd commonly gathered to watch, for bones might be broken in the fall.[2]

No laws regulated what happened in the slaughterhouses. Pigs being fattened might be kept for weeks in spaces so confined that they could not turn or lie down, for this was thought to make their feet more delectable to the palate. Shelley called it a "horrible process of torture."[3] To tenderize the meat, pigs had formerly been whipped to death with knotted ropes, but this was dying out by 1800. Calves might be slowly bled to death, a little each day, in order to make their flesh white. When this method was preferred,

116

"an iron rod, hooked at one end, was used. One end of this instrument was driven through the flesh under the tail of the calf and the other through the nose. The head was thus drawn upwards and to one side." The mouths of the calves were "kept closely muzzled with straps lest the public be attracted by their moans."[4]

Of course animals were also kept and slaughtered in the backyard. Whatever cruelties this involved were completely visible and familiar. Poultry that were being "crammed" – fattened for the table – might have their feet nailed to a board, be confined in a small cage, or be forcibly fed. Turkeys might be slaughtered in the same way as veal. Reformers also condemned the boiling of live lobsters, the skinning and grilling of live eels, and the cutting of collops out of live fish.

Vegetarians allied themselves with the protest of animal rights as part of their polemic against the eating of meat. Vegetarian arguments, apart from the points about cruelty, were medical, ethical, economic, and ethological. I cite Shelley's "Vindication of Natural Diet" and "On the Vegetable System of Diet," since they are well known, but the arguments Shelley voices were common in his age. The medical considerations dated from classical times, and were emphasized in the main source of Shelley's essays, John F. Newton's *The Return to Nature, or a Defence of the Vegetable Regimen* (1811). It was asserted that vegetables are the natural human diet, as is shown by human physiology, for we lack carnivorous teeth and claws. A meat diet "heats the blood," said William Smellie, "and makes it circulate with rapidity." As a result, continues Smellie in his *Philosophy of Natural History* (1790), a compendium of scientific knowledge, persons who eat meat become "much more choleric, fierce and cruel in their tempers than those who live chiefly on vegetables."[5] Smellie was only bringing scientific support to a common observation. As an argument for vegetable diet, Shelley suggests that Napoleon would not have had "the inclination or the power to ascend the throne of the Bourbons" if he had descended "from a race of vegetable feeders" (VI, 11). Because it is unnatural, a meat diet causes disease. Medical authorities also mentioned ancillary considerations. In his *Essay on Health and Long Life* (1724), George Cheyne had pointed out that animals have diseases too, and "diseased Animals can never be proper or sound Food for Men."[6] In his *Reports [on] . . . Cancerous Ulcers*, the well-known doctor William Lambe (a vegetarian Lambe consulted by Keats) argued that a meat diet increases the incidence of cancer. Among the reasons were that meat is harder to digest than vegetables, and accordingly the body must divert more energy into the process.[7]

Medical arguments were augmented by ethical ones. In Thomas Day's *History of Sandford and Merton*, the virtuous Sophron, hero of an inserted story, keeps sheep but only for fleece, and cows only for milk, for he will not take life to "gratify a guilty sensuality."[8] Farmers, butchers, and cooks, said Shelley and many others, "trifle with the sacredness of life." "Accustomed to the sight of wounds and anguish," they become less fitted "for the benevolence and justice" that a civilized society requires (VI, 343). Merely to see the doomed cattle in a field hardens the heart (VI, 154). David Hartley commented that the "taking away the Lives of Animals, in order to convert them into Food, does great Violence to the Principles of Benevolence and Compassion." One sees this, Hartley adds, in "the frequent Hard-heartedness and Cruelty found amongst those persons, whose Occupations engage them in destroying animal Life, as well as from the Uneasiness which others feel in beholding the Butchery of Animals."[9]

Meat eating was economically wasteful. Shelley notes that "the quantity of nutritious vegetable matter, consumed in fattening the carcase of an ox, would afford ten times the sustenance . . . if gathered immediately from the bosom of the earth" (VI, 13). Furthermore, a nation of vegetarians would be egalitarian with respect to diet, or would, at least, lack a marker of hierarchy that, by Shelley's time, was becoming prominent. For meat had social meaning. By the end of the eighteenth century, more cattle were raised than previously, and improvements in fodder made it possible to keep them through the winter. More meat was available to be eaten, and the regular eating of meat spread down from the wealthy to the lower middle classes. The diet of the poor remained largely bread, milk, porridge, potatoes, and vegetables. In Thomas Day's *History of Sandford and Merton*, Tommy, a child of the gentry, finds himself in the kitchen of a poor family. "You must at least want roast meat every day," says Tommy. "No," said the impoverished housewife, "we seldom see roast meat in our house; but we are very well contented, if we can have a bit of fat pork every day, boiled in a pot with greens or turnips; and we bless God that we fare so well; for there are many poor souls, who are as good as we, that can hardly get a morsel of dry bread."[10] Needless to say, not all the poor were so namby-pamby. Under the new conditions, the inability to afford meat became a grievance.

Intellectual vegetarians, such as Shelley, conflated myths of the golden age or of the state of nature with quasi-anthropological reports of various "primitive" peoples and their diets. According to classical authorities such as Hesiod and Ovid, humans in the Golden Age had not eaten animals, just as they had not in the biblical Garden of Eden.[11] Both myths could be interpreted as cultural memories of the state of nature, of *ur*-historical man, who would have been horrified to kill an animal for food. The quasi-anthropological literature of the day was ransacked for traces of this feeling still surviving among primitive peoples. I cite for example John Oswald's *The Cry of Nature* (1791). Oswald had been a soldier in India and, on returning to England, became an itinerant lecturer. He maintained that the diet of the Hindu Brahmans continued "the lovely prejudice of nature" from earliest times.[12] In James Adair's *History of the American Indians* (1775) Oswald read that these tribes "abstain from eating the blood of any animal," a remnant of the primeval feeling in a meat-eating people.[13] Lord Monboddo thought the orang-utan a species of early man; "though they use sticks, [they] do not hunt, but live upon the fruits of the earth, as in the primitive ages all nations did."[14]

II

If one's name is Lamb, does one relish a lamb chop less or more? Presumably neither. Most Lambs (Salmons, Trouts, Veals, etc.) are not affected by the pun at all, especially at dinner. When Mary Lamb remarked that she was "cooking a shoulder of Lamb," no doubt the capital letter meant nothing.[15] Charles Lamb habitually peppered his discourse with puns, including ones on his name, as when he referred to himself as "the Lamb of God" (VI, 409) and "Pope Innocent" (VI, 409). He also punned on his name as food: "Leg of Lamb at 4," he says, inviting Thomas Allsop to dinner, "And the heart of Lamb ever" (VII, 551).

In his writings Lamb posed as a gourmet and no doubt he was one in actual life. To me his gourmet enthusiasms, as he expresses them, seem psychologically defensive against feelings of disgust in eating and particularly in eating flesh. His name may have contributed to this if, in his case, the mental boundary between Lamb and lamb was thinner and more permeable than it usually is. In writing about food Lamb associated remote ranges of experience, and I suppose that he did so also in eating, so that lamb or any meat on the table would bring to mind its life as an animal and its cultural associations – the young creature in the farmer's field, the innocent lamb of literary pastoral, the sacrificial lamb of religious tradition. However, other factors determined his peculiar attitude to meat more traceably: the age-old association between food and sexuality and the contemporary campaign against cruelty to animals. Charles Lamb was strongly exposed to arguments of the latter kind.

How conscious Lamb was of his meaty name can perhaps be seen in his farce, "Mr. H —," which turns on a similar surname. The wealthy, handsome gentleman known in society as Mr. H. conceals his name until, inadvertently, he lets slip that it is Hogsflesh. We can interpret that his name signifies the fleshy or, as might have been said in Lamb's time, the "animal" side of Mr. H., and the sudden disclosure of it agitates the drawing-room. Ladies find it "Disgusting!" "Vile!" "Shocking!" and "Odious!" (v, 202), and other characters speak of or to Mr. H. as though he were a pig. As Hogsflesh, Mr. H. is universally rejected as a suitor. When his name is changed to Bacon, his social and marital prospects are restored. He is now edible, we might say. In other words, Lamb's farce turns on the points that raw realities underlie social manners and customs and that if such realities are brought to mind, they arouse disgust, at least in conventional sensibilities. The relevance of this in the dietary sphere is obvious.

In 1810 Charles's older brother, John, published a fiery pamphlet, partly quoted in chapter 1, denouncing cruelty to animals, including cruelties in cooking. The attitude of Charles Lamb to his brother's pamphlet is not easy to determine. It seems that he abundantly shared the sympathy for suffering animals. On the other hand, this sympathy seems suspended in his famous "Dissertation upon Roast Pig" and in many similar passages of gourmet relish in his letters. But on still another hand, if one had three, a persona (Elia) speaks in the "Dissertation" and is the object of Lamb's satire. In other essays this persona addresses usual humanitarian causes – Africans (ii, 62), chimney sweeps (ii, 108–14), beggars (ii, 114–20), the game laws (ii, 262) – and sidesteps the conventional humanitarian attitude. As in the "Dissertation," the perspectives of Elia are so personal, oblique, paradoxical, obliviously selfish or relentlessly aesthetic that his arguments undermine themselves. (However, this is not always the case: see Elia's brief but hard-hitting indictment of the treatment of women [ii, 79–80].) Even in his private letters Lamb often adopts a pose, and if there are still readers who wish to encounter an author's "identical nature," in Keats's phrase,[16] Lamb would be unusually elusive and baffling.

He commented on his brother's pamphlet in a letter and in an Elia essay on "My Relations," where John is called James Elia. In both passages he more or less dismisses John's concern for animals as an amiable Shandyism. In the letter to Crabb Robinson, attempting to get the pamphlet reviewed, he calls it a "book about humanity," and jokes that it should not be shown to the cook. "For I remember she makes excellent Eel soup, and the leading points of the Book are directed against that very process" (vi, 412). On this occasion, Lamb's attitude was influenced by embarrassment at having to ask for a review. In "My Relations" he portrays James Elia as a bundle of peculiarities, his feeling for suffering animals being one of them. "The contemplation of a lobster boiled, or eels skinned *alive* ... will take the savour from his palate, and the rest from his pillow, for days and nights" (II, 74). I believe that "A Dissertation upon Roast Pig" was partly stimulated by John's attitude. Be this as it may, the "Dissertation" plays with and against the multifarious discourse of which John Lamb's pamphlet was one example.

In his own person, Charles Lamb was tender-hearted to animals. Though he loved Izaak Walton's *Complete Angler*, he would not fish, calling it barbarous (VI, 148). Fishermen were "meek inflictors of pangs intolerable, cool devils" (VI, 146). He described a hunted hare sympathetically (I, 344), and so far as is known, he never hunted. He hoped Southey would write a series of "animal poems, which might have a tendency to rescue some poor creatures from the antipathy of mankind." Among the torments from which such poems might preserve animals were "cooks roasting lobsters, fishmongers crimping skates, etc." (VII, 145–6). In writings for children he argued that toads and frogs must be beautiful because God made them (III, 320), and he presumably approved of the poems for children by Mary Lamb against taking the nests and eggs of wild birds, against tormenting flies, wasps, and butterflies, and in favor of feeding crumbs to birds (III, 286, 353–54, 355–56, 373, 410). He translated from Latin an epitaph on a beggar's faithful dog (II, 117–18), and in a Letter to the Editor of the *Every Day Book* he spoke as a dog on behalf of dogs who were taken up on suspicion of rabies merely, he says, if they look up in a stranger's face or do not wag their tail (I, 383).

On the other hand, Lamb did not, like Shelley, regard bread and raisins as a sufficient feast, and he did not limit his meals to vegetables or to hard biscuits and soda water, as Byron did periodically. In "New Year's Eve," Elia lists among life's best things "the delicious juices of meats and fishes" (II, 29). Whether this sentiment would also have been Lamb's is uncertain. In "Grace Before Meat" Elia confesses that a splendid meal is incompatible with religious devotion: "With the ravenous orgasm upon you, it seems impertinent to interpose a religious sentiment. It is a confusion of purpose to mutter out praises from a mouth that waters. The heats of epicurism put out the gentle flame of devotion ... You are startled at the injustice of returning thanks – for what? – for having too much, while so many starve" (II, 92). The criticism is of "the ravenous orgasm," "the mouth that waters," "having too much."

Food is a major signifier in Lamb's essays and it is surprising that critics have not analyzed it more extensively and thoughtfully. There are three surveys of Lamb's writings about food, by Fred V. Randel in 1975, briefly by D. C. Saxena in 1983, and by J. R. Watson in 1986.[17] Randel thinks that swallowing and digesting represent for Lamb a desirable way of apprehending and dealing with the world. Saxena and Watson sympathize with what they see as Lamb's simple pleasure in food, and for Watson this is an instance of Lamb's "interest in the goings on of common life, the ordinary things that make up our day-to-day existence" (p. 161). "A Dissertation upon Roast Pig" gives Watson difficulties as he tries to read it in this light, and I come back to this. In general, I think that food reminded Lamb of our creaturely being, and that his utterances about food ranged accordingly from expressions of comfort and pleasure at the satisfaction of needs to satire of human material dependence, selfishness, and animality. Clearly, however, food as a signifier in his writings is too polysemous, profound, and ambivalent for brief discussion, and the present essay explores only his attitude to gourmet meat dishes.

As his letters describe this or that palatal pleasure, his enthusiasm, as he represents it, seems exaggerated, and often the pleasure is made to seem vicious or perverse. He writes to Wordsworth, "I have been on the Continent since I saw you. I have eaten frogs" (VII, 592). Frogs represent, of course, a long-desired delight that many might find disgusting: to relish them is to overcome a natural revulsion, that is, to cultivate a perversity. Gloating on this, Lamb tells other correspondents how nice frogs taste – rabbity (VII, 570) – and in describing how to seethe them, he is reminded of the drowning of Shelley, who has gone down "by water to eternal fire!" (VII, 573). If pursued, this remarkable association not only turns Shelley into a cooking frog but also the frog in its broth into a creature in hell. The eating of it becomes cannibalistic and demonic. Lamb emphasizes the sexual pleasure of "cod's head and shoulders" – "that manly firmness, combined with a sort of womanish coming-in-pieces . . . You understand me – these delicate subjects are necessarily obscure" (VII, 681). He loves the "fat unctuous juices of deer's flesh & the green unspeakable of turtle"; the note of guilt or perversion sounds in "unspeakable." He has kept secret, as a taste peculiar to himself, the "exceeding deliciousness of the marrow of boiled knuckle of veal," but now it is "prostitute & common." Still, he has another secret delight that he has never imparted; it is a "little square bit . . . near the knuckle bone of a fried joint of" – here he breaks off, keeping his secret (VII, 682). According to a letter to Thomas Manning, thanking him for a gift of brawn, this food was his supreme palatal pleasure, and he writes an extravagant page in praise of it (VI, 302–03). He does not allude to the "horrible process of torture," in Shelley's phrase, by which brawn was improved. Given Lamb's interest in pork and in brawn, he presumably knew of these cruelties, and his fantastical praise of brawn could be a perverse pose. This may be the place to mention that, according to Shelley, suckling pigs were formerly roasted alive.[18]

Lamb might suggest that food is not only a secret and perverse delight but a solitary one. In "Christ's Hospital Five and Thirty Years Ago," Elia describes a boy of whom, misquoting Shakespeare's *Antony and Cleopatra* (I, iv, 67–68), he writes " 'Twas said / He ate strange flesh." He was "a *gag-eater*," a gag being boiled beef fat, which most boys found revolting, and as a gag-eater, he was excommunicated by his schoolmates. "None saw when he ate them. It was rumoured that he privately devoured them in the night." He was a "*goul*," a creature that feeds on corpses (II, 15–16). It turns out that the boy was taking these morsels to his poor and hungry parents, but the association of food with solitary vice is characteristic of Lamb. Dinner has arrived, he concludes a letter to Thomas Manning: "All that is gross and unspiritual in me rises at the sight! Avaunt friendship and all memory of absent friends!" (VI, 189). The latter sentence reverberates to the remarkable one in "Christ's Hospital, Five and Thirty Years Ago," where Elia remembers how as a schoolboy he would himself guiltily devour, rather than share, the extra food that his aunt brought him: "hunger (eldest, strongest of the passions!) predominant, breaking down the stony fences of shame, and awkwardness, and a troubling over-consciousness" (II, 13). Everything I have quoted was, of course, intended by Lamb as humor, and is all the more revealing for this reason.

Some speculators in Lamb's time attributed sensation and perception to vegetables, raising qualms about eating them also. In this connection I note a characteristic passage of "My Relations," in which Elia remembers his aunt preparing green beans for supper – "the splitting of French beans, and dropping them into a China basin of fair water. The odour of these tender vegetables to this day comes back upon my sense, redolent of soothing recollections. Certainly it is the most delicate of culinary operations" (II, 71). The phrase "culinary operations" occurred in the pamphlet of John Lamb, who wrote that the body of an eel is "convulsed during the culinary operations" (VI, 412), but if we do not recall the parallel, the terms "splitting" and "operations" still suggest an injury. That the performance is "delicate" implies that the injury, if there is one, is dealt deliberately and carefully. The child felt pleasurably protected, not only by the promise of food but also by the order, care, and skill in his aunt's kitchen, and these are still soothing in recollection. Mixed feelings are most present in the word "tender." It tells that the beans are young, therefore easily bruised. Gentle vulnerability arouses sympathy in gentle souls, but when it is perceived in a food, we are ruthless, and prepare the food more cautiously. Such ambiguities and ironies are pursued to the limit in "A Dissertation upon Roast Pig," where the suckling pig is a fragile innocent and is therefore to be roasted with the utmost care. Lest I be thought to have ignored the point, I mention that a lamb is also a young, gentle, innocent, vulnerable, tender victim of "culinary operations."

In vegetarian sentiment, all vegetables had the nostalgic and soothing associations that beans have for Elia. For, as I noted, vegetables were the diet of Paradise or, in the primitivist perspective, of early man. This diet stilled passions; more exactly, it did not arouse them. But, to repeat, meat was said to conduce, both physically and psychologically, to aggression and cruelty, psychologically because in order to obtain meat you have to hunt or slaughter, physiologically because it heats the blood. As for sex, meat eating does not augment the physical pleasure, for given their perfect health, this must have been more intense among the primitive root eaters than it now is. But the aggression, dominance, cruelty, and other psychological disorders that are promoted by a meat diet manifest themselves in condemnable sexual feeling and conduct. The age-old analogies between erotic behavior, hunting, and warfare, illustrate what is meant. My point, however, is not merely that meat was said to inflame a guilty sexuality, but that the one appetite was analogous to the other and could express it in code.

Remarking the human uneasiness with eating animals, Hazlitt noted that our strongest revulsions are against that to which we are also attracted.[19] Lamb parceled this conflict into a pair of would-be humorous essays published simultaneously in 1812: "Edax on Appetite" and "*Hospita* on the Immoderate Indulgence of the Pleasures of the Palate." Both Edax and Hospita, the personae who are supposedly writing the essays, are objects of satire. The unfortunate Edax has a bottomless appetite for food. Merely to mention this fact is, he fears, an offense against delicacy (I, 119). His excesses were first found out in boarding school, where they were manifest in his looks and inanition after meals, and though he was "only following the blameless dictates of nature," he suffered "the penalties of guilt." If he were given gingerbread, he retired to "some silent corner . . . to mumble" it, rather than sharing it, as he ought to have done, with another boy (VI, 120). In adult life Edax's appetite has brought him social opprobrium and cost him an inheritance. His complaint is that an impulsion against which he is helpless is socially punished. Edax's appetite is specifically for meat. Vegetables do not fill him up. He reveals his sense of guilt by quoting from Bernard Mandeville's *Fable of the Bees*, where the Lion says that " 'Tis only Man, mischievous Man, that can make Death a sport. Nature taught your stomach to crave nothing but Vegetables," and you destroy "Animals without Justice or Necessity" (I, 121). "Generally speaking," says Edax, the Lion is "in the right," but he, Edax, is a "lusus naturae" (I, 122). The notion that one is a "lusus naturae" while yielding to natural impulse used to be a characteristic paradox of sexual guilt in youth. Its origin lay in social disapproval of sex combined with hypocrisy and silence about it, so that the "lusus naturae" did not know that others did it also.

In the companion essay we hear from a lady who has had Edax to dinner. Though she and her family are strict vegetarians, they provide meat for him as a guest, and "his way of staring at the dishes as they are brought in, has absolutely something immodest in it: it is like the stare of an impudent man of fashion at a fine woman" (I, 125). She mentions usual vegetarian arguments and adds that her children have never heard of "the dressing of animal food," and do not know "that such things are practised." She calls this a "happy state of innocence," with an allusion, no doubt, to the diet of Adam and Eve but also with an analogy to the (pre-Freudian) sexual innocence of children. For, she adds, "a state of innocence is incompatible with a certain age," and she is trying little by little to prepare her eldest daughter for the shock of finding that people eat meat. "The first hint I gave her upon the subject, I could see her recoil from it with the same horror with which we listen to a tale of Anthropophagism . . . Such being the nature of our little household, you may guess . . . what revolutions and turnings of things upside down, the example of such a feeder as Mr. — is calculated to produce" (I, 126). To treat the appetite for meat as analogous to sexual desire or as encoding it was, then, to make it natural but suspect and, when excessive, perverse and condemnable.

Galen had observed a resemblance between the tastes of human flesh and pork, and this ancient finding had more recently been confirmed by the newly discovered cannibals of the South Seas, who enjoyed "long pig." After he had published "A Dissertation upon Roast Pig," Lamb received this commodity from time to time as a present, for which he wrote thank-you notes. He refers to himself as a "pig lover" (VII, 581); recurring to the theme of sharing food, he tells Coleridge, who had been given a pig, that though he would himself make presents of foods, he would not give a pig, for "pigs are pigs, and I myself therein am nearest to myself." Did "the eyes [of the roast pig] come away kindly with no Oedipean avulsion?" he asks Coleridge, thus associating violence and guilt with the meal (VII, 561). "It was a dear pigmy," he tells a donor, and figures the feast not only as cannibal but as though he had eaten the pig alive. "In spite of his obstinacy . . . I contrived to get at one of" the ears. Alluding to its small feet and "pretty toes," he supposes the pig was "Chinese and a female" (VII, 592). In "Popular Fallacies" Elia speaks of dining on food sent by a friend as though it were dining on the friend: he loves to taste his friend "in grouse or woodcock; to feel him gliding down in the toast peculiar to the latter; to concorporate him in a slice of Canterbury brawn. This is indeed to have him within ourselves; to know him intimately" (II, 262). The suggestions of guilt and perversion (as Lamb would have viewed it) are both cannibalistic and homosexual.

In *Don Juan* Byron also deploys the cannibal joke. The shipwrecked sailors eat Pedrillo, Juan's tutor, for "Man is a carnivorous production / And must have meat" (II, 67, lines 529–30).[20] The situation is a usual one in Byron: body and spirit conflict, and in the comic mode of *Don Juan*, the body overrules. The emphasis on meat in this passage was perhaps Byron's tease of his friend Shelley, since any food would have served in the sailors' extremity. I cite Byron in order to point out that Lamb's jokes about food also turn on material compulsion but in a different register. For the foods Lamb or his personae irresistibly crave are luxury items, such as roast suckling pig, brawn, widgeon, sturgeon, and potted char. Within the usual historical and economic theories of the Enlightenment, luxuries such as these exemplified the unnatural wants created by civilization, and within a primitivist perspective, they were medically and morally condemnable.

Moreover, a craving for gourmet luxuries could not be politically in-nocent. In "Grace Before Meat" Elia describes extreme social inequality in terms of food: the poor man "hardly knows whether he shall have a meal the next day or not," while the courses of the rich are "perennial" (II, 92). These courses were expensive. "A Dissertation upon Roast Pig" highlights this in its fantastic way: in order to cook a pig, the ancient Chinese installed it in their house and burnt the house down. Poor people in Lamb's England could not afford meat, as I noted, though they dearly wished to eat it. (Vegetarians were to be found almost exclusively among middle-class in-tellectuals.) Their hunger prompted Malthus to comfort the wealthy with his dialectic of food supply and population, and it also stimulated the poor to more direct arguments in the form of food riots. Thus the gourmet indulgences of which Lamb writes might be seen not only as unnatural, unhealthy, and perverse, but as socially heedless. A person so myopic and ruthless in pursuit of his pleasures as Elia is in passages of "A Dissertation upon Roast Pig" might be a caricature of the rich as perceived by radicals. But Elia assumes the complicity of the reader. We are like him.

"A Dissertation upon Roast Pig" brings to mind Swift's "Modest Proposal." In Swift also the humor turns on cannibalism and on the peculiar character of the speaker. Among the salient differences are that Swift's speaker proposes literal cannibalism; in the "Dissertation" it is metaphorical. Literally the food is suckling pig, an acceptable food to most people, but figuratively it is a human infant: "a child-pig," "a young and tender suckling . . . his voice as yet not broken"; the serving dish is "his second cradle." Elia applies to the slaughtered suckling pig some lines from Coleridge's "Epitaph on an Infant" (II, 123–24). Hence the shock of, "*He must be roasted*" (II, 123). Nevertheless, that the proposal of Swift's speaker is literal, of Lamb's metaphorical, means that we are free to enjoy Elia's wit and fantasy. We can partly share his enthusiasm; we can laugh at him with a certain fondness, for this is the English comedy of character – he has a humor in the old, theatrical sense. Yet even though the essay is comic, we are chilled at moments by the cruelty lurking in Elia's gourmandise. Compared with the "Modest Proposal," Lamb's essay dissolves clear demarcations and leaves us in ambivalence.[21]

In Swift eating means economic exploitation. In Lamb eating is not a figure for economic exploitation but for sensual pleasure. The pleasure is so extreme that humans inflict cruelties (roasting pigs alive) and incur economic harm (burning down their own houses) for the sake of it. As the speaker reveals his obsession in all its colors, the "Dissertation" falls into the genre of Romantic confession, unfolding an interestingly peculiar, shocking state of mind. Parallels would be with DeQuincey's *Confessions of an English Opium-Eater* and Hazlitt's *Liber Amoris*, which also depict irresistible cravings. Passages in the "Dissertation" bring to mind Humbert Humbert:

the coy, brittle resistance – with the adhesive oleaginous – O call it not fat – but an indefinable sweetness growing up to it – the tender blossoming of fat – fat cropped in the bud – taken in the shoot – in the first innocence – the cream and quintessence of the child-pig's yet pure food. (II, 123–24)

Among the ancient Chinese, Elia says, the idea of eating roast pig aroused horror. Ho-ti "cursed himself that ever he should beget a son that should eat burnt pig." As with the suspected gag-eater among the boys in Christ's Hospital, the food was an abomination, the eater "an unnatural young monster." When Ho-ti, having tasted, succumbs, and eats roast pork himself, his pleasure becomes a secret. His son was "strictly enjoined not to let the secret escape," since "the neighbours would certainly have stoned them." Nevertheless, as with the suspected gag-eater, "strange stories got about," they were watched, the horrid fact was discovered, and soon everyone was doing it, at first, presumably, in secret (II, 122).

The first pigs were roasted alive, and figuratively, as Elia continues, suckling pigs are still cooked in this way. "Behold him, while he is doing – it seemeth rather a refreshing warmth, than a scorching heat, that he is so passive to . . . To see the extreme sensibility of that tender age, he hath wept out his pretty eyes – radiant jellies – shooting stars" (II, 124). The literary strategy is of course to make the reader feel the cruelty while pretending to believe that it is not cruel ("a refreshing warmth"), thus illustrating Elia's obsessional myopia. A long passage on pineapple develops the parallel of palatal and sexual delight, and compares pineapple invidiously to the "no less provocative" pig, even though pineapple offers a ravishing "pleasure bordering on pain from the fierceness and insanity of her relish" (II, 124).

If one has dipped into the various discourses of Lamb's time that condemned cruelty to animals, one sees that his "Dissertation" often alludes to them. Human beings in a state of nature were said to have lived on raw vegetables, and did not eat meat until they invented cooking. John F. Newton's *The Return to Nature* reinterpreted the myth of Prometheus as an allegory of this dire step in the history of mankind. As Shelley summarized, when Prometheus first "applied fire to culinary purposes," a meat diet became more digestible and less disgusting (VI, 6). Lamb's "Dissertation" plays with such arguments and, according to Thomas Allsop, the essay suggested itself to Lamb after a conversation with Thomas Manning on the origin of cooking. Manning had lately returned from China with speculative solutions "of some of the most interesting questions concerned with the early pursuits of men."[22]

But unlike Newton and Shelley, Elia assumes that in the course of history meat was eaten before it was cooked. The ancient Chinese obtained their meals as the Abyssinians still did, slicing or biting them from living cattle. This tidbit from Bruce's travels was a stand-by in vegetarian tracts. Yet, ironically, to eat cooked meat makes Bo-bo all the more into an animal, as is shown by his table manners: "tearing up whole handfuls of the scorched skin with the flesh . . . cramming it down his throat in beastly fashion . . . His father . . . could not beat him from the pig, till he had fairly made an end of it" (II, 121). The horror of the Chinese when they see someone eating cooked meat resembles that of Hospita's daughter, whose innocence is violated by such appetites, which seem as bad to her as "Anthropophagism." As for cruelties in slaughtering, Elia notes that pigs were formerly whipped to death in order to tenderize their flesh, and he is ready to make the experiment: it "might impart a gusto."

A traditional argument against what we now call animal rights was that God had given the creatures to man for his use (Genesis 1. 26–28; 9. 2–3). Within the traditional way of thinking there was wide latitude to argue either that the animals were to be used as humanely as possible – and what would this mean in practice? – or that their sufferings were irrelevant. In the casuistry of conscience it was possible to weigh the degree of use against the degree of suffering, and Lamb parodies this way of thinking as Elia writes,

I remember an hypothesis, argued upon by the young students, when I was at St. Omer's, and maintained with much learning and pleasantry on both sides, 'Whether, supposing that the flavour of a pig who obtained his death by whipping (*per flagellationem extremam*) superadded a pleasure upon the palate of a man more intense than any possible suffering we can conceive in the animal, is man justified in using that method of putting the animal to death?' I forget the decision. (II, 126)

The "pleasantry on both sides," the touch of Latin, the setting in a Jesuit college, and the forgetting of the decision indicate that for the disputants as for Elia the argument was merely an academic trial of wits. The satire is directed against intellectuals lacking in feeling, in sympathy, and is the more telling if we remember that Lamb alludes to fact: pigs had been slaughtered by being whipped to death.

So far as Lamb's "Dissertation" can be read as a positive contribution to the campaign against cruelty to animals, the campaign that inspired John Lamb, it redescribes the eating of flesh not as a need but as a sensual, obsessive, and cruel pleasure, aligned with sexual lasciviousness. However, I think readers generally took the "Dissertation" in a different way, as a fanciful and charming *étalage du moi*, a witty, agreeable confession of Elia's (conflated with Lamb's) peculiarity and humor. Thus in gratitude for the "Dissertation" John Kenyon could send Lamb both a hamper and some verse:

> Elia! Thro' irony of hearts the mender,
> May this pig prove like thine own pathos – tender.[23]

The second line undermines the first by showing that Elia's irony had no effect. It confirms Elia's low opinion of humanity, especially of our sensitivity to the sufferings of animals and the question of their rights.

8

Caged birds and wild

The plea for kindness to animals extended also to birds, the most familiar and loved of wild animals. A typical burst of rhetoric, from James Grahame's *The Birds of Scotland*, affirms that God "who hears the heavenly choirs" listens with equal pleasure to "the woodland song."[1] Protest on behalf of wild birds, especially in poems and in literature for children, focused on the taking of eggs, nests, or nestlings of wild birds and the keeping of caged birds as parlor ornaments and pets. Song birds were also eaten, needless to say. In the 1860s Henry Mayhew estimated that 300,000 larks were sold annually for food in the London market.[2] Georgian cookbooks include recipes for roasting, spitting, or stewing blackbirds, thrush, lapwings, magpies, larks, sparrows, and woodpeckers. Frequently they were served on toast. Various birds, notably sparrows and jays, were viewed as agricultural pests and a bounty might be paid for their corpses. However, these practices did not disturb reformers as much as taking nests and caging. Their protest was part of the matrix of famous high Romantic poems such as Wordsworth's "To a Cuckoo," Shelley's "To a Skylark," and Keats's "Ode to a Nightingale." In these poems, birds are elusive and inviolable. They represent a nature man cannot subjugate or harm, the compensatory dream of Romantic poetry.

I

The hedgerows and heaths, groves and fens of England swarmed with boys. At least, the children's literature of the age leaves this impression. Boys peered everywhere; the densest thicket could not keep them out; the highest or most hidden place was not safe from them. They were "nesting," that is, looking for birds' nests. If boys found one, they would take it, or would crack the eggs together, or blow them empty, or kill the helpless chicks, or give them to a girl, or sell the nest with its eggs. Mayhew mentions a gypsy boy who sold about twenty a week during the four months of the year when the birds were active.[3] Nests with eggs were valued as curios, ornaments, and conversation pieces. A professional dealer might try to rear the chicks until they were old enough to sell. No wonder, in E. A. Kendall's *The Canary Bird*, the chaffinch prays,

> May no idle thoughtless boy
> Rob me of my dearest joy!
> O, guarded be this little shade,
> Wherein my fondest hopes are laid![4]

Original Poems for Infant Minds (1804), a book so popular that it went through fifty editions (it included "Twinkle, twinkle, little star . . ."), tells in one of its poems that

> One day the young birds were all crying for food,
> So off flew their mother away from her brood;
> And up came some boys, who were wicked and rude.
>
> So they pull'd the warm nest down away from the tree;
> And the little ones cried, but they could not get free;
> So at last they all died away, one, two, and three.[5]

A passage in James Grahame's *Birds of Scotland* illustrates how poems for adults typically narrated an episode of nesting. The victims are blackbirds, and the poem previously describes the pair building and guarding the nest in a hawthorn and then incubating and feeding the chicks until they are ready for their first flight, a moment that fills "with joy the fond parental eye."

> The truant schoolboy's eager, bleeding hand,
> Their house, their all, tears from the bending bush;
> A shower of blossoms mourns the ruthless deed!
> The piercing anguish'd note, the brushing wing,
> The spoiler heeds not; triumphing, his way
> Smiling he wends: the ruin'd, hopeless pair,
> O'er many a field follow his townward steps,
> Then back return; and, perching on the bush,
> Find nought of all they loved, but one small tuft
> Of moss, and withered roots.[6]

Figuratively, then, the "warm nest" was the home, the protected place in which children were raised. Birds were the loving parents. Their self-abnegation, as they brood their eggs and feed their chicks, was extolled. James Thomson, in *The Seasons*, compared birds to poor humans who give their own food to their offspring.[7] In Sarah Trimmer's *Fabulous Histories*, the robin remembers how once he helplessly followed a clutch of his nestlings as three boys carried them off and his mate expired of grief.[8] To die of grief is human, and this was the point. The birds feel just as we do. If boys were tempted to carry off nestlings, they should think how their parents would feel if a monster snatched them from their beds.[9] The virtuous boy Harry, in Thomas Day's *History of Sandford and Merton*, "would never go into the fields to take the eggs of poor birds, or their young ones, nor practice any other sort of sport which gave pain to poor animals; who are as capable of feeling as we are ourselves."[10]

Nesting was viewed as a common, typical cruelty of children, like sticking pins through beetles or sicking dogs on cats. It might be merely thought-lessness, but if uncorrected, it led on to worse doings, and it caused agony to the creatures. In *Fabulous Histories* Miss Jenkins pays a visit. She has "no kind mamma to give her instructions," and she has never before heard that there is harm in taking nests. "To toss the young birds about" is, she says, a "nice diversion."[11] Joanna Baillie explained to the children of Hampstead School that "the very wriggling of their bodies, by which their tormentors are sometimes so much diverted, is their natural manner of expressing pain, as weeping or groaning is in human creatures." Should children to whom her pamphlet has been read still find pleasure in destroying nests, they are not "children of God, or even of men – but children of the Devil."[12]

Women especially were protectors of birds, but, as we have seen, male poets also wrote against nesting. Thomson describes the ruses by which birds try to keep the "unfeeling schoolboy" from noticing their nest. They do this from "exalting Love / By the great Father of the Spring inspir'd."[13] As Burns tells it in a letter, he was listening to the "feathered Warblers," and said to himself, "he must be a wretch indeed, who . . . can eye your elusive flights, to discover your secret recesses, and rob you of all the property Nature gives you; your dearest comforts, your helpless, little Nestlings."[14] In "The Daemon of the World" Shelley affirms that at the millennium nesting will cease. Birds will

> prune their sunny feathers on the hands
> Which little children stretch in friendly sport
> Towards these dreadless partners of their play.[15]

John Clare wrote brilliantly and frequently about endangered nests.

> Boys thread the woods
> To their remotest shades
> But in these marshy flats these stagnant floods
> Security pervades.[16]

Nests had many meanings for Clare's imagination. In Freudian terms, the nest was mother. It might also represent the feminine genital organ. Much of Clare's excitement over nests is predatory, and much of the predatory excitement is erotic. But in other poems, nesting figures social predation. Nests are dwellings of the poor, and boys are wealthy persons who destroy merely to feel their power. Such allegories may allude to the enclosure acts and the pulling down of cottages, sometimes merely for the sake of opening the view from the manor house. Yet with a different social bias, Clare also scorns the nesting boys as "clowns" and "louts," village boys, and thus, as I said in an earlier chapter, he repudiates his own past, class, and self. In other poems the ruthlessness of the boys shows the human heart in general. As with Cowper and Wordsworth, Clare's love of nature was partly motivated by fear and repudiation of human nature. He attributes so much cunning, tenacity, and malice to the boys that his reader suspects paranoia. An unreachable nest in a swamp means safety and escape. Apart from "the haunts of men," life is still innocent and Edenic.[17]

Nesting was a gendered activity. Only boys did it, no doubt with the same pleasures that they now find in catching frogs. Dirt, briars, creeping, and climbing were not for girls. Because it was a joy of childhood, ambivalence was possible in poems about nesting. Clare can remember it fondly while deploring it. Near the start of the *Prelude*, Wordsworth recalled times when, as a boy, he would clamber about the ridges, plundering the nests of ravens. The impulses to this were morally troubling, the adult poet feels, but the end was glorious, for nature used the occasion to impress on him its sublimity.[18] Because nesting was boyish, it was also incipient manliness, and to some persons the protest against it seemed emasculating. In *Agnes Grey*, Anne Brontë brought on a wicked uncle who countered the governess's good work. She attempted to teach the evil of bird-nesting, but uncle Robson encouraged Tom's barbarities, which included tormenting nestlings. When she prevented this, Tom had a tantrum. "Damme," said the uncle, "but the lad has some spunk in him . . . He's beyond petticoat government already."[19]

Naturalists collected nests and eggs for their purposes. Scientific study of birds had begun in something like its modern form toward the end of the seventeenth century and flourished thereafter.[20] In cabinets along with skins, feathers, and stuffed birds, nests were useful for classifications and descriptions of the species and in studies of their distribution. Field observation of behavior was also going forward, famously in Gilbert White, and information about birds was conveyed in magazines and in large, beautifully illustrated books. Besides the several redactions of Buffon listed in an earlier chapter, there were, among others, Thomas Pennant's *British Zoology* (1768–70), William Lewin's *Birds of Great Britain* (1789–91), Edward Donovan's *Natural History of British Birds* (1794), and Thomas Bewick's *History of British Birds* (1797 and 1804). The knowledge thus communicated fostered wonder at avian instincts and adaptations, ultimately at the creative benevolence of God that inspired them. In *The Village Curate* (1788) James Hurdis typically marveled at a nest:

> Mark it well within, without.
> No tool had he that wrought, no knife to cut,
> No nail to fix, no bodkin to insert,
> No glue to join; his little beak was all,
> And yet how neatly finish'd. What nice hand,
> With ev'ry implement and means of art,
> And twenty years apprenticeship to boot,
> Could make me such another?[21]

Much of the scientific lore, however, could only have been gathered by repressing imaginative sympathy, by intruding destructively on the creatures, on their God-given happiness, and for this reason it might be read with ambivalent feelings. This did not hinder most scientists, but a poet who was also a naturalist was in a bind.

This was the case with John Clare. He prided himself on his close, detailed knowledge of the natural world and its creatures, and he rightly felt that this was valued by his readers. He even aspired to emulate Gilbert White by writing a natural history of the flora and fauna of his region. In the literary culture of Clare's time, close description of nature would generally have been understood as the poet's act of love, but not when Clare as a naturalist showed himself still a boy, peering and penetrating to get at nests.

Clare's remarkable sonnet, "Birds in Alarm," reports the different responses of birds to threatening intrusions, how the "fire tail . . . tweets and flyes," "the yellow hammer never makes a noise," and "the nightingale keeps tweeting churring round / But leaves in silence when the nest is found."[22] But how does the poet know? Clare must have felt the imputation, for in many poems he introduces persons other than himself to cause the fear reactions and make the discovery. In "The Yellowhammers Nest" the poet just happens to be looking on as a cow boy scrambles down a bank. The boy frightens a bird into flying up, revealing its hidden nest, in which the poet then sees "Five eggs pen-scribbled over lilac shells / Resembling writing scrawls." In "The Pettichaps Nest" the poet causes the nest-disclosing alarm, but he does so inadvertently as he walks along, since the nest was built dangerously close to a public way. "The Wrynecks Nest" is exposed by "peeping idlers." In "The Firetails Nest" the blue eggs are uncovered by a hedger.[23] Similarly in "The Sparrow's Nest" Wordsworth is careful to remark that the "bright blue eggs together laid" is a "chance-discovered sight."[24]

"The Nightingale's Nest," a fine poem, reveals Clare's conflicting impulses with regard to nests. The poem narrates a successful search. It concludes with splendid verses describing the nest and the eggs. This description is the scientific profit of the expedition. The imagery at this point is closely particular and detailed, specifying the number and color of the eggs, the materials and layered construction of the nest – the sort of information that can now be found in Audubon encyclopedias. Clare's contemporaries would have recognized the scientific character of this description – that Clare knew more positivistic truth about nightingales than Keats.

To find the nest, the speaker draws on lore and cunning. That he has to force his way through difficult thickets enhances the excitement. If in this respect Clare seems boyish, other figuration in the poem suggests that the quest is post-pubertal. Let us follow him. He guesses that a nest might be hidden in "this black thorn clump" (line 43). He wades through grass and parts hazel branches to get at it. With its hazels, thorns, and brambles, nature resists. Imagery of penetration, even forceful penetration describes the nester. When, hunting through the clump, Clare finds "her secret nest . . . Upon this white thorn stulp" (stump, lines 53–54), he urges his companion to "put that bramble bye / Nay trample on its branshes and get near" (lines 55–56). Though at first the speaker would approach "in a gentle way" (line 45), his feelings coarsen as he draws close. The bird raises a "Plaintive note of danger nigh" (line 59) and then stops in "choaking fear" (line 60). Only at this point does the speaker reveal that he is finally not a boy, a hunter, a naturalist, or a lover, but a sympathizing poet, as he reassures that "Well [we'll] leave it [the nest] as we found it" (line 62) and invites the bird to "sing on" (line 67). But he has brought fear into the hidden bower of joy (lines 22–23).[25]

II

In *Fabulous Histories*, to take another incident from this story, the young Frederick wants to cage robins so that he can feed them. "Should you like to be always shut up in a little room," his mother asks. "It must be a dreadful life for a poor bird to be shut up in a cage, where he cannot so much as make use of his wings – where he is excluded from his natural companions – and where he cannot possibly receive that refreshment, which the air must afford to him when at liberty to soar."[26] Despite such arguments, Gerard Manley Hopkins' great lines about a "dare-gale skylark scanted in a dull cage" describe a sight that was common until the Parliamentary bill of 1880. Birds were kept as pets for their songs, looks, naturalness, and companionship, and, as with other pets, an astonishing variety of desires and fears were projected upon them. They were particularly appreciated by persons such as weavers, barbers, and small shopkeepers who could listen to them as they worked. Grahame describes a pitiful lark whose song lightened a "pale mechanic's tedious task," and the poem draws the inevitable comparison between the avian captives and the child workers in cotton mills who had themselves so little of natural light and air.[27] Doves, canaries, bullfinch, linnets, goldfinch, larks, nightingales, starlings, thrushes, and robins were the most frequent victims, though other species were also used. Mayhew, surveying Victorian London, estimates that over 300,000 birds were sold for this purpose annually.[28] But this figure is only for London and for regular transactions of shops and street vendors. For all England the number was much larger.

Unlike pets such as dogs, cats, and lambs, the caged bird was thought to desire its freedom. If given the chance, it would fly away. This provided an inexhaustible theme for poems in which the speaker either granted or withheld liberty, always for tender-hearted reasons. In her fine anthology of Romantic women poets, Paula Feldman suggests, as others have also, that in such poems women explored their "conflicting desires for free- dom and safety," debated "the virtues of domesticity measured against the excitement of liberty and its attendant danger."[29] Caged birds were ad- dressed and caressed as though they were children, and maternal themes were an alternative or sometimes a simultaneous subtext in these poems. The smallness, harmlessness, and chirpiness of birds especially qualified them for the infant role. William Blake drew the parallel in "On Another's Sorrow":

> And can he who smiles on all
> Hear the wren with sorrows small,
> Hear the small bird's grief & care,
> Hear the woes that infants bear,
>
> And not sit beside the nest,
> Pouring pity in their breast;
> And not sit the cradle near,
> Weeping tear on infant's tear.[30]

Within Romantic culture a cruel poet was a contradiction, most especially if the cruelty were to animals. Hence a poem about your own caged bird was problematic. There had to be a strongly sympathetic, loving reason for keeping the bird captive. To some poets, such as Cowper, the world seemed so perilous that there could be no question of releasing loved creatures into it. The cage expressed love as protection. This is the theme of Mary Hays's "Ode to Her Bullfinch" (1785); given the lurking prevalence of fowlers and boys, the bullfinch, she tells it, should bless its cage, where at least there is "sympathy and tenderness." The poem obscurely suggests that the speaker may herself have suffered from too much liberty; something, at any rate, has caused "pangs which do my bosom wound."[31] With Hays as with Cowper, incidentally, the woes of animals in the wild come from human beings.

If a bird were exotic, injured, or otherwise unable to survive in English countryside, to keep it in a cage might be the best one could do, hence poetically acceptable as an act of pity. This presumably was the case with Cowper's two goldfinch that, he implies in "The Faithful Bird," were born in a cage. So also with Wordsworth's turtledove, which cooed whenever the poet began to compose aloud.[32] In "The Mistress's Reply to Her Little Bird," Ann Taylor answers "The Little Bird's Complaint" of its cage by explaining that a "cruel boy" took the bird as a nestling and gave it to the poet. It would die if set free.[33] In most poems, however, the bird was released to liberty, for example, in Mary Robinson's "The Linnet's Petition" and Elizabeth Bentley's "To a Redbreast, That Flew into the House and Suffered Itself to be Taken by the Hand of the Authoress." Since the English robin will come indoors for crumbs and pick about the table or hearth, or even the bosom, it especially endeared itself. This behavior permitted a relationship with the wild thing that was not harmful and guilty. Birds in the poetry of Felicia Hemans are typically high Romantic ones, a species to which I come later. They are proud, soaring creatures, symbols of poetry or of the spirit. "The Sea-Bird Flying Inland" refuses the soft allures of countryside and hies back "To his throne of pride on the billow's crest." In "The Freed Bird," Hemans stages a debate between the bird and its former mistress, who vainly pleads with it to return to the cage. The bird is

> of a tameless race,
> With the soul of the wild-wood, my native place!
> With the spirit that panted through heaven to soar:
> Woo me not back – I return no more.[34]

The pet that wings its way to the bosom might also figure a lover. In William Blake's "How sweet I roam'd from field to field," the caged bird suggests complex feelings about love's cost in freedom. The "prince of love" has caught the speaker "in his silken net, / And shut me in his golden cage."

> He loves to sit and hear me sing,
>   Then, laughing, sports and plays with me;
> Then stretches out my golden wing,
>   And mocks my loss of liberty.[35]

A caged robin in Blake's "Auguries of Innocence" "puts all Heaven in a Rage," maybe because Heaven shares Blake's indignation at love – the phallus – being confined.[36] For the feminine "blossom" in Blake's *Songs of Innocence*, the sparrow is both phallus and infant:

> A happy Blossom
> Sees you swift as arrow
> Seek your cradle narrow
> Near my Bosom.[37]

Blake was not the only writer to make this association. In Helen Leigh's "The Linnet: A Fable," Celia's "bosom, with love, and with tenderness glow'd" for her caged linnet, who displaced her lover. The bird flies off, returns, and is "faithful" thereafter.[38] A 1755 *Connoisseur* essay against over-valuing pets jokes that the "slighted gallant" envies "the caresses given to a lap-dog, or kisses bestowed on a squirrel! And 'I would I were thy bird!' has been the fond exclamation of many a Romeo."[39] James Thomson compares caged birds to "pretty slaves" languishing in a harem. He also compares them to poets, and amid these projections, he does not forget – neither should we – the main point. Caging of birds, Thomson writes, is inhuman and impious:

> Oh then, ye Friends of Love and Love-taught Song,
> Spare the soft Tribes, this barbarous Art forbear!
> If on your Bosom Innocence can win,
> Music engage, or Piety persuade.[40]

III

The most famous of all poems on cruelty to a bird is of course Coleridge's "Rime of the Ancient Mariner." The poem has now been interpreted so often and variously that for academic critics its suggestions spread and diverge endlessly. But most readers have thought that the mariner commits a crime, undergoes punishment, and is partially redeemed. The crime is said to be the shooting of the albatross and, in this view, the punishment consists of the subsequent bodily and psychological sufferings of the Mariner, his thirst and fatigue and his feelings of isolation, abandonment, constriction, guilt, and self-disgust. The severity of the punishment gives status to the crime, and the poem becomes a didactic utterance when the Mariner draws his moral:

> He prayeth best, who loveth best
> All things both great and small;
> For the dear God who loveth us,
> He made and loveth all.
> (lines 614–17)[41]

Many moments in the poem have caused difficulty, but the main puzzle has been that the punishment seems in excess of the crime to the point of paradox. Interpreters feel challenged to explain how it is appropriate to visit so much on a human being merely for shooting a bird. Inability to answer this question lent some plausibility to the Aesthetic reading of the poem at the end of the nineteenth century, when it was said to be amoral like all great art. The same bafflement compelled John Livingston Lowes, the chief authority of the 1920s and 1930s, to argue that the poem was irrational like a dream.[42] The quandary could also be a factor in more recent commentary that finds the poem uninterpretable, though much else also makes this reading acceptable at the present time.

I also find the poem enigmatic but hope that this book throws a bit of light on some points. By 1797–98, when Coleridge wrote his poem, sophisticated readers might be imbued with a strong feeling of God's immanence in nature, including animals. Poets described the beauty of animals in order to evoke love for them. The habitual religious argument was exactly the Mariner's moral: the Father loves *all* his children. Cruelty to animals was portrayed as serious, socially dangerous, and literally damnable. In poems, novels, and literature for children it was regularly represented as evidence of an evil character. As Dorothy Kilner put it, "Every action that is cruel . . . and gives pain to *any* living creature, is wicked, and is a sure sign of a *bad* heart."[43] In books for children, boys who snared birds or stole eggs from their nests (crimes Wordsworth confessed in *The Prelude*), or any children who pulled wings from flies, were dreadfully punished. The punishment might come naturally in the course of things. Or cruelty to an animal might be revenged by Heaven, as is menaced at the start of Blake's *Auguries of Innocence* and in Christopher Smart's "A Story of a Cock and a Bull."

If we still consider the Mariner's punishment excessive, we may recall, as Robert Penn Warren did long ago, Coleridge's own ethical and religious philosophy: an action does not become evil by its consequences but by the malign will to which it gives expression.[44] From this point of view, fiendlike malice may be as much present in the shooting of a bird as of any other creature, including a human one.

However, it is not necessary to take the Mariner's sufferings as punishment for a crime. If we apply the thought of Coleridge in his later years, what befalls the Mariner may not be a consequence of what he has done, but a "sign," to use Kilner's word, of what he is. Coleridge was uneasy about attempts to express spiritual truths in temporal narrative form. In Wordsworth's famous ode on "Intimations of Immortality," the myth of pre-existence was, for Coleridge, such a case. Coleridge certainly believed what the myth conveyed, that on earth a human being is partly alien, an immortal, spiritual creature involved in a temporal, material existence. But when Wordsworth told how the soul comes to earth from heaven and, for a while, still recollects its former home, Coleridge added a warning gloss: "the ode was intended for such readers only as had been accustomed to watch the flux and reflux of their inmost nature, to venture at times into the twilight realms of consciousness, and to feel a deep interest in the modes of inmost being, to which they know that *the attributes of time and space are inapplicable and alien, but which yet can not be conveyed, save in symbols of time and space.*"[45]

Coleridge was troubled in the same way by the biblical story of the Fall of Man in the garden of Eden, for the Fall, in his theology, "stood in no relation whatever to time, can neither be called in time nor out of time."[46] Original sin was a spiritual state that was not explainable or even expressible in a narrative structure. "The first acts and movements of our own will . . . can neither be counted, coloured, nor delineated. Before and after, when applied to such subjects, are but allegories."[47] These comments date from long after Coleridge composed "The Rime of the Ancient Mariner," but the problem they address was much on his mind in 1797–98, for at that time he was contemplating a poem on the origin of evil. The comments suggest how Coleridge might have read his poem in later years and possibly when he first wrote it. If the shooting of the albatross manifests a "motiveless malignity," to quote Coleridge's phrase about Iago, a "*bad* heart," in the language of children's literature, the mystery of the poem would be less the excessive punishment than the Mariner's evil will. Coleridge could not account for it in narrative or any other terms, but he could depict it. Though in the narrative they follow after the shooting, lines 232–62 of the "Rime of the

Ancient Mariner" describe a person who would shoot the albatross. They are the picture or, better, the analysis of a heart without love – its isolation, constriction, and self-loathing. The act and the state of mind are presented at different moments of the poem, but (to use Coleridgean terms) they manifest the same "personeity" or self. The punishment cannot be called excessive unless it is a punishment to be what you are.

IV

Like all poems, the lyrics of high Romanticism about birds – Wordsworth's "To the Cuckoo," Coleridge's "The Nightingale," Shelley's "To a Skylark," Keats's "Ode to a Nightingale" – were shaped by previous ones. Either they continued or they deliberately corrected images of birds that were traditional in poetry. From simple facts – birds fly, they sing in the dark or from high near heaven, they reflect light – the poetic imagination had spun metaphors marvelously. There were poetic traditions with respect to particular species. Owls were mournful graveyard mopers. Nightingales were "most musical, most melancholy," as Milton expressed it in "Il Penseroso."

Whatever else they also represented or were associated with, between roughly 1750 and 1850 birds in poetry always represented "nature" by metonymy or synecdoche. Birds, obviously, could seldom be made to embody exactly the same qualities as daffodils, clouds, mountains, or lakes, though all may be equally "nature." The object – bird, cloud, or whatever – offers itself to the poet as a nexus of expressive possibilities and limitations, and a poet chooses his image for the sake of what can be said with it. Of all animals a wild bird especially could represent nature as poets dearly wished nature to be – inviolable – and this is one reason why birds were the central image in so many poems. Romantic poems about birds may also involve feelings about the widespread trapping, netting, nesting, and caging of these animals.

Living their lives in close proximity to mankind, in sheds, gardens, hedgerows, and fields, songbirds were maybe the most familiar, studied, and loved of all the wild creatures. Yet their lives were the most habitually intruded upon. The persecution of such harmless, innocent creatures belied the hope that humans could live in harmony with the natural world, a cherished ideal of Enlightened and Romantic intellectuals. We have long recognized that the Romantic idealization of nature was itself partly compensatory, a response at the ideological level to increasingly crass and visible exploitation. Nowhere was this idealization more extreme than in poems on birds.

In the famous lyrics I mentioned, the birds are wild and at a safe distance from the poet. They are not pets, not caged, and not catchable, though there is a sense, to which I return, in which the poem itself might be considered an exploitation. If we ask how, in general, birds are seen in this poetry, they are unseen. The owls in Wordsworth's "There Was a Boy" shout to him across the lake. They are just voices. In Wordsworth's "To the Cuckoo" the bird is sought but "never seen," a stock thought in poetry about this bird. In Wordsworth's "The Green Linnet" the bird is elusive to the eye as it flits in the leaves. Keats's nightingale is perceived only by the ear and the imagination. Shelley's skylark is lost in distance and light. Seeing is grasping at a distance, according to Eric Ericson, and the unseeable is inviolable. To the poets, invisibility also suggested that the birds were disembodied. They merged wholly into the natural world or into the heavens, becoming spirit.

As the birds call or sing in these poems, their sounds convey to the poet their gladness but otherwise are not interpretable. Psychologically, even ontologically, the birds are alien to human beings. (But this is not always the case in Wordsworth, in poems that imagine the separation from nature being overcome – for example, in memories of childhood in which the child is a natural creature among others.) The meaning of their songs transcends human knowing. It is very noticeable, to repeat, that in most high Romantic poems the feelings of wild birds are not humanized (except for the attribution of gladness) as they were in countless earlier poems and writings for children.

As the invisibility, unknowability, and otherness of the birds is emphasized, imaginative space is opened for the subjective outpouring of human emotion in the lyric. It cannot really focus on the bird, for the bird is hardly there. The poet perceives only himself, and taking the bird as other, he bestows on it whatever he himself lacks and deeply desires. Hence the birds may be endowed with spontaneity, unity of being, unconsciousness of death, immortality, and immediacy to the divine. This is the poets' way of exploiting animals.

For example, Keats's "Ode to a Nightingale," assumes that the wild creature is happy (line 6), a state that the poem later intensifies to "ecstasy" (line 58).[48] Among the many reasons why the nightingale must be happy is that the animal is designed throughout the poem as a contrast to the poet. The bird sings with "full-throated ease" (line 10), pouring forth its soul in its song (line 57) with spontaneity and unity of being, while the consciousness of the poet is numbed (line 1) and divided, partly listening to the nightingale and partly conscious of human sorrows (lines 23–30). As a figure of nature ("among the leaves," line 22), the nightingale has never known "weariness," "fever" (both sickness and desire), "fret," change, age, time, and satiety. Already in the first stanza, amid the shadows of the trees, the nightingale is unseen. In the course of the poem, the nightingale recedes deeper into the forest and the scene darkens. At the end, the bird flies still further from the listening poet (lines 76–78). The growing physical distance corresponds to an ontological one. The nightingale is "pouring forth its soul" without dying (lines 57–59) – "immortal" (line 61). The moment when the poet attributes immortality to the bird is a climax, the most intense outpouring in the poem of the poet's subjectivity. It is also the most extreme assertion in the poem of the bird's alien being. The song of the bird consoles, but not because it is "beautiful," whatever that might mean, but because it belongs to this alien existence. Hearing the song, the poet can dwell with it, or try to, for the moment that the song is present.

We are very far, with this ode, from the view of animals, of nature, that we find in Cowper's fine poem on his pet hare, for example, and in John Clare on the nightingale. "His diet was of wheaten bread," writes Cowper, "with sand to scour his maw";[49] if you approach its nest, Clare observes, the nightingale "keeps tweeting churring round."[50] These poets knew too much about animals to write what Keats did. But Keats's construction of the nightingale was not idiosyncratic. It drew on common assumptions of Romantic intellectuals about animal subjectivity, that, to repeat, animals experience no self-division, are wholly present in each moment, do not live in time, have no awareness of their own mortality, and are happy. Without these assumptions, poets would not have written some of their famous and moving poems.

We can consider, for example, the belief that animals are happy. In an earlier chapter I stressed that this derived logically from the cutting-edge, natural theology of the age. Since a benevolent God made the creatures or, in a stronger version, was immanent in them, they must of course be full of joy in every moment unless humans make this impossible. High Romantic poems express this belief as perception. In Wordsworth's "The Green Linnet," the poet's orchard is one of those wishful places where animals and humans live together in loving harmony, as if in a restored Eden.[51] As the poet speaks, a festival is going on, "the revels of the May" (line 15), in which the flowers and birds celebrate the return of spring. The poet is a host who greets his returning "friends" (line 8) and guests (line 11). All the creatures are happy, even "blest," a locution with religious overtones. Their joy is rendered, as it commonly is in Wordsworth's poetry, in imagery of light and motion, light glancing off things in motion: "brightest sunshine" (line 3), the "twinkle" of "dancing" leaves in the breeze (lines 26, 34), "sunny glimmerings" (line 31) of birds' wings. This happiness is unifying and erotic: "birds, and butterflies, and flowers, / Make all one band of paramours" (lines 17–18). But the linnet, the "happiest" of the creatures (line 9), is "Too blest with any one to pair; / Thyself thy own enjoyment" (lines 23–24) – lines only Wordsworth could have written. Whatever other interpretations also suggest themselves, it is clear that by a bold metonymy the linnet becomes a figure of the divine being immanent everywhere: it is "A Life, a Presence, like the Air, / Scattering thy gladness" (lines 21–22). There is a propriety in what might seem stale convention when the poet addresses the humble bird as though it were a superior being: "Hail to Thee, far above the rest / In joy of voice and pinion" (lines 11–12). The poem dwells, with marvelous delicacy, on the elusiveness of the bird, how it is almost seen, or unseen, and then seen, as it moves among the leaves and finally sings from the cottage roof. The poet feels wonder and gratitude that all this is present in his orchard, a place so near and familiar. The linnet has undergone a Romantic idealization that makes it altogether different from, say, "Little Trotty Wagtail," the bird John Clare so affectionately describes, that lives in the "warm pigsty." "Hail to Thee!" even suggests a reversal of the human/animal hierarchy.

In poetry the hoots of owls had regularly been mournful and associated with death. The first readers of Wordsworth's "There Was a Boy" must have been surprised, therefore, at the description of owls shouting across a lake:

> With quivering peals,
> And long halloos, and screams, and echoes loud
> Redoubled and redoubled; concourse wild
> Of jocund din! [52]

The lines are magnificently cacophonous, with diverse long vowels and many plosives and dentals, and the mere sounds convey the immense vitality of these birds. Connotatively the hoots are passionate, like loud bells, or hunting calls, or cries of pain or terror. The uproar might even seem somewhat intimidating, except that in the end, the sounds run together ("concourse") and express a reassuring glee – "jocund." In this poem the natural gladness of the birds (and the boy) is counterpointed by a more solemn imagery of natural forms surrounding the boy, of lake, hills, and sky in twilight. This imagery of quiet, calm, majestic, impending things associates itself in the poem with death, even forecasts the death of the boy. Thus though the owls embody joyful, passionate vitality, they are still linked to death as traditionally they were in eighteenth-century poetry.

The "peals" they make might even recall, subliminally, the bell towers of the church, the locus whence owls are heard in many an eighteenth-century poem.

In his "conversation poem" on "The Nightingale" Samuel Taylor Coleridge redescribed this bird. In naturalist fact, so to speak, the nightingale is a seldom-seen, brown-buff bird that nests close to the ground in dense thickets. In England it sings from mid-April, when it returns from North Africa and southern Europe, and it can be heard by day as well as night, though its name, derived from Anglo-Saxon, means "night singer." Its Latin name, *luscinia*, conveys that it sings lamentations, and so does its poetic name, "Philomel," whose myth tells how she was raped by king Tereus. A long poetic tradition affirmed the melancholy of the nightingale, and it was continued in Coleridge's time in lyrics by Charlotte Smith, Ann Radcliffe, and Mary Robinson. "Child of the melancholy song," Ann Radcliffe addresses the bird,

> O yet that tender strain prolong!
> . . .
> To mourn, unseen, the boughs among;
> When Twilight spreads her pensive shade.[53]

"Poor melancholy bird," writes Smith, "that all night long / Tell'st to the Moon thy tale of tender woe."[54] Like the bird they address, both poets confide their sorrows in their song. So also does Mary Robinson in her two odes "To the Nightingale."[55] But according to Coleridge, in nature "there is nothing melancholy."[56] Milton, Smith, Radcliffe, and so forth, wrote falsely of the bird. At the origin of the traditional fallacy, some unhappy person "filled all things with himself," and "made all gentle sounds tell back the tale / Of his own sorrow" (lines 19–21). (Coleridge was later to call this psychological process "imagination" and consider it the essentially poetic act, but in 1798, when he wrote "The Nightingale," he had a different theory of poetry.) Thus "these notes" were named "a melancholy strain" (line 22) and "many a poet echoes the conceit" (line 23). In other words, the "melancholy" nightingale is what Wordsworth, in his Preface written about the same time as Coleridge's poem, called "a family language which Writers in metre seem to lay claim to by prescription."[57] Continuing in Wordsworthian vein, Coleridge writes that a poet should leave "ball-rooms and hot theatres" (line 37), forget about "building up the rhyme" (line 24), and go outdoors, "surrendering his whole spirit" to the "influxes" of nature (line 29). Coleridge offers "Philomela's pity-pleading strains" (line 39) as an example of the false phrasing of the indoors poet, and, as a contrast,

composes several descriptions of the nightingale's song that are supposed
to be more accurate:

> 'Tis the merry Nightingale
> That crowds, and hurries, and precipitates
> With fast thick warble his delicious notes,
> As he were fearful that an April night
> Would be too short for him to utter forth
> His love-chant, and disburthen his full soul
> Of all its music!   (lines 43–49)

Like Wordsworth's lines on the vocal owls, this is a relatively extended
description of a transient sensation, and such writing was still unusual in
poetry. The terms of it – "crowds," "hurries," "precipitates," "fast thick
warble" – must have seemed exact and fresh, as though the poet were
listening attentively and trying carefully to express what he heard. In a later
moment of the poem Coleridge describes several nightingales singing in a
grove:

> With skirmish and capricious passagings,
> And murmurs musical and swift jug jug,
> And one low piping sound more sweet than all.
>   (lines 59–61)

And in a still later moment, a nightingale perches on a breezy twig,

> And to that motion tune[s] his wanton song
> Like tipsy Joy that reels with tossing head.
>   (lines 85–86)

Obviously these lines include just the sort of subjective projection that
the poem condemns in other poets. The song is a "love-chant." The bird
is anxious lest the night be too short. (Despite the Romantic lore that
wild creatures do not live in time!) The "melancholy" nightingale is, for
Coleridge, a subjective and conventional fallacy, but the "merry" one is
truth. Other passages also humanize the bird. As the poet departs, the
bird sings as though "it would delay me" (line 91). At the end, the poet
addresses it, "Sweet Nightingale!" (line 110). Is it only by sentimentally
humanizing, by filling the creatures with ourselves, that we can feel affection
and compassion for them?

These high Romantic poems transform natural behavior of the birds
into metaphors of human desires. Nowhere is this more explicit than in
Shelley's "To a Skylark."[58] This bird soars, often too high to be seen, and
sings as it flies, so that its song may fall as though disembodied. It may

become invisible in light. At dawn or sunset, the rays of sun may reflect like fire from its wings. From this observable basis Shelley exalts the bird into a spirit singing from heaven, an "unbodied joy" whose voice fills "all the earth and air," a poet whose utterance transcends human knowledge. The gladness, delight, or joy of the bird is the most emphatic theme of the poem, repeatedly asserted (lines 15, 20, 60, 65, 72, 76, 95, 97, 101). As in Wordsworth's poem on the linnet, the happiness of this "spirit" is also conveyed in images of swift motion and bright glitter. Like Keats's nightingale, the lark is a being without the woes inherent in human being – desire, regret, languor, satiety, self-division, the feeling of *lacrimae rerum* that comes with thought (76–80, 86–90). The animal is not said to be immortal, as happens in the emotional climax of Keats's ode, and it is not said to lack consciousness of mortality, as most intellectuals would have assumed, but it knows something about death that humans do not – some truth that makes death not final or, at any rate, not fearful. How without such knowledge could it sing so joyously?

> Thou of death must deem
> Things more true and deep
> Than we mortals dream,
>
> Or how could thy notes flow in such a crystal stream?
> (lines 81–85)

As the poem laments the human condition, the sense of animal difference is wistful. Like Keats's ode, the poem finally reverses hierarchy, locating the animal above the human:

> Teach me half the gladness
> That thy brain must know.

Shelley elevates the animal in order to bewail the human condition. I find the device dubious.[59] Thus exalted, an animal cannot be viewed with fellow feeling, much less with compassion. The real object of pity in such poems is the poet, the human being. The animal is just a metaphor, with little character or life of its own that the poet values.

Notes

PREFACE

1 For surveys of writings about animals see Keith Thomas, *Man and the Natural World: Changing Attitudes in England 1500–1800* (London: Allen Lane, 1983), pp. 92–191, and for a work more oriented to *belles lettres*, Christine Kenyon-Jones, *Kindred Brutes: Animals in Romantic-Period Writing* (Aldershot: Ashgate Publishing Limited, 2001).

2 G. J. Barker-Benfield, *The Culture of Sensibility: Sex and Society in Eighteenth-Century Britain* (Chicago: Chicago University Press, 1992), p. 236.

3 Carol J. Adams, *The Sexual Politics of Meat* (New York: Continuum Publishing Co., 1990), p. 13.

4 Moira Ferguson, *Animal Advocacy and Englishwomen, 1780–1900: Patriots, Nation, and Empire* (Ann Arbor: Michigan University Press, 1998). For example, when Sarah Trimmer's story for children about a family of robins is "transposed to a human context, the cultural position of the robins is that of the beautiful and the weak in need of protection." The robins also represent soldiers (redcoats), tradition (for they live amid ivy), and the poor, patronized by the genteel children who are their benefactors (p. 24).

5 George Gordon, Lord Byron, *Don Juan*, Canto x, Stanza 50, in *Works: Poetry*, ed. Ernest Hartley Coleridge, 7 vols. (London: John Murray, 1903), VI, 415.

6 General histories, such as that of Keith Thomas, *Man and the Natural World*, do not emphasize regional differences. Robert W. Malcolmson, *Popular Recreations in English Society 1700–1850*, explains that "Because the sources are so scattered and fragmentary, and so thinly available in local materials, it is necessary to draw one's evidence from all parts of the country in order to offer a reasonably thorough account" (p. 3).

7 Roy Porter, *English Society in the Eighteenth Century* (London: Allen Lane, 1982), p. 68.

8 Leonore Davidoff and Catherine Hall, *Family Fortunes: Men and Women of the English Middle Class, 1780–1850* (London: Hutchinson, 1987), p. 24.

9 William Wordsworth, "Home at Grasmere," lines 264–89, in *Poetical Works*, ed. Ernest de Selincourt and Helen Darbishire (Oxford: Clarendon Press, 1949), V, 323; Percy Bysshe Shelley, "Peter Bell the Third," fn. to line 131, in *Complete*

Works, ed. Roger Ingpen and Walter E. Peck (New York: Gordian Press, 1965), III, 280.

10 The *Norwich Mercury*, quoted in *Norfolk and Norwich Notes and Queries*, series 2 (1896–99), 396 and quoted from this source by Robert W. Malcolmson, *Popular Recreations in English Society 1700–1850*, p. 120.

11 George Barton, *Chronology of Stamford* (Stamford: Robert Bagley, 1846), pp. 51–52, quoted in Martin Walsh, "November Bull-Running in Stamford, Lincolnshire," *Journal of Popular Culture*, 30:1 (1996), 234. The effort, lasting almost a century, to terminate the ancient custom of bull-running in Stamford is described by Malcolmson, *Popular Recreations*, pp. 66–68, 126–36.

12 For example, Keith Thomas, *Man and the Natural World*; Robert W. Malcolmson, *Popular Recreations in English Society 1700–1850*; Richard H. Thomas, *The Politics of Hunting* (Aldershot: Gower Publishing Co., 1983); James Turner, *Reckoning with the Beast: Animals, Pain, and Humanity in the Victorian Mind* (Baltimore: The Johns Hopkins University Press, 1980).

13 J. M. Golby and A. W. Purdue, *The Civilisation of the Crowd: Popular Culture in England 1750–1900* (London: Batsford Academic and Educational, 1984), p. 74.

14 The tract by Lewis Gompertz is quoted in Charles D. Niven, *History of the Humane Movement* (London: Johnson Publications, 1967), pp. 69–70.

15 Roy Porter, *English Society in the Eighteenth Century*, p. 287.

16 Richard H. Thomas, *The Politics of Hunting* (Aldershot: Gower Publishing, 1983), pp. 188–89.

I IN THE BEGINNING OF ANIMAL RIGHTS

1 Postscript to James Granger, *An Apology for the Brute Creation; or Abuse of Animals Censured*, 2nd edn. (London: T. Davies, 1773).

2 *Monthly Review*, 44 (1772), 491; *Critical Review*, 34 (1772), 468; *Letters Between Rev. James Granger and Many of the Most Eminent Literary Men of His Time*, ed. J. P. Malcolm (London: Longman, 1805), p. 55.

3 James Granger, *An Apology for the Brute Creation*, pp. 9–10, 12–13, 21, 15.

4 *Clemency to Brutes: The Substance of Two Sermons Preached on a Shrove-Sunday . . . to Dissuade from that Species of Cruelty, annually practiced in England, the Throwing at Cocks* (London: Dodsley, 1761).

5 *Monthly Review*, 24 (1761), 307–15; *Critical Review*, 12 (1761), 49–53.

6 Quoted in Richard D. Ryder, *Animal Revolution* (Oxford: Basil Blackwell, 1989), p. 67.

7 *Critical Review*, 41 (1776), 143.

8 Primatt was excerpted in John Toogood, *The Book of Nature: A Discourse on some of those Instances of the Power, Wisdom, and Goodness of God . . . To which is added, The Duty of Mercy and Sin of Cruelty to Brutes, taken chiefly from Dr. Primatt's Dissertation*, 4th edn. (Boston: Samuel Hall, 1802).

9 James Plumptre, *Three Discourses on the Case of the Animal Creation and the Duties of Man to Them* (London: Darton, Harvey, and Darton, 1816), p. 55.

Humphry Primatt had also emphasized God's command that cattle should not work on the sabbath. (John Toogood, *The Book of Nature*, pp. 40–41.)

10 James Plumptre, *Three Discourses*, pp. v–vi.

11 Samuel Taylor Coleridge, *Notebooks*, ed. Kathleen Coburn, 3 vols. (Princeton: Princeton University Press, 1957–73), II, entry no. 2666.

12 Iris Origo, *The Last Attachment* (London: Cape and Murray, 1949), II, 87.

13 John Keats, *Letters*, ed. Hyder E. Rollins, 2 vols. (Cambridge, MA: Harvard University Press, 1958), I, 86.

14 William E. A. Axon, *Shelley's Vegetarianism* (New York: Haskell House, 1971), pp. 5–6.

15 Percy Bysshe Shelley, *Complete Works*, ed. Roger Ingpen and Walter E. Peck, 10 vols. (New York: Gordian Press, 1965), II, 280.

16 Charles and Mary Lamb, *Works*, ed. E. V. Lucas, 7 vols. (London: Methuen & Co., 1905), VII, 637–38.

17 Charles Lamb, *Works*, I, 304.

18 William Blake, "Auguries of Innocence," lines 19–20, in *Complete Writings*, ed. Geoffrey Keynes (London: Oxford University Press, 1966), p. 431.

19 George Gordon, Lord Byron, *Works*, ed. Ernest Hartley Coleridge, 10 vols. (London: John Murray, 1903), I, 280–81. For extended commentary on Byron's "Inscription," see Christine Kenyon-Jones, *Kindred Brutes: Animals in Romantic-Period Writing* (Aldershot: Ashgate Publishing, 2001), pp. 13–38.

20 Catherine Ann Dorset, "To the Lady-Bird," in *British Women Poets of the Romantic Era*, ed. Paula R. Feldman (Baltimore: The Johns Hopkins University Press, 1997), p. 230.

21 William Blake, *Milton*, 26, lines 2–5, in *Complete Writings*, p. 512.

22 Thomas Percival, *A Father's Instructions* (London: R. Dodsley, 1784), pp. 4–5. Percival also had qualms about dining on vegetables, which he surmised were capable of feeling.

23 Thomas Day, *The History of Sandford and Merton* (1783–89; New York: Hurd and Houghton, 1865), pp. 13–14.

24 William H. Drummond, *The Rights of Animals and Man's Obligation to Treat Them with Humanity* (London: John Mardon, 1838), p. 189.

25 Alexander Pope, "Essay on Man," I, 217–18, *An Essay on Man*, ed. Maynard Mack (London: Methuen and Co., 1950), p. 41.

26 William Blake, "The Fly," lines 5–8, in *Complete Writings*, p. 213.

27 John Aikin and Letitia Barbauld, *Evenings at Home* (1792–96: Boston: D. Lothrop, 1872), p. 233.

28 William Wordsworth, "Written in Germany on One of the Coldest Days of the Century"; James Thomson, *The Seasons*, "Summer," line 280, *The Seasons*, ed. James Sambrook (Oxford: Clarendon Press, 1981), p. 72.

29 Laurence Sterne, *Tristram Shandy* (New York: Penguin, 1997), p. 131.

30 William Blake, "Vala," lines 459–60, in *Complete Writings*, p. 277.

31 Sarah Trimmer, *Fabulous Histories, or, The History of the Robins Designed for the Instruction of Children Respecting Their Treatment of Animals* (1786; London: J. F. Dove, 1833), pp. 150–51.

32 Robert Southey, "To a Spider," *Poetical Works*, 10 vols. (Boston: Little, Brown and Co., 1864), II, 180–81.

33 Charles Lamb, *Works*, VI, 146.

34 Quotations from "To a Mouse" are from *The Poems and Songs of Robert Burns*, ed. James Kinsley, 3 vols. (Oxford: Clarendon Press, 1968), I, 127.

35 Dix Harwood, *Love for Animals and How It Developed in Great Britain* (New York: np, 1928), p. 344.

36 Anna Letitia Barbauld, "The Mouse's Petition Found in the Trap where he had been confin'd all Night," in *British Women Poets of the Romantic Era: An Anthology*, pp. 56–58.

37 Cf. John Young, *Robert Burns: A Man for All Seasons* (Aberdeen: Scottish Cultural Press, 1996), p. 75: "There seems little doubt that Burns . . . used the poignant moment to reflect on the human situation of 'home' eviction with all the tragedy and trauma that that evokes." Marilyn Butler remarks that the poem "lightly addresses the human experience of homelessness" ("Burns and Politics," in *Robert Burns and Cultural Authority*, ed. Robert Crawford [Edinburgh: Edinburgh University Press, 1997], p. 89).

38 Carol McGuirk, *Robert Burns and the Sentimental Era* (Athens: Georgia University Press, 1985), p. 9.

39 Seamus Heaney, "Burns's Art Speech," in *Robert Burns and Cultural Authority*, p. 220.

40 See e. g. Erasmus Darwin, *Zoonomia: or, the Laws of Organic Life*, 2 vols. (New York: AMS Press, 1974, reprinting the edition of 1794–96), I, 184.

41 Carol McGuirk, *Robert Burns and the Sentimental Era*, p. 9.

42 Norbert Elias, "An Essay on Sport and Violence," in Norbert Elias and Eric Dunning, *Quest for Excitement: Sport and Leisure in the Civilizing Process* (Oxford: Basil Blackwell, 1986), pp. 166, 162–63. Unfortunately, Elias weakens his thesis by his example, for he thinks that practices in fox hunting showed "an advance in people's revulsion against doing violence" because the actual killing was done by the hounds rather than the hunters. One might make the same argument with respect to the Roman arena, where Christians were slaughtered by lions rather than people.

43 James Turner, *Reckoning with the Beast: Animals, Pain, and Humanity in the Victorian Mind* (Baltimore: The Johns Hopkins University Press, 1980), pp. 30–34.

44 John Lawrence, *A Philosophical and Practical Treatise on Horses, and on the Moral Duties of Man towards the Brute Creation*, 2 vols. (London: T. N. Longman, 1796–98), I, 141.

45 John Gay, *Trivia*, II, 229–32, *Poetry and Prose*, ed. Vinton A. Dearing, with the assistance of Charles E. Beckwith, 2 vols. (Oxford: Clarendon Press, 1974), I, 150.

46 Donald B. Kelley, "Friends and Nature in America," *Pennsylvania History*, 53 (1986), 266.

47 Thomas Erskine, speech in Parliament, May 15, 1809, *Parliamentary Debates; From 1803 to 1809* (London: Hansard, 1812), XIV, column 562.

48 *The Every-Day Book*, ed. William Hone (London: W. Tegg, 1835), September 19, 1835, p. 1304.

49 John Lawrence, *A Philosophical and Practical Treatise on Horses*, I, 132–33.

50 Samuel Johnson, *The Idler and The Adventurer*, ed. W. J. Bate, J. M. Bullitt, and L. F. Powell (New Haven: Yale University Press, 1963), pp. 55–56. Cf. the strong condemnation of vivisectors in Johnson's comment on Shakespeare's *Cymbeline*, I, 5. 23, in *Johnson on Shakespeare*, ed. Arthur Sherbo (New Haven: Yale University Press, 1968), p. 881.

51 *Monthly Review*, 39 (1768), 573.

52 For example, the *Monthly Review*, 43 (1771), 212–14, reports a series of experiments by Dr. John Caverhill. He thought that chalky swellings of gout were composed of an "earth" which was first secreted in the brain and then transmitted to the limbs through the "nervous tubes." As this "earth" rubbed against the sides of the tubes, it produced "animal heat." Caverhill reasoned that if one destroyed nerves, the temperature of an animal would be reduced. He confirmed this hypothesis by sticking awls into the spinal columns of rabbits, scores of them, and they indeed got colder, but still lived for ten to nineteen days in much pain, sometimes until their bladders burst because they could no longer urinate.

53 Thomas Bewick, *A Memoir of Thomas Bewick Written by Himself*, ed. Iain Bain (Oxford: Oxford University Press, 1979), p. 6.

54 Peter Beckford, *Thoughts Upon Hunting: In a Series of Familiar Letters to a Friend* (Sarum: P. Elmsly, 1781), pp. 221–27.

55 William Somerville, *The Chase* (1735), IV, 145–56, in *English Poets*, ed. A. Chalmers (London: Booksellers of London, 1810), II, 167.

56 E. V. Lucas, *The Life of Charles Lamb*, 2 vols. (London: Methuen, 1905), II, 79–80.

57 For an extended survey, see George Nicholson, *On the Conduct of Man to Inferior Animals* (Stourport: G. Nicholson, 1819).

58 Arthur W. Moss, *Valiant Crusade: The History of the RSPCA* (London: Cassell, 1961), p. 13.

59 John Trusler, *The Works of William Hogarth in a Series of Engravings with Descriptions and a Comment on Their Moral Tendency*, 2 vols. (London: Jones and Co., 1800), II, 188.

60 Robert W. Malcolmson, *Popular Recreations in English Society 1700–1850* (Cambridge: Cambridge University Press, 1973), p. 124.

61 Henri Misson, *M. Misson's Memoirs and Observations in His Travels over England, with some Account of Scotland and Ireland*, ed. John Ozell (London: 1719), p. 27, quoted in Robert W. Malcolmson, *Popular Recreations in English Society 1700–1850*, p. 46.

62 Arthur W. Moss, *Valiant Crusade*, p. 14.

63 William Howitt, *The Rural Life of England*, 2 vols. (London: Longman, Orme, Brown, Green, and Longmans, 1838), II, 271.

64 William Hazlitt, *Collected Works*, ed. P. P. Howe, 21 vols. (London: Dent, 1930–34), III, 158n.; XII, 273.

65 *Hansard's Parliamentary Debates* (London: Longman, 1819), XXXV (1800–01), column 206.

66 *Hansard's Parliamentary Debates*, XXXV (1800–01), column, 211.

67 George Nicholson, *On the Conduct of Man to Inferior Animals*, p. 256.

68 Quoted in Arthur W. Moss, *Valiant Crusade*, pp. 34–35. For a similar story, this one in a book for children, see Thomas Day, *The History of Sandford and Merton*, pp. 48–51.

69 Quoted in Arthur W. Moss, *Valiant Crusade*, p. 15.

70 *Hansard's Parliamentary Debates* (1812), XIV, June 13, 1809, cols. 1036, 1034, 1026, 1040.

71 *Hansard's Parliamentary Debates*, VII, May 24, 1822, cols. 758–59.

72 Arthur W. Moss, *Valiant Crusade*, p. 16.

2 GROUNDS OF ARGUMENT

1 Francis Hutcheson, *System of Moral Philosophy* (London: A. Miller, 1755), p. 314. Immanuel Kant put it this way: "we can judge the heart of a man by his treatment of animals, for he who is cruel to animals becomes hard also in his dealings with men." (Quoted by Keith Tester, *Animals and Society: The Humanity of Animal Rights* [London and New York: Routledge, 1991], p. 99.)

2 John Locke, *Thoughts on Education* (1693), in *Works* (London: T. Tegg, 1823), IX, 112–13.

3 *Monthly Review*, 36 (1767), 79–80. Cf. the review of William Jay, *Short Discourses to be read in Families*, *Monthly Review*, 51 (1806), 379.

4 James Granger, *An Apology for the Brute Creation; or Abuse of Animals Censured*, 2nd edn. (London: T. Davies, 1773), p. 22.

5 Gotthilf Salzmann, *Moralisches Elementarbuch* (1782), trans. Mary Wollstonecraft, *Elements of Morality, for the Use of Children; with an Introductory Address to Parents* (1791; Baltimore: Joseph Robinson, 1811), p. 195.

6 Joanna Baillie, *A Lesson Intended for the Use of the Hampstead School* (Camden Town: L. Miller, 1826), p. 10.

7 John Trusler, *The Works of William Hogarth in a Series of Engravings with Descriptions and a Comment on their Moral Tendency*, 2 vols. (London: Jones and Co., 1800), II, 185.

8 Dorothy Kilner, *The Life and Perambulation of a Mouse* (London: John Marshall, 1780), p. 24.

9 George Nicholson, *On the Conduct of Man to Inferior Animals* (Stourport: G. Nicholson, 1819), p. 249. In *A Philosophical and Practical Treatise on Horses, and on the Moral Duties of Man towards the Brute Creation*, 2 vols. (London: T. N. Longman, 1796–98), I, 136–37, John Lawrence tells a story about a boy who was pulling legs from flies. His father, to teach a lesson, pulled hairs from his child's head.

10 Thomas Day, *The History of Sandford and Merton* (1783–89; New York: Hurd and Houghton, 1865), pp. 111–12.

11 Sarah Trimmer, *The Robins: or, Fabulous Histories, Designed for the Instruction of Children, respecting Their Treatment of Animals* (1786; Boston: Munroe and Francis, 1822), p. 229. This work went through a great many editions, and in some it was entitled *Fabulous Histories* and in others *The Robins*. For the sake of consistency, I have referred to it in the text as *Fabulous Histories* thoughout, whichever edition I was using.

12 Mary Wollstonecraft, *Original Stories from Real Life* (1791; facsimile Oxford and New York: Woodstock Books, 1990), p. 19.

13 John Locke, *Essay Concerning Human Understanding*, ed. P. H. Nidditch (Oxford: Clarendon Press, 1975), pp. 159–60. Even insects were said to have a memory and to draw conclusions from experience. Samuel Taylor Coleridge learned this from Pierre Huber's *Natural History of Ants* (1820) and might have learned it from H. S. Reimar's *Physical and Moral Observations on the Instinct of Animals, on their Industry, and Manners*, which had been translated in 1771.

14 David Hartley, *Observations on Man, his Frame, his Duty, and his Expectations*, 2 vols. (London: S. Richardson, 1749, facsimile, New York: Garland, 1971), I, 406.

15 David Hume, *Treatise of Human Nature* (1739–40), ed. L. A. Selby-Bigge (Oxford: Clarendon Press, 1978), p. 397.

16 John Lawrence, *A Philosophical and Practical Treatise on Horses*, I, 80.

17 John Lawrence, *A Philosophical and Practical Treatise on Horses*, I, 83.

18 John Lawrence, *British Field Sports* (1818; 2nd edn.: London: Sherwood, Neely, and Jones, 1820), p. 113. To see the distinctions between man and animal explained to a child, one might turn to John Aikin and Letitia Barbauld, *Evenings at Home; or, The Juvenile Budget Opened* (1792–96; Boston: D. Lothrop, 1872), pp. 118–22. These authors dwell on the human power of speech and the degree to which this makes man "an *improvable* being" (p. 119), able to accumulate knowledge from one generation to the next.

19 John Locke, *Essay Concerning Human Understanding*, pp. 159–60.

20 David Hartley, *Observations on Man*, I, 409.

21 Dugald Stewart, *Elements of the Philosophy of the Human Mind* (1792), in *Works*, ed. W. Hamilton (Edinburgh: T. T. Clark, 1877), IV, 207n.

22 David Hume, *A Treatise of Human Nature*, p. 176.

23 Erasmus Darwin, *Zoonomia; or, the Laws of Organic Life* (1794–96; 2 vols., New York: AMS Press, 1974), I, 184.

24 *Monthly Review*, Second Series, 4 (1791), 534.

25 David Hartley, *Observations on Man*, I, 413–14.

26 David Hume, *A Treatise of Human Nature*, pp. 326–98, *passim*.

27 William Wordsworth, "Essay on Epitaphs," *The Prose Works of William Wordsworth*, ed. W. J. B. Owen and Jane Worthington Smyser, 3 vols. (Oxford: Clarendon Press, 1974), II, 50.

28 John Oswald, *The Cry of Nature; or, An Appeal to Mercy and to Justice, on Behalf of the Persecuted Animals* (London: J. Johnson, 1791), p. 11; John F. Newton, *The Return to Nature, or, A Defence of the Vegetable Regimen* (London: T. Cadell and W. Davies, 1811), pp. 17–18; Percy Bysshe Shelley, Notes to *Queen Mab*,

in *Complete Works*, ed. Roger Ingpen and Walter E. Peck, 10 vols. (New York: Gordian Press, 1965), I, 159. It was, in fact, long doubtful in the eighteenth century whether or not the orang-utan should be classified as a human species. For discussion see Richard D. Ryder, *Animal Revolution* (Oxford: Basil Blackwell, 1989), pp. 72–73.

29 Erasmus Darwin, *Zoonomia*, I, 184.

30 Jeremy Bentham, *An Introduction to the Principles of Morals and Legislation* (1789), in *Works*, ed. John Bowring, II vols. (New York: Russell and Russell, 1962), I, 143n.

31 Jeremy Bentham, *Principles of Penal Law*, *Works*, I, 562.

32 Thomas Young, *An Essay on Humanity to Animals* (1789, 2nd edn., London: 1809), quoted in Richard D. Ryder, *Animal Revolution*, p. 69.

33 Humphry Primatt, *The Duty of Mercy and Sin of Cruelty to Animals*, quoted in James Turner, *Reckoning with the Beast: Animals, Pain, and Humanity in the Victorian Mind* (Baltimore: The Johns Hopkins University Press, 1980), p. 11.

34 George Nicholson, *On the Conduct of Man to Inferior Animals*, p. 124.

35 Mary Wollstonecraft, *Original Stories*, p. 3.

36 Percy Bysshe Shelley, *Prometheus Unbound*, I, i, 305, in *Complete Works*, II, 188.

37 Henry Brooke, *The Fool of Quality*, 5 vols. (New York: Garland, 1979, reprinting the 4 vol. edn. of 1766), V, 78, 80–81.

38 Mary Wollstonecraft, *Original Stories*, p. 15.

39 David Hume, *A Treatise of Human Nature*, p. 398.

40 David Hume, *An Enquiry concerning the Principles of Morals*, ed. Tom L. Beauchamp (Oxford: Clarendon Press, 1998), p. 93.

41 Katherine M. Rogers, *The Cat and the Human Imagination: Feline Images from Bast to Garfield* (Ann Arbor: Michigan University Press, 1998), pp. 157–58.

42 John Lawrence, *A Philosophical and Practical Treatise on Horses*, p. 79.

43 Sarah Trimmer, *The Robins*, pp. 36–37.

44 Christine Kenyon-Jones, *Kindred Brutes: Animals in Romantic-period Writing* (Aldershot: Ashgate Publishing, 2001), p. 24, cites this from *Goody Two-Shoes: A Facsimile Reproduction of the Edition of 1766*, ed. Charles Welsh (London: Griffith and Farran, 1881).

45 William Wordsworth, *Poetical Works*, ed. Ernest de Selincourt and Helen Darbishire, 5 vols. (Oxford: Clarendon Press, 1947), IV, 81.

46 Debate on this subject from ancient Greece and Rome to the modern era is briefly summarized by Christine Kenyon-Jones, *Kindred Brutes*, pp. 15–27.

47 David-Renaud Boullier, *Essai Philosophique sur L'Âme des Bêtes*, 2nd edn. (Amsterdam: François Changuion, 1737; reprinted Paris: Fayard, 1985), p. 237. Voltaire similarly deployed the findings of vivisection to argue against Descartes that animals feel pain: nail a dog to a table, "dissect him alive, in order to show you his veins and nerves. And what you then discover in him are *all the same organs of sensation that you have in yourself.* Answer me, mechanist, has Nature arranged all the springs of feeling in this animal *to the end that he might not feel*? Has he nerves that he may be incapable of suffering?" Quoted in Richard D. Ryder, *Animal Revolution*, p. 60.

48 Alexander Pope, *An Essay on Man*, ed. Maynard Mack (London: Methuen, 1958), I, lines 99–112, pp. 27–28.

49 Joseph Spence, *Observations, Anecdotes, and Characters of Books and Men*, ed. J. M. Osborn, 2 vols. (Oxford: Clarendon Press, 1966), I, 118–19.

50 Samuel Taylor Coleridge, *Collected Letters*, ed. Earl Leslie Griggs, 6 vols. (Oxford: Clarendon Press, 1956–71), II, 703.

51 Robert Southey, *Poems* (Bristol: Joseph Cottle, 1797; reprinted Oxford: Woodstock Books, 1989), p. 133.

52 William Wollaston, *The Religion of Nature Delineated* (1724; New York: Garland, 1978), p. 203.

53 Richard Dean, *An Essay on the Future Life of Brute Creatures*, 2 vols. (London: G. Kearsley, 1768), I, 21. Pierre Bayle made the same point in possibly ironic support of Descartes. Bayle cites harms humans inflict on animals and asks, would it not be "cruelty and injustice to subject an innocent soul to so many miseries? The opinion of Des Cartes frees us from all these difficulties," for a creature without a soul cannot suffer. *Mr. Bayle's Historical and Critical Dictionary, the second edition, to which is prefixed the Life of the Author revised, corrected and enlarged by Mr Des Maizeaux*, 5 vols. (London: Knapton, etc., 1734), IV, 902, cited in Christine Kenyon-Jones, *Kindred Brutes*, p. 20.

54 John Wesley, *Sermons*, II, 60 (The General Deliverance), in *Works* (1958), VI, 251; cited in Matt Cartmill, *A View to a Death in the Morning: Hunting and Nature through History* (Cambridge, MA: Harvard University Press, 1993), p. 103.

55 Peter Buchan, *Scriptural & Philosophical Arguments . . . that Brutes Have Souls* (Peterhead: n.p., 1824), p. 17.

56 David Hume, "Of the Immortality of the Soul," *Essays: Moral, Political and Literary*, ed. Eugene F. Miller (Indianapolis: Liberty Classics, 1985), p. 597.

57 James Boswell, *Life of Johnson*, ed. George Birkbeck Hill, rev. L. F. Powell, 6 vols. (Oxford: Clarendon Press, 1934), II, 54.

58 Samuel Taylor Coleridge, *On the Constitution of the Church and State*, ed. John Colmer (Princeton, NJ: Princeton University Press, 1976), p. 47n.

59 Samuel Taylor Coleridge, *Shorter Works and Fragments*, ed. H. J. Jackson and J. R. de J. Jackson, 2 vols. (Princeton, NJ: Princeton University Press, 1995), II, 958n. Anya Taylor, *Coleridge's Defense of the Human* (Columbus: Ohio University Press, 1985), pp. 35–60, emphasizes how firmly Coleridge maintained that there is an essential distinction between humans and animals.

60 David-Renaud Boullier, *Essai Philosophique sur L'Âme des Bêtes*, p. 434.

61 Ibid., p. 441.

62 T. R. Malthus, *Essay on the Principle of Population* (1798), quoted in Matt Cartmill, *A View to a Death in the Morning*, p. 103.

63 E. P. Thompson, *Witness Against the Beast: William Blake and the Moral Law* (New York: The New Press, 1993), p. 79.

64 George Nicholson, *On the Conduct of Man to Inferior Animals*, p. 96.

65 Oliver Goldsmith, *The Citizen of the World, Works*, ed. Arthur Friedman, 5 vols. (Oxford: Clarendon Press, 1966), II, 66.

66 Quoted in Samuel F. Pickering, Jr., *John Locke and Children's Books in Eighteenth-Century England* (Knoxville: Tennessee University Press, 1981), p. 25.

67 Quoted in Samuel F. Pickering, *John Locke and Children's Books in Eighteenth-Century England,* p. 25.

68 Sarah Trimmer, *The Robins,* p. 75.

69 Robert Burns, *Letters,* ed. J. De Lancey Ferguson, 2nd edn. ed. G. Ross Roy (Oxford: Clarendon Press, 1985), pp. 417–18.

70 Henry Brooke, *The Fool of Quality,* 1, 56–57.

71 Anthony Ashley Cooper, 3rd Earl of Shaftesbury, *Shaftesbury's Characteristics,* ed. J. M. Robertson (London: G. Richards, 1900), bk. 2, part 2, section 3.

72 Richard E. Brantley, *Locke, Wesley, and the Method of English Romanticism* (Gainesville: Florida University Press, 1984), p. 90.

73 William Paley, *The Principles of Moral and Political Philosophy,* 2 vols. (London: R. Faulder, 1785; reprint New York: Garland, 1978), 1, 84.

74 Sarah Trimmer, *The Robins,* pp. 69–70.

75 Roy Porter, *English Society in the Eighteenth Century* (London: Allen Lane, 1982), p. 187.

76 Thomas Paine, *Age of Reason* (1794), ed. P. S. Foner (Secaucus, NJ: Citadel Press, 1974), p. 98.

77 James Granger, *Apology for the Brute Creation,* p. 10.

78 Thomas Young, *An Essay on Humanity to Animals* (1798), quoted in Samuel F. Pickering, Jr., *John Locke and Children's Books in Eighteenth-Century England,* p. 37.

79 Edward Augustus Kendall, *Keeper's Travels in Search of His Master* (1799; Philadelphia: B. and J. Johnson, 1801), p. v.

80 William Cowper, *The Task,* Book VI, "The Winter Walk at Noon," lines 442–43, 600, *Poetical Works,* ed. H. S. Milford, 4th edn. (London: Oxford University Press, 1934), pp. 229, 232.

81 William Blake, "The Book of Thel," Plate 5, lines 9–10; "Auguries of Innocence," lines 5–6, *Complete Writings,* ed. Geoffrey Keynes (London: Oxford University Press, 1966), pp. 130, 431.

82 *Clemency to Brutes,* pp. 11, 13.

83 William H. Drummond, *The Rights of Animals and Man's Obligation to Treat Them with Humanity* (London: John Mardon, 1836), p. 49.

84 Sarah Trimmer, *The Robins,* p. 224; Edward Augustus Kendall, *Keeper's Travels In Search of His Master* (1799; Leipzig: Breitkopf and Haertel, 1816), p. 22.

85 For example, Mary Wollstonecraft, *Original Stories,* p. 3; Edward Augustus Kendall, quoting another author in *The Canary Bird: A Moral Story, Interspersed with Poetry* (Philadelphia: B. Johnson and J. Johnson, 1801), p. 54; John Woolman, quoted in Richard D. Ryder, *Animal Revolution* (Oxford: Basil Blackwell, 1989), p. 66; Joseph Priestly, *Three Tracts,* p. 177, quoted in Thomas McFarland, *Coleridge and the Pantheist Tradition* (Oxford: Clarendon Press, 1969), p. 312.

86 Thomas Reid, *Lectures on Natural Theology* (1780), ed. Elmer H. Duncan (Washington, DC: University Press of America, 1981), p. 86.

87 David Hume, *Dialogues Concerning Natural Religion*, ed. Nelson Pike (New York: Bobbs-Merrill, 1970), p. 22.

88 William Paley, *Natural Theology* (New York: American Tract Society, nd), p. 163.

89 William Paley, *Natural Theology*, p. 295.

90 Thomas Erskine, Speech in Parliament, May 15, 1809, *Parliamentary Debates; From 1803 to 1809* (London: Hansard, 1812), xiv, column 555.

91 Edward Augustus Kendall, *The Canary Bird: A Moral Story*, p. 54.

92 William H. Drummond, *The Rights of Animals and Man's Obligation to Treat Them with Humanity*. The theme sounds throughout his book, but one might see especially pp. 188–89.

93 David Hume, *Dialogues Concerning Natural Religion*, pp. 72–73.

94 William Paley, *Natural Theology*, pp. 311–12.

95 For quotations and discussion see A. O. Lovejoy, *The Great Chain of Being* (1936; New York: Harper, 1960), pp. 187–88.

96 John Aikin and Letitia Barbauld, *Evenings at Home*, p. 234.

97 Lovejoy, *The Great Chain of Being*, p. 183.

98 John Aikin and Letitia Barbauld, *Evenings at Home*, p. 234.

99 William Wordsworth, "Michael," line 77, *Poetical Works*, ii, 83.

100 William Wordsworth, lines 13–20, *Poetical Works*, iv, 58.

101 William Paley, *Natural Theology*, pp. 296–97.

102 Henry Needler, "Letter to D," *Works* (London: J. Watts, 1724), pp. 201–02.

103 James Thomson, *The Seasons*, "Spring," line 901, *The Seasons*, ed. James Sambrook (Oxford: Clarendon, 1981), p. 46.

104 William Wordsworth, lines 93–94, 96, 100–02, *Poetical Works*, ii, 261–62.

105 Alexander Pope, *An Essay on Man*, ed. Maynard Mack (New Haven: Yale University Press, 1950), p. 47, lines 267–68 and n.

106 William Cowper, *The Task*, Book vi, "The Winter Walk at Noon," lines 184–85, 222, pp. 223–24.

107 William Blake, *The Marriage of Heaven and Hell*, in *Complete Writings*, p. 160.

108 William Blake, "Spring," lines 3–9, in *Complete Writings*, p. 123.

109 William Cowper, *The Task*, Book vi, "The Winter Walk at Noon," lines 327–29, 339–40, pp. 226–27.

110 William Wordsworth, "Resolution and Independence," line 11, *Poetical Works*, ii, 235.

111 James Thomson, *The Seasons*, "Winter," pp. 198–99; William Cowper, *The Task*, Book v. "The Winter Morning Walk," lines 65–95, pp. 201–02.

112 Thomas Day, *The History of Sandford and Merton*, pp. 162–63.

113 William Cowper, *The Task*, Book vi, "The Winter Walk at Noon," p. 172.

114 William Blake, *Milton*, plate 31, lines 34–38, in *Complete Writings*, p. 520.

115 Thomas Tryon, *Wisdom's Dictates* (London: T. Salisbury, 1691), p. 94.

116 Cited in Clifford J. Sherry, *Animal Rights: A Reference Handbook* (Santa Barbara, CA: ABC–CLIO, Inc., 1994), p. 62.

117 Samuel J. Pratt, *The Lower World: a Poem in Four Books* (London: Sharpe and Hailes, 1810), p. i.

118 Humphry Primatt, *The Duty of Mercy and Sin of Cruelty to Beasts*, excerpted in John Toogood, *The Book of Nature: Discourse on Some of the Instances of the Power, Wisdom, and Goodness of God . . . To which is added, The Duty of Mercy and Sin of Cruelty to Brutes, Taken Chiefly from Dr. Primatt's Dissertation*, 4th edn. (Boston: Samuel Hall, 1802), p. 37.

119 Francis Hutcheson, *System of Moral Philosophy*, pp. 311–14.

120 William H. Drummond, *The Rights of Animals and Man's Obligation to Treat Them with Humanity*, pp. 208, 92. Cf. the anonymous *Three Dialogues on the Amusements of Clergymen*, a pamphlet against parsons who hunt, in which Dr. Stillingfleet observes that "there are laws also to be observed between man and beast, which are equally coercive, though the injured party has no power of appeal." (*Three Dialogues on the Amusements of Clergymen*, 2nd edn. [London: T. Cadell, jun. and W. Davies, 1797], pp. 60–61.)

121 Margaret Cullen, *Mornton* (Philadelphia: Carey, Wells, and Lilly, 1816, reprinting the Edinburgh edn. of 1814), p. 119.

122 John Lawrence, *A Philosophical and Practical Treatise on Horses*, pp. 132–33.

123 Thomas Paine, "Cruelty to Animals Exposed," *Pennsylvania Magazine* (March, 1775), I, 231–32.

124 Sarah Trimmer, review of E. A. Kendall, *Keeper's Travels in Search of His Master*, quoted in Samuel F. Pickering, *John Locke and Children's Books in Eighteenth-Century England*, p. 38.

3 KEEPING PETS: WILLIAM COWPER AND HIS HARES

1 Samuel Taylor Coleridge, *Collected Letters*, ed. Earl Leslie Griggs, 6 vols. (Oxford: Clarendon Press, 1956–71), III, 179, 119.

2 As the text suggests, my estimate of Cowper's influence is an impression based on reading his contemporaries and the next generations. What reception study has been made supports my claim. See the investigation of diaries, commonplace books, libraries, and the like in Birmingham and in Sussex farm country by Leonore Davidoff and Catherine Hall, *Family Fortunes: Men and Women of the English Middle Class, 1780–1850* (London: Hutchinson, 1987), pp. 157–58. Cf. the commentary on this work in Julie Ellison, "News, Blues, and Cowper's Busy World," *MLQ*, 62, no. 2 (Sept. 2001), 220–24.

3 Leonore Davidoff and Catherine Hall, *Family Fortunes*, p. 157.

4 William Cowper, *The Task*, III, 41–42, in *Poetical Works*, ed. H. S. Milford, 4th edn. (London: Oxford University Press, 1934), p. 165. Subsequent citations of this poem are identified in the text by book and line number.

5 Leonore Davidoff and Catherine Hall, *Family Fortunes*, p. 158.

6 William Cowper, *The Gentleman's Magazine* (June, 1784), reprinted in *Poetical Works*, p. 652.

7 Georges Louis Leclerc Buffon, *Buffon's Natural History*, trans. William Smellie, 10 vols. (London: Barr, 1797), VI, 98.

8 John Bowring, *Memoir of Jeremy Bentham*, in Jeremy Bentham, *Works*, ed. Bowring, 11 vols. (New York: Russell and Russell, 1962), XI, 81.

9 *The Letters and Prose Writings of William Cowper*, ed. James King and Charles Ryskamp, 4 vols. (Oxford: Clarendon Press, 1979–81), II, 469.

10 This list is based on passages in Cowper's letters and on a letter from Lady Hesketh cited in Dix Harwood, *Love for Animals and How it Developed in Great Britain* (New York: no publisher listed, 1928), p. 215.

11 John Lawrence, *A Philosophical and Practical Treatise on Horses, and on the Moral Duties of Man toward the Brute Creation*, 2 vols. (London: T. N. Longman, 1796–98), I, 22.

12 William Cowper, "Epitaph on a Hare," lines 13–20, in *Poetical Works*, p. 352.

13 Keith Thomas, *Man and the Natural World*, (London: Allen Lane, 1983), p. 119.

14 Joanna Baillie, "The Kitten," lines 100–126, *Fugitive Verses* (1790; London: Moxon, 1840), pp. 199–200.

15 For discussion see Christine Kenyon-Jones, *Kindred Brutes: Animals in Romantic-Period Writing* (Aldershot: Ashgate Publishing Limited, 2001), pp. 23–27.

16 George Gordon, Lord Byron, "The Prisoner of Chillon," lines 381–88, *Works*, ed. E. H. Coleridge and R. E. Prothero, 13 vols. (London: John Murray, 1898–1904), IV, 28.

17 Edward Augustus Kendall, *The Canary Bird* (London: E. Newbery, 1799), pp. 69–70.

18 Alexander Pope, "Epigram. Engraved on the Collar of a Dog which I gave to his Royal Highness," *Minor Poems*, ed. Norman Ault and John Butt (London: Methuen, 1954), p. 372.

19 *Poems and Songs of Robert Burns*, ed. James Kinsley, 3 vols. (Oxford: Clarendon Press, 1968), I, 32–36. Subsequent references to these poems are by title and line number in the text.

20 Kenneth Simpson, *The Protean Scot: The Crisis of Identity in Eighteenth Century Scottish Literature* (Aberdeen: Aberdeen University Press, 1988), p. 189.

21 John Aikin and Letitia Barbauld, *Evenings at Home; or, The Juvenile Budget Opened*, 2nd edn., 3 vols. together (Philadelphia: T. Dobson, 1797), I, 84.

22 In *Poems and Songs of Robert Burns*, I, 165–68, lines 1–2.

23 Christopher Smart, *Poetical Works*, ed. Karina Williamson, 6 vols. (Oxford: Clarendon Press, 1980–96), I, 87–90. Quotations from this work are identified in the text by verse number.

24 William Blake, "The Marriage of Heaven and Hell," *Complete Writings*, ed. Geoffrey Keynes (London: Oxford University Press, 1966), p. 160.

25 Joanna Baillie, "The Kitten," lines 97–100, *Fugitive Verses*, pp. 199–200.

26 William Hargrave, *History and Description of the Ancient City of York*, 3 vols. (York: William Alexander, 1818), III, 542.

27 *The Philanthropist* (London: Longman 1813), III, 330, reviewing Samuel Tuke, *Description of the Retreat, an Institution Near York for Insane Persons* (1813). Samuel Tuke was a grandson of William Tuke, who had founded the Retreat.

28 Thomas Bewick and Ralph Beilby, *A General History of Quadrupeds* (Newcastle Upon Tyne: S. Hodgson et al., 1790), p. 321.

29 Edward Topsell, *The Historie of Four-footed Beastes* (London: 1607), p. 269.

30 George Ewart Evans and David Thomson, *The Leaping Hare* (London: Faber and Faber, 1972), p. 28; Henry Tegner, *Wild Hares* (London: John Baker, 1969), pp. 36–37.

31 Thomas Bewick, *A Memoir of Thomas Bewick Written by Himself*, ed. Iain Bain (Oxford: Oxford University Press, 1979), p. 6; William Somerville, *The Chase*, II, 270–72, describes a hare dying "with infant screams"; Tegner, *Wild Hares*, p. 23. William Blake (*Complete Writings*, lines 13–14, p. 431) alludes to this in "Auguries of Innocence," in the monitory couplet on the hunted hare: "Each outcry of the hunted Hare A fibre from the Brain does tear." With the infant scream of its outcry, the hare becomes an innocent child like the ones in Blake's *Songs of Innocence*. Even hardened and joyous hunters were disturbed by the hare's scream, as though the animal they were killing had transformed itself into a baby.

32 *Letters and Prose Writings*, III, 522–23.

33 Edward Topsell, *The Historie of Four-footed Beastes*, p. 266.

34 Georges Louis Leclerc Buffon, *Buffon's Natural History*, VI, 95.

35 William Cowper, *Letters*, I, 153.

36 David Cecil, *The Stricken Deer: The Life of Cowper* (London: Constable, 1929), p. 21; Charles Ryskamp, *William Cowper of the Inner Temple, Esq.* (Cambridge: Cambridge University Press, 1959), pp. 135–44. The statement that Cowper was a hermaphrodite was made by John Newton in a letter to John Thornton. Newton's letters to Thornton were sent to Robert Southey in 1834, when Southey was writing a biography of Cowper. Southey did not publish this statement, but he referred to it in his own private correspondence, making clear that he did not believe it. Charles Greville, who had seen Newton's letters, also refers in his diary to Cowper's supposed deformity. Everyone who has written on this topic assumes that if he made the statement to Newton, Cowper meant by "hermaphrodite" a genital malformation.

37 Leonore Davidoff and Catherine Hall, *Family Fortunes*, pp. 111–12. Cf. the discussion of similar tendencies in the religious life of the age in Colin Campbell, *The Romantic Ethic and the Spirit of Modern Consumerism* (Oxford: Basil Blackwell, 1987), pp. 131–35.

38 James Thomson, *The Seasons*, ed. James Sambrook (Oxford: Clarendon, 1981), p. 216.

39 James Thomson, *The Seasons*, "Autumn," lines 401–25, p. 160.

40 John King, *William Cowper: A Biography* (Durham: Duke University Press, 1986), p. 9n.

41 Alexander Pope, *Windsor Forest*, lines 101–02, in *Pastoral Poetry and An Essay on Criticism*, ed. Audra Williams (London: Methuen, 1961), p. 160.

42 John Gay, *Rural Sports*, in *Poetry and Prose*, ed. Vinton A. Dearing with the assistance of Charles E. Beckwith, 2 vols. (Oxford: Clarendon Press, 1974), I, 52.

43 *Letters and Prose Writings*, III, 118–19.

44 William Cowper, *Letters and Prose Writings*, I, 382.

45 John King, *William Cowper*, pp. 274–75.

46 William Cowper, *Letters*, IV, 374–75.

47 For brief discussion see Matt Cartmill, *A View to a Death in the Morning: Hunting and Nature through History* (Cambridge, MA: Harvard University Press, 1993), pp. 123–26.

48 William Cowper, *Letters and Prose Writings*, IV, 56.

49 William Cowper, "Adelphi: an Account of the Conversion of W. C. Esquire," in *Letters and Prose Writings*, I, 5.

50 William Cowper, *Letters and Prose Writings*, III, 106–07.

51 Ibid., IV, 469.

52 Ibid., IV, 468.

53 Ibid., III, 337.

4 BARBARIAN PLEASURES: AGAINST HUNTING

1 William Howitt, *The Rural Life of England*, 2 vols. (London: Longman, Orme, Brown, Green, and Longmans, 1838), I, 63–64.

2 E. W. Bovill, *English Country Life 1780–1830* (London: Oxford University Press, 1962), p. 174; Richard H. Thomas, *The Politics of Hunting* (Aldershot: Gower Publishing Co., 1983), p. 18.

3 In Thomas Day's *History of Sandford and Merton*, which dates from the 1780s, the horse-courser demands two hundred guineas for a handsome, well-trained, gentle, tractable horse that is "full of spirit" (Thomas Day, *The History of Sandford and Merton* [New York: Hurd and Houghton, 1865], p. 222). Roger Longrigg, *The English Squire and his Sport* (London: Michael Jordan, 1977) p. 117, says that a good hunter in 1760 cost at least £150. David C. Itzkowitz, *Peculiar Privilege: A Social History of English Foxhunting 1753–1885* (Hassocks, Sussex: John Spiers, 1977), pp. 31–32, says that through most of the nineteenth century "an average hunter cost around £75 to £150, and £300 to £400 was generally considered a high price." Hunting horses could cost as much as a thousand guineas.

4 John Lawrence, *The Horse in All His Varieties and Uses; His Breeding, Rearing, and Management; with Rules, Occasionally Interspersed, for his Preservation from Disease* (London: M. Arnold, 1829), p. 228.

5 Roger Longrigg, *The English Squire and his Sport*, p. 116.

6 John Lawrence, *British Field Sports*, (1818; 2nd edn. London: Sherwood, Neely, and Jones, 1820), p. 300.

7 Peter Beckford, *Thoughts Upon Hunting*, new edn. (Sarum: P. Elmsly et al., 1782), p. 218.

8 William Somerville, *The Chase*, Book I, lines 14–15, in *The Poetical Works of Joseph Addison; Gay's Fables; and Somerville's Chase*, ed. George Gilfillan (Edinburgh: James Nichol, 1859).

9   Quoted by Peter Beckford, *Thoughts on Hunting*, p. 11. Miguel de Cervantes
    Saavedra, *Don Quixote*, 2 vols. (London: Dent, 1906), 11, 224.
10 Georges Louis Leclerc Buffon, *Buffon's Natural History*, trans. William Smellie,
    10 vols. (London: Barr, 1797), VI, 28.
11 Francis Noel Clarke Mundy, *Needwood Forest* (Lichfield: John Jackson, 1776),
    p. 38.
12 Quoted in David C. Itzkowitz, *Peculiar Privilege*, p. 20.
13 John Cook, *Observations on Fox-Hunting*, new edn. (London: Edward Arnold,
    1922), p. 101.
14 Quoted in David C. Itzkowitz, *Peculiar Privilege*, p. 121.
15 John Henry Walsh, *British Rural Sport*, 14th edn. (London: Frederick Warne,
    1878), p. viii.
16 John M. MacKenzie, *The Empire of Nature: Hunting, Conservation and British
    Imperialism* (Manchester: Manchester University Press, 1988), p. 44.
17 John Aikin and Letitia Barbauld, *Evenings at Home* (Boston: D. Lothrop, 1872),
    p. 332.
18 John Lawrence, *British Field Sports*, pp. 2–3.
19 Thomas Day, *The History of Sandford and Merton*, p. 48.
20 William Howitt, *The Rural Life of England*, 1, 67.
21 Peter Beckford, *Thoughts on Hunting*, pp. 129–30.
22 "Essay on the Diversions of Hunting, Fishing, &c," in *Memoirs of the Manchester
    Literary and Philosophical Society* (London: Warrington, 1781–83), 1, 349–51.
23 Quoted in E. W. Bovill, *English Country Life 1780–1830*, p. 220n.
24 Preface to William Chafin, *Anecdotes and History of Cranborne Chase* (1818;
    Stanbridge, Wimborne, Dorset: The Dovecote Press, 1991), p. xix.
25 William Shenstone, *Essays on Men and Manners* (1791; London: Bradbury and
    Evans, 1868), p. 176.
26 Samuel Johnson, *Johnsonian Miscellanies*, ed. George Birkbeck Hill, 2 vols.
    (1897; rpt. New York: Barnes and Noble, 1966), 11, 170.
27 Samuel Johnson, *Johnsonian Miscellanies*, 1, 288.
28 Percy Bysshe Shelley, "On the Game Laws," *Prose Works*, ed. E. B. Murray
    (Oxford: Clarendon Press, 1993), 1, 280–81.
29 Percy Bysshe Shelley, letter to Thomas Jefferson Hogg, October 22, 1821, in
    The Letters of Percy Bysshe Shelley, ed. Frederick L. Jones, 2 vols. (Oxford:
    Clarendon Press, 1964), 11, 361. But Shelley had shot birds as a teenager (see
    Letters, 1, 4).
30 *Don Juan*, Canto XIV, st. 35, in George Gordon, Lord Byron, *The Works
    of Lord Byron: Poetry*, ed. Ernest Hartley Coleridge, 7 vols. (London: John
    Murray, 1900–04), VI, 525; George Gordon, Lord Byron, letter to Augusta
    Leigh, December 14, 1808, in *The Works of Lord Byron: Letters and Journals*, ed.
    Rowland E. Prothero, 6 vols. (London: John Murray, 1900–04), 1, 205.
31 George Gordon, Lord Byron, *Letters and Journals*, 11, 405.
32 George Nicholson, *On the Conduct of Man to Inferior Animals* (Stourport: G.
    Nicholson, 1819), p. 69.

33 *Three Dialogues on the Amusements of Clergymen*, 2nd edn. (London: T. Cadell and W. Davies, 1797), pp. 23–32. The Preface says this was written by Josiah Frampton and found among his manuscripts after his death. Keith Thomas, *Man and the Natural World: Changing Attitudes in England, 1500–1800* (London: Allen Lane, 1983), p. 362, guesses that the author was William Gilpin.

34 *The Hare; or, Hunting Incompatible with Humanity: Written as a Stimulus to Youth Towards a Proper Treatment of Animals* (London: Vernor and Hood, 1799), p. 81.

35 T. Fry, *Domestic Portraiture: or the Successful Application of Religious Principles in the Education of a Family* (1833; New York: J. Leavitt, 1833), pp. 29–30.

36 Edward, Second Duke of York, *The Master of Game* (1406–13), ed. Wm. A. and F. Baillie-Grohman (New York: Duffied and Co., 1919), p. 15.

37 *The Monthly Review* 65 (Sept. 1781), 210, 217.

38 John Cook, *Observations on Fox-Hunting*, p. 16.

39 William Somerville, *The Chase*, Book II, lines 115–17.

40 Ibid., Book III, lines 118–23. E. W. Bovill, *English Country Life, 1780–1830*, p. 207, mentions the "appalling tale of dead and foundered horses which marred every great hunt." Things improved for horses around 1800, when Lord Sefton, who was overweight, introduced the practice of bringing two or three spare horses to the field.

41 William Wordsworth, *Poetical Works*, ed. E. de Selincourt, 2nd edn., 5 vols. (Oxford: Clarendon Press, 1952–59), IV, 61; lines 17–18.

42 "Essay on the Diversions of Hunting, Fishing, &c," I, 353.

43 James Granger, *An Apology for the Brute Creation, or Abuse of Animals Censured: In a Sermon on Proverbs xii, 10* (London: T. Davies, 1773), p. 16.

44 See, for example, Robert Burns's "On Seeing a Wounded Hare limp by me . . . " and "The Briggs of Ayr," lines 34–41, and, in *The Letters of Robert Burns*, ed. J. De Lancey Ferguson, 2nd edn. by G. Ross Roy, 2 vols. (Oxford: Clarendon Press, 1985), the letters of 21 April 1789, 4 May 1789, and 21 June 1789, I, 397–98, 404–05, and 417–18.

45 John Clare, "Sports of the Field," lines 7–8, *Early Poems 1804–1822*, ed. Eric Robinson with David Powell and Margaret Granger, 2 vols. (Oxford: Clarendon Press, 1989), I, 378–79.

46 Robert Burns, "On Seeing a Wounded Hare limp by me . . . ," lines 1, 13–16, in *The Poems and Songs of Robert Burns*, ed. James Kinsley, 3 vols. (Oxford: Clarendon Press, 1968), I, 465–66.

47 James Thomson, *The Seasons*, "Spring," line 1161, *The Seasons*, ed. James Sambrook (Oxford: Clarendon Press, 1981), p. 56.

48 James Thomson, *The Seasons*, "Spring," lines 853–54, p. 26.

49 James Thomson, *The Seasons*, "Autumn," lines 454–57, pp. 161–62.

50 *Cooper's Hill*, in *The Poetical Works of Sir John Denham*, ed. Theodore Howard Banks, Jr. (New Haven: Yale University Press, 1928), p. 85, lines 305–06. Shelley took up this topic in his "Orpheus," lines 46–50, in *The Complete Works of Percy Bysshe Shelley*, ed. Roger Ingpen and Walter E. Peck, 10 vols. (New York: Gordian Press, 1965), IV, 69.

51 Thomas Bewick, *A General History of Quadrupeds* (Newcastle: S. Hodgson, 1790), p. 109.

52 James Thomson, *The Seasons*, "Autumn," lines 473–76, p. 162.

53 Ibid., "Autumn," lines 502–69, pp. 164–66.

54 José Ortega y Gasset, *Meditations on Hunting*, trans. Howard B. Wescott (New York: Charles Scribner's Sons, 1972), p. 89.

55 William Wordsworth, *The Prelude*, ed. Ernest de Selincourt, rev. Helen Darbishire, 2nd edn. (Oxford: Clarendon Press, 1959), Book 1 (1850), lines 435–37. In *Wordsworth: Play and Politics: A Study of Wordsworth's Poetry, 1787–1800* (New York: St. Martin's Press, 1986), pp. 175–76, John Turner quotes from the 1805 version of the lines on stealing woodcocks (*Prelude* [1805–06], Book 1, lines 309–21) and notes a comparison between the boy as a "fell destroyer" and Sir Walter.

56 Dorothy Wordsworth, *Journals of Dorothy Wordsworth*, ed. E. de Selincourt, 2 vols. (London: Macmillan, 1959), I, 417. Wordsworth referred to stag hunting in a few other writings: "The Tuft of Primroses" (*Poetical Works*, V, 354, 360; lines 248, 501–02); "Miscellaneous Sonnets," no. 29 (*Poetical Works*, III, 34); and "Hart's Horn Tree, near Penrith" (*Poetical Works*, III, 177). In these verses the attitude to the sport seems neutral or ambivalent. On three occasions Dorothy Wordsworth's *Journals* (I, 204, 350, 416) refer to hunters, including stag hunters, that she had met or had been told about. She makes no criticism of their sport.

57 "Preface to 'Lyrical Ballads,'" in *Poetical Works*, II, 389.

58 William Wordsworth, *The Prelude* (1850), Book 1, lines 349–50, p. 23.

59 *Home at Grasmere: Part First, Book First, of "The Recluse,"* ed. Beth Darlington (Ithaca: Cornell University Press, 1977), p. 52 (MS B, lines 254–56).

60 Don H. Bialostosky, *Making Tales: The Poetics of Wordsworth's Narrative Experiments* (Chicago: Chicago University Press, 1984), pp. 90–91.

61 John Jones, *The Egotistical Sublime: A History of Wordsworth's Imagination* (London: Chatto and Windus, 1954), p. 139.

62 Don H. Bialostosky, *Making Tales*, p. 95.

63 James H. Averill, *Wordsworth and the Poetry of Human Suffering* (Ithaca: Cornell University Press, 1980), pp. 222, 214.

64 Geoffrey Hartman, "False Themes and Gentle Minds," *Philological Quarterly*, 47 (1968), 67.

65 John A. Hodgson, *Wordsworth's Philosophical Poetry 1797–1814* (Lincoln, NB: Nebraska University Press, 1980), pp. 75–82.

66 Turner, *Wordsworth: Play and Politics*, pp. 189–90.

67 However, the recent environmental/ecological influence in literary criticism may be bringing a welcome change. In addition to my 1998 article on the poem, there are Peter Mortenson, "Taking Animals Seriously: William Wordsworth and the Claims of Ecological Romanticism," *Orbis Litterarum*, 55(4) (2000), 296–311, which is mostly on "Hart-Leap Well," and brief remarks on the poem in Onno Oerlemans, *Romanticism and the Materiality of Nature* (2002).

68 "*Lyrical Ballads, with Other Poems*: in Two Volumes by William Wordsworth," *British Critic*, 17 (Feb. 1801), 128.

69 *Poetical Works*, II, 211, lines 22–23.

70 As John Hodgson puts it, in *Wordsworth's Philosophical Poetry*, p. 80, Sir Walter "literally makes over the spot into a physical emblem of his pleasures and his pride."

71 Mary Moorman, *William Wordsworth: A Biography*, 2 vols. (Oxford: Clarendon Press, 1957), I, 454–56.

72 *Poetical Works*, II, 514n.

73 David Chandler, "Hart-Leap Well: A History of the Site of Wordsworth's Poem," *Notes & Queries*, 49 (March, 2002), 22.

74 Cited by David Chandler, "Hart-Leap Well . . . ," p. 21, from George Young, *A History of Whitby, and Streoneshalh Abbey*, 2 vols. (Whitby, 1817), II, 797.

75 On this association see Marcelle Thiébaux, *The Stag of Love: The Chase in Medieval Literature* (Ithaca: Cornell University Press, 1974).

76 Dorothy Wordsworth, *Journals*, I, 123.

77 Wordsworth, *Home at Grasmere*, p. 60 (Ms B, lines 375–78).

5 SAVAGE AMUSEMENTS OF THE POOR: JOHN CLARE'S BADGER SONNETS

1 Quoted in William E. H. Lecky, *A History of England in the Eighteenth Century*, 8 vols. (New York: D. Appleton, 1878–90), I, 589.

2 Thomas Day, *The History of Sandford and Merton* (1783–89; New York: Hurd and Houghton, 1865), pp. 317–26.

3 Thomas Bewick, *A General History of Quadrupeds* (Newcastle: S. Hodgson, 1790), p. 291. The text was written by Bewick's partner, Ralph Beilby.

4 Ernest Neal, *The Badger* (London: Collins, 1948), p. 128.

5 Thomas Bewick, *A General History of Quadrupeds*, pp. 238–39.

6 Thomas Bewick, *A Memoir of Thomas Bewick Written by Himself*, ed. Iain Bain (London: Oxford University Press, 1975), p. 6.

7 Nicholas Cox, *The Gentleman's Recreation*, (1637; London: The Cresset Press, 1928), p. 97.

8 Daniel Defoe, *Journey Through England* (1724), quoted in George Ryley Scott, *The History of Cockfighting* (Hampshire, England: Spur Publications, 1975), p. 79.

9 John Clare, "The Badger," line 54, in *John Clare* (Oxford Authors), ed. Eric Robinson and David Powell (Oxford: Oxford University Press, 1984), p. 247.

10 William Chafin, *Anecdotes and History of Cranborne Chase* (1818; Stanbridge, Wimborne, Dorset: The Dovecote Press, 1991), p. 51.

11 *The Poetical Works of George Crabbe*, 8 vols. (London: J. Murray, 1834), II, 151.

12 William Blake, "Auguries of Innocence," lines 17–18, in *Complete Writings*, ed. Geoffrey Keynes (London: Oxford University Press, 1966), p. 431.

13 James Plumptre, *Three Discourses on the Case of the Animal Creation and the Duties of Man to Them* (London: Darton, Harvey, and Darton, 1816),

pp. 60–61. The interpolated quotation is from William Cowper, *The Task*, Book VI, "The Winter Walk at Noon," line 379, *Poetical Works*, ed. H. S. Milford, 4th edn. (London: Oxford University Press, 1934), p. 228.

14 *The Medusa; or, Penny Politician*, 1 (1820), pp. 18–19, quoted in Timothy Morton, *Shelley and the Revolution in Taste* (Cambridge: Cambridge University Press, 1994), pp. 36–37.

15 *Cock-Fighting and Game Fowl from the Note-Books of Herbert Atkinson of Ewelme together with the Life and Letters of John Harris, the Cornish Cocker*, ed. Game Cock (Samuel J. Looker) (Bath: George Bayntun, 1938), p. 152.

16 Richard King, *The Frauds of London Detected* (1770), pp. 29–30, quoted in George Ryley Scott, *The History of Cockfighting*, pp. 144–45.

17 Joseph Strutt, *Sports and Pastimes of the People of England* (London: J. White, 1801), p. 193.

18 *The Sporting Magazine*, 60 (Apr. 1822), 38–40, quoted in *Hounds in the Morning: Sundry Sports of Merry England, Selections from The Sporting Magazine 1792–1836*, ed. Carl B. Cone (Lexington, KY: Kentucky University Press, 1981), pp. 172–73.

19 John Lawrence, *A Philosophical and Practical Treatise on Horses, and on the Moral Duties of Man towards the Brute Creation*, 2 vols. (London: T. N. Longman, 1796–98), II, 148.

20 *Hansard's Parliamentary Debates; from 1803 to 1809* (London: Hansard, 1812), May 15, 1809, column 554.

21 Edward Augustus Kendall, *Keeper's Travels in Search of His Master* (Leipzig: Breitkopf and Haertel, 1816), p. 10.

22 Mary Wollstonecraft, "Vindication of the Rights of Women," *Works* (New York: New York University Press, 1989), V, 243.

23 John Lawrence, *A Philosophical and Practical Treatise on Horses*, I, 149.

24 Henry Crowe, *Zoophilos: or, Considerations on the Moral Treatment of Inferior Animals* (London: printed for the author, 1819), p. 5, quoted in Timothy Morton, *Shelley and the Revolution in Taste*, p. 28.

25 George Gordon, Lord Byron, *Works: Poetry*, ed. Ernest Hartley Coleridge, 7 vols. (London: John Murray, 1900–04), II, 72, stanza 80.

26 John Clare, draft Introduction for his poems: "the ensuing Trifles are nothing but the simple productions of an Unlettered Rustic"; John Taylor, the publisher, in his Introduction to Clare's *Poems Descriptive of Rural Life and Scenery* (1820): The poems are "the genuine productions of a young Peasant, a daylabourer . . . who has had no advantages of education beyond others of his class" (*Clare: The Critical Heritage*, ed. Mark Storey [London: Routledge & Kegan Paul, 1973], pp. 29, 43).

27 See John Lucas, "Clare's Politics," in *John Clare in Context*, ed. Hugh Haughton, Adam Phillips, and Geoffrey Summerfield (Cambridge: Cambridge University Press, 1994), pp. 148–77. See also the first four essays in *The Independent Spirit: John Clare and the Self-Taught Tradition*, ed. John Goodridge (Helpston: The John Clare Society and the Margaret Grainger Memorial Trust, 1994).

28 John Clare, "The Village Minstrel," line 57, in *Early Poems 1804–1822*, ed. Eric Robinson with David Powell and Margaret Granger, 2 vols. (Oxford: Clarendon Press, 1989), II, 125.

29 Introduction by Eric Robinson to John Clare, *Later Poems*, ed. Eric Robinson and David Powell, 2 vols. (Oxford: Clarendon Press, 1984), I, ix. Robinson's interpretation of "The Badger" is shared by Seamus Heaney, "John Clare: A Bicentenary Lecture," in *John Clare in Context*, p. 137, and by David Constantine, "Outside Eden: John Clare's Descriptive Poetry," in *An Infinite Complexity: Essays in Romanticism*, ed. J. R. Watson (Edinburgh: Edinburgh University Press, 1983), p. 190, but Constantine wisely adds that Clare was "slow to identify himself... with figures in a landscape, animal or human, in whom he might be expected to see an image of himself. That is characteristic of his humility: the landscape and its figures are not at his disposal."

30 Alan Porter, review of *Madrigals and Chronicles*, ed. Edmund Blunden, in *Spectator*, 5017 (23 August 1924), reprinted in *Clare: The Critical Heritage*, p. 368.

31 Line 63 reads "They let him out and turn a barrow down." "Barrow" is presumably a slip for "barrel," since a barrel, placed horizontally, was often used in the way I describe as a substitute den for the badger, and I imagine that Clare had this in mind.

32 John Clare, *Natural History Prose Writings*, ed. Margaret Grainger (Oxford: Clarendon Press, 1983), p. 264. A fragment by Clare entitled "Badger Catchers" presumably begins a poem that would have told how catchers in the woods heard this noise and were afflicted with superstitious terror (*Poems of the Middle Period 1822–1837*, ed. Eric Robinson, David Powell, and P. M. S. Dawson [Oxford: Clarendon Press, 1996], II, 242).

33 George Darley, Introduction, *The Works of Beaumont and Fletcher*, 2 vols. (London: Edward Moxon, 1840), I, xlv.

6 WORK ANIMALS, SLAVES, SERVANTS: COLERIDGE'S YOUNG ASS

1 Anthony Burgess, *Coaching Days in England* (London: Paul Elek, 1966), pp. 14–18.

2 Robert Bloomfield, *The Farmer's Boy; A Rural Poem* 3rd edn. (London: Vernor and Hood, 1800), pp. 86–88, in Robert Bloomfield and Nathaniel Bloomfield, *The Farmer's Boy, Rural Tales, Good Tidings, with An Essay on War*, ed. Donald H. Reiman (New York: Garland Publishing, 1977).

3 John Stuart Mill, *Principles of Political Economy*, 3rd edn., 2 vols. (London: John W. Parker and Son, 1852), II, 546.

4 Humphry Primatt, *The Duty of Mercy and Sin of Cruelty to Brutes*, quoted in Richard D. Ryder, *Animal Revolution* (Oxford: Basil Blackwell, 1989), pp. 66–67.

5 Keith Thomas, *Man and the Natural World* (London: Allen Lane, 1983), p. 46.

6 James Turner, *Reckoning with the Beast: Animals, Pain, and Humanity in the Victorian Mind* (Baltimore: The Johns Hopkins University Press, 1980), p. 54,

mentions the workings of this analogy in the Victorian period. Cf. Harriet Ritvo, *The Animal Estate: The English and Other Creatures in the Victorian Age* (Cambridge, MA: Harvard University Press, 1987), pp. 15ff.

7 James Granger, *An Apology for the Brute Creation* (London: T. Davies, 1773), p. 24. Cf. the anonymous sermon on *Clemency to Brutes* addressing the lower classes: "Do you therefore to whom Providence hath assigned the lower stations in Life amongst us learn to attender your Hearts towards the Creatures inferior to you by Nature, as the Hearts of your Superiors in point of Fortune are seen already attendered towards you" (*Clemency to Brutes* [Dublin: Peter and William Wilson, 1769], p. 20).

8 Sarah Trimmer, *Fabulous Histories, or, The History of the Robins* (1786; London, J. F. Dove, 1833), pp. 170–71.

9 George Nicholson, *On the Conduct of Man to Inferior Animals* (Stourport: G. Nicholson, 1819), p. 13.

10 Robert Bloomfield, *The Farmer's Boy: A Rural Poem*, pp. 77–78.

11 William Wordsworth, "Peter Bell," lines 1128–30, in *Poetical Works*, 2nd edn., ed. Ernest de Selincourt, 5 vols. (Oxford: Clarendon Press, 1952), II, 382.

12 Percy Bysshe Shelley, Preface to *Prometheus Unbound* (1820), in *Works*, ed. Roger Ingpen and Walter E. Peck, 10 vols. (New York: Gordian Press, 1965), II, 174.

13 Francis Hutcheson, *System of Moral Philosophy*, 2 vols. (London: A. Miller, 1755), Book II, chap. 6, "Adventitious Rights," I, 313.

14 Samuel Taylor Coleridge, "To a Young Ass," in *Poems*, ed. E. H. Coleridge (Oxford: Clarendon Press, 1912), pp. 74–76. Hereafter in this chapter cited parenthetically in the text by line number.

15 Samuel Taylor Coleridge, *Lectures 1795 On Politics and Religion*, ed. Lewis Patton and Peter Mann (Princeton, NJ: Princeton University Press, 1971), p. 247.

16 Dagobert De Levie, *The Modern Idea of the Prevention of Cruelty to Animals and Its Reflection in English Poetry* (New York: S. F. Vanni, 1947), p. 76.

17 George Gordon, Lord Byron, "English Bards, and Scotch Reviewers," line 262, in *Works*, ed. E. H. Coleridge and Rowland E. Prothero, 12 vols. (London: John Murray, 1903), I, 317.

18 Thomas Bewick, *A General History of Quadrupeds* (Newcastle: S. Hodgson, 1790), p. 15.

19 Samuel Taylor Coleridge, *Collected Letters*, ed. E. L. Griggs, 3 vols. (Oxford: Clarendon Press, 1956–71), I, 121.

20 For literary tradition and folklore regarding asses, see Lean Sinanoglou Marcus, "Vaughan, Wordsworth, Coleridge and the *Encomium Asini*," *ELH*, 42 (1975), 224–41.

21 Ernest S. Turner, *All Heaven in a Rage* (New York: St. Martin's Press, 1965), p. 127.

22 Coleridge, *Letters*, I, 103.

23 Ibid., I, 83.

24 Ibid., I, 143.

25 For convenience I quote this from Appendix C in Coleridge's *Poetical Works*, ed. James Dykes Campbell (London: Macmillan, 1898), p. 478.

26 See Keith Thomas, *Man and the Natural World*, p. 187; and for a similar displacement of compassion from humans to animals in the Victorian age, Harriet Ritvo, *The Animal Estate*, pp. 134–35; and James Turner, *Reckoning with the Beast*, pp. 36–37, 54–55.

27 Coleridge, *Letters*, I, 125–28.

7 THE SLAUGHTERHOUSE AND THE KITCHEN: CHARLES LAMB'S
"DISSERTATION UPON ROAST PIG"

1 Alec Forshaw and Theo Bergstrom, *Smithfield, Past and Present* (London: Heineman, 1980), p. 34.

2 John Lawrence, *A Philosophical and Practical Treatise on Horses, and on the Moral Duties of Man towards the Brute Creation*, 2 vols. (London: T. N. Longman, 1796–98), I, 159.

3 Percy Bysshe Shelley, *Complete Works*, 10 vols., ed. Roger Ingpen and Walter E. Peck (New York: Gordian Press, 1965), VI, 340. Subsequent quotations from Shelley are from this edition and are identified parenthetically in the text.

4 Lewis Gompertz in a tract of 1829 quoted in Charles D. Niven, *History of the Humane Movement* (London: Johnson Publications, 1967), p. 70.

5 Quoted in Timothy Morton, *Shelley and the Revolution in Taste* (Cambridge: Cambridge University Press, 1994), p. 144.

6 George Cheyne, *An Essay of Health and Long Life* (Dublin: George Ewing, 1725), p. 20.

7 Timothy Morton, *Shelley and the Revolution in Taste*, p. 160.

8 Thomas Day, *The History of Sandford and Merton* (1783–89; New York: Hurd and Houghton, 1865), p. 356.

9 David Hartley, *Observations on Man, His Frame, His Duty, and His Expectations*, 2 vols. (London: S. Richardson, 1749; reprint New York: Garland, 1971), II, 222–23.

10 Thomas Day, *The History of Sandford and Merton*, p. 131. Cf. David Davies, *The Case of Labourers in Husbandry Stated and Considered* (1795), p. 21: "bread makes the principal part of the food of all poor families and almost the whole of the food of . . . large families," quoted in D. J. Oddy, "Food, drink, and nutrition," in *The Cambridge Social History of Britain 1750–1950*, ed. F. M. L. Thompson, 2 vols. (Cambridge: Cambridge University Press, 1990), II, 255. Roy Porter, *English Society in the Eighteenth Century* (London: Allen Lane, 1982), p. 234: "The common people could afford little meat, and that was mainly fat bacon . . . The higher in the social scale, the larger the amount of meat eaten."

11 According to a once-common interpretation of Hesiod, a meat diet came in with the age of brass (*Works and Days*, trans. David W. Tandy and Walter E. Neale [Berkeley: California University Press, 1996], p. 69). For Ovid see *Metamorphoses*, Book 15. For diet in Paradise, see Genesis 1. 29.

12 John Oswald, *The Cry of Nature; or, An Appeal to Mercy and Justice on Behalf of the Persecuted Animals* (London: J. Johnson, 1791), pp. 78–79.

13 John Oswald, *The Cry of Nature*, p. 153, quoting p. 134 in Adair.

14 Quoted in John Oswald, *The Cry of Nature*, p. 92, from James Burnett, Lord Monboddo, *Of the Origin and Progress of Language* (1773–92).

15 Charles and Mary Lamb, *Works*, ed. E. V. Lucas, 7 vols. (London: Methuen & Co., 1905), VI, 358. Subsequent references to this edition are given in the text.

16 To Richard Woodhouse, October 27, 1818, in *The Letters of John Keats*, ed. Hyder E. Rollins, 2 vols. (Cambridge, MA: Harvard University Press, 1958), I, 386.

17 Fred V. Randel, *The World of Elia: Charles Lamb's Essayistic Romanticism* (Port Washington, NY: Kennikat Press, 1975); D. C. Saxena, "The Autobiographical Content of Lamb's Letters: Romancer of the City Streets; Conoisseur of Food and Fellowship," *Charles Lamb Bulletin* (Richmond, Surrey, England), 41 and 42 (January and April, 1983), 16–21, 36–42; J. R. Watson, "Lamb and Food, *Charles Lamb Bulletin*, 54, ns (April, 1986), 160–75.

18 Percy Bysshe Shelley, "On the Vegetable System of Diet," *Complete Works*, VI, 340.

19 William Hazlitt, "Hot and Cold," *Complete Works*, ed. P. P. Howe, 21 vols. (London: J. M. Dent, 1931), XII, 171–74.

20 George Gordon, Lord Byron, *Works*, ed. E. H. Coleridge and Rowland E. Prothero, 13 vols. (London: John Murray, 1903), VI, 101.

21 This is the reaction both of Randel and of Watson. In *The World of Elia* Randel thinks the "Dissertation" is "distinct from satire" because it both "exposes and embraces" (p. 124). Watson, in "Lamb and Food," conflates Elia and Lamb, but the "Dissertation" gradually unsettles this assumption. At first Watson speculates that "Lamb's imagination has got out of control in this essay" (p. 171), then he suggests that the "Dissertation" can be read "as an exercise in playing the role of a thoughtless gourmet" (p. 172), and then again he modifies this view: "Possibly Lamb is trying to have it both ways . . . he relishes suckling pig, but he feels guilty about it" (p. 172).

22 Quoted in Watson, "Lamb and Food," p. 169. Manning told Lamb the Chinese story that is retold in the "Dissertation" (II, 389).

23 *The Letters of Charles and Mary Lamb*, ed. E. V. Lucas, 3 vols. (London: Methuen, 1935; reprint New York: AMS Press, 1968), III, 403.

8 CAGED BIRDS AND WILD

1 James Grahame, *The Birds of Scotland* (1806), in *Poetical Works of Henry K. White and James Grahame*, ed. Charles Cowden Clarke (Edinburgh: W. P. Nimmo, 1868), p. 283.

2 Henry Mayhew, *London Labour and the London Poor*, 4 vols. (London: C. Griffin, 1861–62), II, 68.

3 Ibid., II, 84.

4 Edward Augustus Kendall, *The Canary Bird: A Moral Fiction Interspersed with Poetry* (London: E. Newbery, 1799), p. 88.
5 Ann and Jane Taylor, "Little Birds and Cruel Boys," *Original Poems for Infant Minds* (1804–05), reprinted as *Original Poems*, ed. E. V. Lucas (London: Wells, Gardner, and Darton, 1903), p. 303.
6 James Grahame, *The Birds of Scotland*, pp. 268–69. A similar episode with a lark's nest appears on pp. 252–53.
7 James Thomson, *The Seasons*, "Spring," lines 680–86, *The Seasons*, ed. James Sambrook (Oxford: Clarendon, 1981), p. 34.
8 Sarah Trimmer, *Fabulous Histories; or, the History of the Robins* (1786; London: J. F. Dove, 1833), pp. 46–49.
9 Ann and Jane Taylor, *Original Poems*, "The Bird's-Nest," pp. 10–11; cf. Sarah Trimmer, *Fabulous Histories*, pp. 43–45.
10 Thomas Day, *History of Sandford and Merton* (New York: Hurd and Houghton, 1865), p. 13.
11 Sarah Trimmer, *Fabulous Histories*, pp. 52–53.
12 Joanna Baillie, *A Lesson Intended for the Use of the Hampstead School* (Camden Town: L. Miller, 1826), pp. 8–9.
13 James Thomson, *The Seasons*, "Spring," lines 687–88, p. 34.
14 Robert Burns, *Letters*, ed. J. De Lancey Ferguson, 2nd edn. ed. G. Ross Roy (Oxford: Clarendon Press, 1985), pp. 63–64.
15 Percy Bysshe Shelley, *Complete Works*, ed. Roger Ingpen and Walter E. Peck, 10 vols. (New York: Gordian Press, 1965), I, 222.
16 John Clare, "To the Snipe," *John Clare*, ed. Eric Robinson and David Powell (Oxford: Oxford University Press, 1984), p. 206.
17 "The Yellow Wagtails Nest," *John Clare*, pp. 231. My generalizations in this paragraph are also based on "The Fern Owl's Nest," "The Wryneck's Nest," "The Nightingale's Nest," "The Sky Lark," "The Raven's Nest," "The Moorhen's Nest," "Sedge Birds Nest," "The Robin's Nest," "The Landrail," "The Reed Bird," and "Birds in Alarm." I have also drawn on John Clare, *John Clare's Birds*, ed. Eric Robinson and Richard Fitter (Oxford: Oxford University Press, 1982) and John Clare, *Natural History Prose Writings*, ed. Margaret Granger (Oxford: Clarendon Press, 1983).
18 William Wordsworth, *The Prelude; or, Growth of a Poet's Mind*, ed. Ernest de Selincourt, 2nd edn. rev. by Helen Darbishire (Oxford: Clarendon Press, 1959), I (1850), lines 326–39, pp. 21–23.
19 Anne Brontë, *Agnes Grey*, ed. H. Marsden and R. Inglesfield (Oxford: Clarendon Press, 1998), pp. 47–49.
20 For an excellent history see the relevant chapters in Erwin Stresemann, *Ornithology from Aristotle to the Present* (Cambridge, MA: Harvard University Press, 1975).
21 James Hurdis, *The Village Curate: A Poem* (London: J. Johnson, 1788), p. 45.
22 *John Clare*, p. 242.
23 Ibid., pp. 230, 229, 213, 212.

24 William Wordsworth, "The Sparrow's Nest," in *Poetical Works*, ed. Ernest de Selincourt, 2nd edn., 5 vols. (Oxford: Clarendon Press, 1952), I, 227.

25 *John Clare*, pp. 213–14.

26 Sarah Trimmer, *Fabulous Histories*, p. 29.

27 James Grahame, *The Birds of Scotland*, pp. 269, 274.

28 Henry Mayhew, *London Labour and the London Poor*, II, 66–74.

29 Paula R. Feldman, ed., *British Women Poets of the Romantic Era* (Baltimore: The Johns Hopkins University Press, 1997), pp. xxviii–xxix.

30 William Blake, *Complete Writings*, ed. Geoffrey Keynes (London: Oxford University Press, 1966), p. 122.

31 *Universal Magazine*, 77 (Dec., 1785), p. 39; in Paula R. Feldman, ed., *British Women Poets of the Romantic Era*, pp. 273–74.

32 William Wordsworth, "The Poet and the Caged Turtledove," in *Poetical Works*, II, 163.

33 Ann and Jane Taylor, *Original Poems*, pp. 134–39.

34 Felicia Hemans, *Poems* (London and Edinburgh: Blackwood, 1872), "The Sea-Bird Flying Inland," p. 484; "The Freed Bird," p. 521.

35 William Blake, *Complete Writings*, p. 6.

36 William Blake, "Auguries of Innocence," lines 5–6, *Complete Writings*, p. 431.

37 William Blake, "The Blossom," lines 3–6, *Complete Writings*, p. 115.

38 Helen Leigh, "The Linnet: A Fable," in Paula R. Feldman, ed., *British Women Poets of the Romantic Era*, pp. 391–93.

39 *Connoisseur*, 89 (1755), 123.

40 James Thomson, *The Seasons*, "Spring," lines 710–13, *The Seasons*, p. 36.

41 Samuel Taylor Coleridge, "The Rime of the Ancient Mariner," in *Poems*, ed. E. H. Coleridge (Oxford: Clarendon Press, 1912), p. 209.

42 John Livingston Lowes, *The Road to Xanadu: A Study in the Ways of the Imagination*, 2nd edn. (Princeton, NJ: Princeton University Press, 1964), pp. 275–77.

43 Dorothy Kilner, *The Life and Perambulation of a Mouse* (London: John Marshall, 1780), p. 24.

44 Robert Penn Warren, "A Poem of Pure Imagination: An Experiment in Reading" (1946), reprinted with an appendix in *New and Selected Essays* (New York: Random House, 1989), pp. 335–423. I discuss and criticize Warren's interpretation in "The 'Ancient Mariner' and Its Interpreters: Some Versions of Coleridge," *Modern Language Quarterly*, 57:3 (September, 1996), 431–38.

45 Samuel Taylor Coleridge, *Biographia Literaria*, ed. James Engell and W. J. Bate, 2 vols. (Princeton, NJ: Princeton University Press, 1983), II, 147. My italics.

46 Samuel Taylor Coleridge, *Aids to Reflection*, in *Complete Works*, ed. William G. T. Shedd, 7 vols. (New York: Harper and Brothers, 1853), I, 287.

47 Coleridge, *Complete Works*, ed. Shedd, I, 49. Cf. V, 204, 448; and Samuel Taylor Coleridge, *Marginalia*, ed. George Whalley, 3 vols. (Princeton, NJ: Princeton University Press, 1980), I, 825.

48 John Keats, "Ode to the Nightingale," in *Complete Poems*, ed. Jack Stillinger (Cambridge, MA: Harvard University Press, 1982), pp. 279–81.

49 William Cowper, "Epitaph on a Hare," in *Poetical Works*, ed. H. S. Milford, 4th edn. (London: Oxford University Press, 1934), p. 352.
50 John Clare, "Birds in Alarm," in *John Clare*, p. 242.
51 William Wordsworth, "The Green Linnet," in *Poetical Works*, II, 139–41.
52 William Wordsworth, "There Was a Boy," lines 13–16, in *Poetical Works*, II, 206.
53 Ann Radcliffe, "To the Nightingale," in *Romance of the Forest* (New York: Arno Press, 1974), pp. 156–57.
54 Charlotte Smith, "To a Nightingale," in *Poems*, ed. Stuart Curran (New York: Oxford University Press, 1993), p. 14.
55 Mary Robinson, *Poetical Works* (London: Jones, 1824), pp. 41–42.
56 Samuel Taylor Coleridge, "The Nightingale," line 56, in *Poetical Works*, ed. James Dykes Campbell (London: Macmillan, 1924), pp. 131–33.
57 William Wordsworth, "Preface to the Second Edition of... 'Lyrical Ballads,'" *Poetical Works*, II, 390.
58 Percy Bysshe Shelley, "To a Skylark," in *Complete Works*, II, 302–05.
59 Cf. Tony Pinkney, "Romantic Ecology," in *A Companion to Romanticism*, ed. Duncan Wu (Oxford: Blackwell, 1998), p. 414: "The skylark's own identity, its actual autonomous being in its indigenous environment, is at once cancelled out. The bird instead is turned into a symbol; it is folded back into the subjectivity of the author rather than respected in its objectivity and otherness."

Bibliographical essay

In *Man and the Natural World: Changing Attitudes in England 1500–1800* (1983), Keith Thomas includes an extensive bibliography of writings, including poems, that expressed attitudes to animals. In this essay I limit myself to primary and secondary publications I have found particularly helpful. I omit specific bibliographic information about the editions used, since this is available in the footnotes.

Keith Thomas's magisterial survey represents all the points of view that were present in England from the early modern period to the end of the nineteenth century. Otherwise, not much has been written about the beginnings of animal rights in the ages of Enlightenment and Romanticism. Several excellent books deal mainly with Victorian and modern developments, but have some preliminary material on earlier ages: Arthur W. Moss, *Valiant Crusade: The History of the RSPCA* (1961); Ernest S. Turner, *All Heaven in a Rage* (1965); Gerald Carson, *Men, Beasts, and Gods* (1972); James Turner, *Reckoning with the Beast: Animals, Pain, and Humanity in the Victorian Mind* (1980); Harriet Ritvo, *The Animal Estate: The English and Other Creatures in the Victorian Age* (1987); Richard D. Ryder, *Animal Revolution* (1989); Keith Tester, *Animals and Society: The Humanity of Animal Rights* (1991); Katharine M. Rogers, *The Cat and the Human Imagination: Feline Images from Bast to Garfield* (1998); Hilda Kean, *Animal Rights: Political and Social Change in Britain Since 1800* (1998); and Moira Ferguson, *Animal Advocacy and English Women, 1780–1900* (1999). Though her topic is much broader than mine, Christine Kenyon-Jones, *Kindred Brutes: Animals in Romantic-Period Writing* (2001), includes much that is relevant to animal rights. Onno Oerlemans, *Romanticism and the Materiality of Nature* (2002), pp. 65–97, has brief comments on many poems of the period on animals. Timothy Morton, *Shelley and the Revolution in Taste* (1994), gives information on vegetarian discourse in the Romantic era. On the contribution of literature to the protest on behalf of animals there are two older studies in the history of ideas: Dix Harwood, *Love for Animals and How It Developed in Great Britain* (1928) and Dagobert De Levie, *The Modern Idea of the Prevention of Cruelty to Animals* (1947). Samuel F. Pickering, Jr., *John Locke and Children's Books in Eighteenth-Century England* (1981), discusses the inculcation of kindness to animals in this literature.

The very extensive discourse of the present on animal rights is generally not concerned with practices and attitudes in the past. A list of books can be found in Clifford J. Sherry, *Animal Rights: A Reference Handbook* (1994). Though it is not itself historical, this discourse is historically interesting because one finds in it the same arguments continuing after two hundred and fifty years. The best single introduction to our contemporary debate is J. M. Coetzee, *The Lives of Animals* (1999).

Information concerning hunting and other sports in the past can be found in social histories: William Howitt, *The Rural Life of England* (1838), Volume 1 of William Lecky's *History of England in the Eighteenth Century* (1878–90), Sir Walter Besant, *London in the Eighteenth Century* (1903), Sir Walter Gilbey, *Sport in the Olden Time* (1912), F. J. Drake-Carmell, *Old English Customs and Ceremonies* (1938), E. W. Bovill, *English Country Life 1780–1830* (1962), Robert W. Malcolmson, *Popular Recreations in English Society 1700–1850* (1973), Roger Longrigg, *The English Squire and his Sport* (1977), and David C. Itzkowitz, *Peculiar Privilege: A Social History of English Foxhunting 1753–1885* (1977). Joseph Strutt's *Sports and Pastimes of the People of England* (1801) was just such a historial work, but since it dates from the period we are studying, it is also a primary source for attitudes then. In *The Empire of Nature: Hunting, Conservation and British Imperialism* (1998) John M. MacKenzie deals mainly with hunting in some parts of Africa and India during the nineteenth century. In *Quest for Excitement: Sport and Leisure in the Civilizing Process* (1986), by Norbert Elias and Eric Dunning, Elias develops a sociological, theoretical argument that fox hunting marked a stage in the civilizing process because dogs rather than humans usually did the killing. Richard H. Thomas, *The Politics of Hunting* (1983), includes historical information on his topic. On another "sport," George Ryley Scott is excellent on *The History of Cockfighting* (1975).

James Serpell, *In the Company of Animals: A Study of Human–Animal Relationships* (1986), is informative on the history of pet keeping. The many works in recent years on the psychological and medical benefits of keeping pets are not concerned with earlier times, but their conclusions may be valid for them. I have been much interested by Alan Beck and Aaron Katcher, *Between Pets and People: The Importance of Animal Companionship* (1983), by the essays gathered by these authors in *New Perspectives on Our Lives with Companion Animals* (1983), and by Bruce Fogle, ed., *Interrelations Between People and Pets* (1981).

Coming now to primary sources for attitudes in the eighteeenth century and the Romantic age, I begin with a selection of sermons that, in most cases, startled their hearers when they were first delivered: *Clemency to Brutes* (1769) was published anonymously; James Granger, *An Apology for the Brute Creation* (1773); Richard Mant, *Reflections on the Sinfulness of Cruelty to Animals* (1807), one of a series of endowed sermons on this topic; and James Plumptre, *Three Discourses on the Case of Animal Creation, and the Duties of Man to Them* (1816). To these may be added clerical books that pleaded the cause of compassion, such as John Hildrop, *Free Thoughts Upon the Brute Creation* (1742), Humphry Primatt, *Duty of Mercy & Sin of Cruelty to Beasts* (1776), and Thomas Young, *An Essay on Humanity to Animals* (1789), the latter showing the strong impact of utilitarian ethics – the duty of diminishing the sum of pain. William Drummond, a Presbyterian minister, published a fiercely committed work, *The Rights of Animals and Man's Obligation to Treat Them with Humanity* (1838). Pamphlets, articles, and books flowed also from lay persons. Letter 15 of Oliver Goldsmith's *The Citizen of the World* (1760–61) attacked cruelties in the slaughter house and kitchen. "Disquisition II" of Soame Jenyns' *Disquisitions on Several Subjects* (1782) deployed the great chain of being to argue that we should view animals as we hope God may us. Thomas Taylor's *A Vindication of the Rights of Brutes* (1792) was intended as a parody of arguments for the rights of man. Taylor deployed many of the same contentions that were used seriously by defenders of animals. These seemed so absurd to Taylor that to state was to satirize them.

Whether animals could be said to have souls and whether, if so, their souls were immortal was a subject of controversy. Descartes had denied this point, and most English philosophers took it up in passing. Several clerics also went into the question: Samuel Colliber, *Free Thoughts Concerning Souls* (1734); David-Renaud Boullier, *Essai Philosophique sur L'Âme des Bêtes*, 2nd edn. (1737); Richard Dean, *Essay on the Future Life of Brute Creatures* (1768); and Peter Buchan, *Scriptural and Philosophical Arguments . . . That Brutes Have Souls* (1824).

Vegetarian polemic dwelt on the cruelties and moral corruption involved in eating animals. As a soldier in the Indian Army, John Oswald became a vegetarian under the influence of Hindu teachings. He wrote *The Cry of Nature; or, An Appeal to Mercy and to Justice, on Behalf of the Persecuted Animals* (1791). George Nicholson's *On the Conduct of Man to Inferior Animals* (1819) denounces not just the eating of animals but every cruelty to them. Joseph Ritson's *An Essay on Abstinence from Animal Food as a Moral Duty* (1802) compiled lore that Ritson had been collecting all his life. John F. Newton's *Return to Nature, or, a Defence of the Vegetable Regimen* (1811) was an important book for Shelley, the most famous of the pamphleteers on this subject: *A Vindication of Natural Diet* (1813), "On the Game Laws" (1816–18), and "On the Vegetable System of Diet."

The character and faculties of animals, their degree of likeness to man, and the ethical problems involved in human use of them are topics in most English philosophers of the eighteenth century. That this is so attests to the widespread concern. The insistence of Anthony Ashley Cooper, 3rd Earl of Shaftesbury, in *Characteristicks* (1711) that kindness is natural and pleasurable to human beings was a significant straw in the current of sentimental benevolence, but Shaftesbury said little about animals. In his treatise *On Education* (1693) John Locke urged that kindness to animals should be taught to children, and in the *Essay Concerning Human Understanding* (1690; Part II, Chapters 10 and 11) Locke discussed the intellectual powers of animals. David Hume continued this topic in the *Treatise of Human Nature* (1739), emphasizing the similarity of humans and animals on their affective sides. In Hume's *Enquiry Concerning the Human Understanding* (1748), Section 9 deals with "the Reason of Animals." There is sporadic but important discussion in Hume's *Enquiry Concerning the Principles of Morals* (1751). In a few pages (1, 404–15) of *Observations on Man* (1749), David Hartley took up similar questions. Hartley had grave doubts about the ethics of eating meat. Francis Hutcheson made a case for this and for other uses of animals in the sections of his *System of Moral Philosophy* (1755) on "Adventitious Rights" (chapter 6, sections 3 and 4). The same question was considered by William Paley in chapter XI, "The

General Rights of Mankind," of his *Principles of Moral and Political Philosophy* (1785). Both Hutcheson and Paley of course argued that animals have at least a right that no useless pain should be inflicted. In his *Elements of the Philosophy of the Human Mind* (1792), Dugald Stewart compared "the Faculties of Man and Those of the Lower Animals" (part III, chapter 2, sections 1–2). Thomas Paine spoke strongly though briefly against cruelty to animals in the *Age of Reason* (1793) and also published in Pennsylvania a poem entitled "Cruelty to Animals Exposed" (1775). The strongest single statement that animals have rights may be found in Jeremy Bentham, *Introduction to the Principles of Morals* (1789), as a footnote in chapter 19. Bentham is still frequently quoted on this subject, but he did not touch on it often. There is an important paragraph in his *Principles of Penal Law* (1811; part 3, chapter 17), and a letter to the *Morning Chronicle* (March 4, 1825) further clarifies his position. The *Memoir* of Bentham by John Bowring, volume II of Bowring's edition of Bentham's *Works* (1843), tells several charming anecdotes to illustrate Bentham's fondness for animals.

No magazines were devoted solely to the cause or question of animals, but relevant articles appeared occasionally in most of the periodicals. The most useful are the *Monthly Review* and the *Critical Review*, for these journals reviewed current books and printed long extracts.

The contemporary understanding of animal nature and of particular animals can also be read in the natural histories of the age. Most of them were translations or redactions of the great *Histoire Naturelle* (1749–88) of Georges Louis Leclerc Buffon: Oliver Goldsmith, *An History of the Earth and Animated Nature* (1774); Thomas Bewick and Ralph Beilby, *A General History of Quadrupeds* (1790); William Smellie, trans., *Buffon's Natural History* (1797). Thomas Pennant's *History of Quadrupeds* (1793) was largely independent of Buffon. Among other scientific or quasi-scientific works of a general kind, William Smellie's *Philosophy of Natural History* (1790) is particularly useful. Erasmus Darwin's *Zoonomia: or, the Laws of Organic Life* (1794–96) was important, and James Burnett, Lord Monboddo, started a long-lived controversy with his contention, in *Of the Origin and Progress of Language* (1773–92), that the orang-utan is a species of human being. William Paley's *Principles of Moral and Political Philosophy* (1785), which I mentioned earlier, was the culmination of the long tradition of natural theology, and it gave much information on the anatomy, physiology, and supposed emotion of animals. For birds there is Thomas Bewick's *History and Description of British Birds* (1794) and other items that are now extremely rare. Henry Mayhew, *London Labour and the London Poor* (1861–62), collects much information about the capture and sale of song birds in his time. The most important book for my subject on horses was John Lawrence's *Treatise on Horses* (1796–98). Lawrence wrote several other books on the management of animals and always advocated kindly treatment.

On hunting practices, Nicholas Cox, *The Gentleman's Recreation* (1674), must be used cautiously, since it reflects an earlier period. The most informative book on fox hunting, including the care and training of dogs, is Peter Beckford's *Thoughts Upon Hunting* (1781), which was used as a manual. John Cook's *Observations on Fox-Hunting* expresses the views of a typical Master of Hounds, and William Chafin's naive, delightful *Anecdotes and History of Cranborne Chase* (1818) record the feelings of another Nimrod. Whether a clergyman should hunt was a disputed question. *Three Dialogues on the Amusements of Clergymen* (1796) offers a decided negative. The pamphlet was published anonymously, but a Preface in the second edition says it was written by Josiah Frampton; Keith Thomas suggests that the author was William Gilpin. Another anonymous pamphlet, *The Hare, or, Hunting Incompatible with Humanity* (1800), denounces the pursuit of this animal. John Lawrence's manual, *British Field Sports* (1818), embraced, as the subtitle says, "Practical Instructions in Shooting, Hunting, Coursing, Racing, Cocking, Fishing, etc. with Observations on the Breaking and Training of Dogs and Horses; also the Management of Fowling Pieces, and all other Sporting Implements." Cockfighters in the eighteenth century probably still also consulted Gervase Markham's *Country Contentments* (1633) for the training and feeding of their birds. *The Sporting Magazine* is a valuable resource for the Romantic period, and Carl B. Cone, *Hounds in the Morning* (1981), is an anthology of extracts from it.

One may read in Hansard the Parliamentary debates of the various bills that were introduced with the purpose of relieving animal suffering. The most revealing passages surround Sir William Pulteney's 1800 bill to prevent bull baiting and Lord Thomas Erskine's 1809 bill to prevent cruelty to animals. On the former occasion William Windham gave a famous speech (April 18, 1800). On the latter, Lord Erskine held forth (May 15, 1809 and May 31, 1809) and, again, William Windham was in opposition (June 13, 1809).

Marvelous passages of sentiment for animals may be found in Lawrence Sterne's *Tristram Shandy* (1760–67) and *A Sentimental Journey* (1768). Among other novels that reveal attitudes about animals are Henry Brooke's *The Fool of Quality* (1766), Margaret Cullen's *Mornton* (1814), and Anne Brontë's *Agnes Grey* (1847).

When writings for children mentioned animals, they invariably urged compassion. Mary Wollstonecraft's *Original Stories from Real Life* (1791) was one such book. Wollstonecraft translated Gotthilf Salzmann's *Moralisches Elementarbuch* (1782) as *Elements of Morality, for the Use of Children* (1791). Often animals were the central characters of a story. Of all such works, the most widely read was Sarah Trimmer's *Fabulous Histories Designed for the Instruction of Children Respecting the Treatment of Animals* (1786). Generally known as *The Robins*, it went through a great many editions until the end of the nineteenth century. Among the many works for children of Edward Augustus Kendall were *The Canary Bird* (1799) and *Keeper's Travels in Search of His Master* (1799), the latter a very popular work that is still touching. Dorothy Kilner told the *Life and Perambulation of a Mouse* (1780), and in her *The Rational Brutes* (1803), published under the pseudonym of M. Pelham, animals are the speakers. In "From Grimalkin to Selima," in Anna Letitia Barbauld's *A Legacy for Young Ladies* (1826), a cat's instruction to its offspring applies also to girls. This was reprinted from John Aikin and Letitia Barbauld, *Evenings at Home; or, The Juvenile Budget Opened* (1792–96), in which a great many of the essays and poems are about animals. More thoughts about animals and adventures with them are set forth in Thomas Day's *History of Sandford and Merton* (1783–89). Robert Southey's charming "Memoir of the Cats of Greta Hall," about his own pets, was written for his children. Many books for children were didacticism unsweetened by narrative. Among those that made a point of behavior to animals were Thomas Percival's *A Father's Instruction* (1784), the little known, unsigned *Lesson* (1826) that Joanna Baillie produced for the school children of Hampstead, and Legh Richmond's *Domestic Portraiture* (1833).

Books of children's poetry usually included poems of sympathy with animals. Blake's *Songs of Innocence* (1789) would originally have been read as such a book. Sara Coleridge's *Pretty Lessons in Verse for Good Children* (1834) was among the better ones. Ann and Jane Taylor's *Original Poems for Infant Minds* (1804) were more typical.

Since the number of poems about animals was very large, I mention only a few famous ones and a few others that particularly influenced attitudes or are now instructive because they describe contemporary lore and practice in detail. At the start of the eighteenth century the great reputation of Alexander Pope was engaged on the side of animals. Passages in his poetry were quoted by advocates of animals throughout the eighteenth century. In the *Guardian* (61; 1713) Pope published an essay against cruelty to animals. James Thomson's *The Seasons* (1726–30) had an even larger impact. William Somerville's *The Chase* (1735) has enthusiastic descriptions of fox and hare hunting, and the same material is used in the same spirit in *Needwood Forest* (1776) by Francis Noel Clarke Mundy. In *Jubilate Agno* (1759–63) Christopher Smart has splendid lines on his cat Jeoffry, but the poem was not published until 1939. The most influential single poet was William Cowper, and the central poem was his *The Task* (1785). It was quoted over and over in sermons and pamphlets, in didactic works, and in Parliament. Robert Burns's "To a Mouse" (1786) is one of the most loved poems of compassion for an animal in the English language, and Burns wrote several others in this vein. Robert Bloomfield's *The Farmer's Boy* (1800), a very popular work, activated sympathy for farm animals and coach horses. In "Auguries of Innocence" (1803) William Blake wrote verses that have been oracular for animal rights advocates ever since the poem was first published in 1863. There are other remarkable passages of sympathy with animals in Blake's *Songs of Innocence* (1789), *Book of Thel* (1789), and *Milton* (1804–08). James Grahame's *The Birds of Scotland* (1806) is a long, blank-verse poem of forty-five pages that pleasantly sets forth lore about the various species. The poetry of John Clare abounds in sympathetic observation of animals and identification with them. Animals and especially pets were a frequent subject in poems by women. This writing may be conveniently sampled in Paula Feldman's fine anthology of *British Women Poets of the Romantic Era* (1997), which includes many poems that would otherwise be difficult to obtain, and in volumes by Anna Letitia Barbauld, Charlotte Smith, Mary Robinson, and Joanna Baillie. William Wordsworth, Samuel Taylor Coleridge, Robert Southey, Lord Byron, and Percy Bysshe Shelley were highly sensitive to the sufferings of animals and occasionally wrote about them. Such poems include Wordsworth's "Hart-Leap Well," Byron's early "Inscription on the Monument of a Newfoundland Dog" and his verses against hunting in Canto 14 of *Don Juan*, and Coleridge's "Rime of the Ancient Mariner," the most famous of all poems on this theme. Felicia Hemans, the greatest of the women poets, had her own, characteristic view of animals; they are sublime in her poetry and evoke awe. This Romantic attitude characterized a great many poems after the turn of the century, including such famous ones as John Keats's "Ode to a Nightingale" and Shelley's "To a Skylark." In such poems the animals are idealized to the point that they transcend mortal limitations and are no longer subjects for compassion.

Index

Unwin, Mary, 47, 56–57, 63
Utilitarianism, 25

vegetables, capable of feeling, 150
vegetarianism, 24, 32–33, 117–19, 126
Verga, Giovanni
  "Story of the Saint Joseph's Ass," 105
vivisection, xv, 14–15, 155
  Samuel Johnson on, 15, 152
  John Lawrence on, 14
Voltaire (François Marie Arouet), 155

Walsh, John Henry ("Stonehenge"), 66
Walton, Izaak
  Complete Angler, 121
Warren, Robert Penn, 140
Watson, J. R., 121, 122, 171
Weeks, Shadrach, 111–12
Wesley, John, 28, 32
Whitaker, Thomas Dunham, 83
White, Gilbert, 133, 134
Wilberforce, William, 44
Windham, William, 16, 17, 93, 179
  opposes Sir William Pulteney's bill against
      bullbaiting, 17–18
  opposes Lord Thomas Erskine's bill for the
      Prevention of Cruelty to Animals, 16,
      18–19
Wollaston, William, 28, 34
Wollstonecraft, Mary, 21, 43
  Elements of Morality, for the Use of Children,
      21, 179
  Original Stories from Real Life, 22, 25, 26, 179
  "Vindication of the Rights of Women," 95
Woolman, John, 14
Wordsworth, Dorothy, 78
  Journals, 165
  "Mary Jones and Her Pet Lamb," 49
Wordsworth, William, x, xiii, 6, 8, 59, 72, 75,
      122, 133, 180
  on emotions of animals, 24

Preface to the Second Edition of *Lyrical
      Ballads*, 145
poems:
  "Fidelity," 27
  "Goody Blake and Harry Gill," 11
  "The Green Linnet," 101, 107, 142, 143–44,
      147
  "Hart-Leap Well," 77–88, 180
  "Hart's Horn Tree, near Penrith," 165
  Home at Grasmere, 79, 82, 86–87
  "Lines Composed a Few Miles above
      Tintern Abbey," 39, 84, 86
  "Lines Written in Early Spring," 38
  "Miscellaneous Sonnets," no. 29, 165
  "Nutting," 81, 86
  "Ode: Intimations of Immortality," 9, 10,
      40, 41; Coleridge on, 140
  "Peter Bell," 94, 107, 110–11
  "The Poet and the Caged Turtledove," 137
  The Prelude, 78, 84, 86, 133, 139
  "Resolution and Independence," 10, 40
  "Simon Lee," 73, 78, 86
  "The Sparrow's Nest," 107, 135
  "There Was a Boy," 86, 142, 144–45,
      146
  "To a Butterfly" ("I've watched you
      now . . ."), 40, 85, 107
  "To a Butterfly" ("Stay near me . . ."),
      84–85, 86
  "To the Cuckoo," 130, 141, 142
  "To a Sky-Lark," 40
  "The Tuft of Primroses," 165

Xenophon, 65

Yorke, James, 66
Young, George
  A History of Whitby, and Streoneshalh Abbey, 83
Young, John, 151
Young, Thomas
  An Essay on Humanity to Animals, 25, 34, 176

CAMBRIDGE STUDIES IN ROMANTICISM

GENERAL EDITORS
MARILYN BUTLER, *University of Oxford*
JAMES CHANDLER, *University of Chicago*